Operation
White Rabbit

Operation White Rabbit

LSD, the DEA, and the Fate of the Acid King

Dennis McDougal

Skyhorse Publishing

Skyhorse Publishing books may be purchased in bulk at special discounts for sales promotion, corporate gifts, fund-raising, or educational purposes. Special editions can also be created to specifications. For details, contact the Special Sales Department, Skyhorse Publishing, 307 West 36th Street, 11th Floor, New York, NY 10018 or info@skyhorsepublishing.com.

Skyhorse® and Skyhorse Publishing® are registered trademarks of Skyhorse Publishing, Inc.®, a Delaware corporation.

Visit our website at www.skyhorsepublishing.com.

10 9 8 7 6 5 4 3 2 1

Library of Congress Cataloging-in-Publication Data is available on file.

Cover design by Brian Peterson

Print ISBN: 978-1-5107-4537-7
Ebook ISBN: 978-1-5107-4538-4

Printed in the United States of America

For each and every gentle soul misplaced inside a jail.

Prologue

Wamego, Kansas—Nov. 6, 2000

WILLIAM LEONARD PICKARD TENSED LIKE a gazelle, all senses alert. He sniffed the air, scanning his surroundings for movement, but remained stock still. Breathe in. Breathe out. Give the adrenaline time to dissipate.

Satisfied that the moment was false alarm, he relaxed, then returned to the task at hand.

On the eve of Election Day at the turn of the twenty-first century, the courtly, silver-haired chemist and his bearded sidekick, Clyde Apperson, loaded boxes containing aluminum canisters and an array of laboratory glassware into the rear of a Ryder truck outside a retired Atlas Missile silo on the edge of Wamego, Kansas. The pair worked with haste and care. The labware was delicate. The canisters looked as harmless as Pringles potato chip cans, but the powder inside could provoke convulsions, delusions—even death. There was no room for false moves.

When they finished loading the truck, Pickard silently directed Apperson to climb behind the wheel and then did the same with his rented Buick LeSabre. Like a wizard trailed by his inelegant apprentice, Pickard angled his silver sedan past the chain link surrounding the former missile base while Apperson followed close behind. They each had a walkie-talkie so they could keep in touch as they prepared to head west on US 24.

Apperson was new to paranoia, but pulling up stakes on a moment's notice was routine to Pickard. For the better part of a decade, staying on the move had been as big a part of his complicated lifestyle as schmoozing with Afghan warlords, hobnobbing with Russian diplomats, or investigating money laundering on the Caribbean resort island of St. Maarten. When he wasn't globetrotting on behalf of the State Department or pushing paper as an academic at UCLA, Pickard synthesized psychedelic sacraments on the fly, lysergic acid diethylamide chief among them.

Leonard Pickard saw himself as heir to Dr. Timothy Leary, even while he slowly morphed into the Walter White of LSD—but with one crucial difference, Pickard would argue: whereas the protagonist of TV's *Breaking Bad* made crystal meth, which ruins lives and kills thousands, Pickard maintained that LSD never killed anyone.

Possessing it *is* illegal, however, and carting around ingredients and lab equipment tends to raise questions. A veteran of many a previous bust, Pickard had grown wary to the point of neurosis: an ounce of prevention was worth a ton of police confrontation. Pickard preferred the serenity of anonymity.

As night fell over the fresh layer of snow that blanketed the Flint Hills, Wamego lit up like a beacon. The farm town that advertises itself as "home of L. Frank Baum's fictional Land of Oz" afforded the only light for a hundred square miles. Once they'd driven beyond its halo, Pickard and Apperson were shrouded in darkness. They stayed well within the speed limit.

Pickard saw the flashing lights before he heard the sirens. He slowed, took a deep breath and waited for squad cars to blow past on their way to some accident on the Interstate.

Panic not. Obey all traffic laws. Draw no attention. Hide in plain sight.

Only this time, the cops didn't fly by. Pickard began to perspire when a black-and-white crept up behind, its high-pitched yelp directing the LeSabre to pull over. Instead, Pickard switched instantly from calm to catastrophic. He whipped the walkie-talkie to his lips: "This is it," he barked. "This is what we talked about."

He gunned his engine. Apperson followed his lead. The chase was on.

It ended soon enough. Within a few hundred yards, the Kansas Highway Patrol overtook and forced both vehicles to the shoulder. Apperson made a half-hearted attempt to bolt before falling to his knees in surrender.

Pickard had different ideas. He left the Buick idling and lit out across an open field. Weapons drawn, the highway patrolmen hollered, "Halt!" They followed in hot pursuit that cooled to lukewarm then frostbitten in minutes.

A veteran marathon runner, Pickard could be seen in silhouette against the horizon. He ran a broken-field pattern well ahead of harriers half his age and did a fast fade into the night.

"I actually waded down streams to elude the bloodhound scents," Pickard recalled months later. "It took a while for those Nikes to dry out. And a full moon to top it all."

Inside the Buick, Pickard left behind a paperback describing how to vanish from public view and establish a new identity. Police also found two pamphlets titled "Escape From Controlled Custody" and "How to Survive Federal Prison Camp." In the trunk were several more instructional brochures: how to obtain an international drivers' license; how to file for a concealed-weapons permit in Florida; strategies for surviving a police interrogation; and how to hide contraband in public places. Were there any further doubt that they had the right suspect, the cops also located a

Department of Justice handbook on controlled substances in the back seat and a catalogue of surveillance equipment in the glove compartment.

Fortified half an hour later by a small army of DEA agents, the Kansas Highway Patrol joined Wamego police and a squadron of Pottawatomie County Sheriff's deputies in a full-on flashlight dragnet, crisscrossing the cornfields. Helicopters with infrared scanners and packs of bloodhounds aided in the search. When that failed, a house-to-house canvas of the rural hinterlands surrounding Wamego lasted through the night.

The following morning, a farmer named Billy Taylor rang the sheriff's office. A stranger claiming car trouble was holed up in Taylor's barn out on Military Road, four miles west of Wamego.

Taylor had found the man snoozing in the cab of his old pickup at daybreak. If it weren't for his dirty sneakers and grubby clothes, Taylor might have bought his story. The fellow seemed more like a professor than a hobo. He was cool as a cucumber when he asked Taylor to drive him to nearby Manhattan. Taylor gave him a nod, but added that he needed to put oil in his rig first. Then he called the sheriff.

With neither lights nor sirens blazing this time, a squad car eased onto Taylor's property. Taylor had engaged the stranger in small talk until he caught sight of the deputies. Pickard saw them at the same time.

Once again, Pickard ran off through the fields, but this time, the deputies stayed in their squad car and kept pace right behind, bumping over irrigation ditches and shorn stumps of cornstalk. After a thousand yards, Pickard collapsed, breathless.

"You've got me," he told them.

Tucson Federal Penitentiary—July 8, 2018

Inside the antiseptic glare of a fluorescent-flooded visiting room the size of an NBA arena, contact is limited to a hug or handshake upon greeting and departure. Khaki-clad inmates sit in one set of chairs and visitors in street clothes on another. They face each other. No touching. The place looks benign, if sterile, but make no mistake: there is violence here.

William Leonard Pickard leans across a four-foot gap that separates him from his visitor.

"While the guards were distracted, inmates circled 'round," Pickard confides. He keeps his voice low, his pale blue eyes tilted down. "One inmate steps in, stabs him *eighty* times." His eyelids flutter. His normally low timbre hitches a notch at "eighty."

"*Eighty* times?" asks his incredulous visitor.

"Eight," says Pickard, pantomiming the jackhammer action of a shiv against his own narrow torso. He blinks twice then glances away, leaving the visitor in doubt as to whether he's heard correctly.

"Eight?" the visitor repeats.

Pickard leaves the question hanging, neither confirming nor denying.

"It was *David Mitchell*!" he hisses. "The guy who kidnapped Elizabeth Smart?" Pickard sits back in horrific triumph. "Blood everywhere."

Pickard looks askance at two correctional officers kibitzing nearby. Bored at having to spend another Sunday afternoon chaperoning, the guards will clock out once visiting hours end and prisoners return to their Spartan quarters.

Pickard has been in residence almost a dozen years. He has lost count of the attacks he has witnessed. David Mitchell is just the most recent. Several were far more grisly. His point: don't let the benign trappings of visiting day fool you. Federal prison is a damned dangerous place.

Tucson isn't the nation's worst. The penitentiary at Florence, Colorado, 800 miles north of here is a Level 5 and houses such criminal elites as Unabomber Ted Kaczynski,[1] World Trade Center mastermind Zacarias Moussaoui, and Silk Road internet wunderkind Ross Ulbricht. Florence is far safer than Tucson. The difference is that everyone is locked down all the time—the equivalent of solitary confinement, 24/7. Not much room for either violence or intimacy.

Pickard's home base is also locked down frequently. It has had its own set of notables: celebrity felons as varied as ex-Black Panther H. Rap Brown, Utah polygamist Warren Jeffs, Boston mobster James "Whitey" Bulger Jr. and, of course, Brian David Mitchell, the sixty-four-year-old street-preaching pedophile who kidnapped fourteen-year-old Elizabeth Smart in 2002 and kept her indentured as a sex slave for nearly a year.

According to Pickard, Mitchell is the latest of Tucson's 1,500 high-risk inmates to fall victim to gang violence and guard indifference.[2]

So was wheelchair-bound Bulger, though the scuttlebutt around the yard was that Whitey had been caught colluding with a prison employee who sold his autograph on eBay. Bulger was summarily shipped out as punishment.

"He was disinclined to walk the yard, but had been seen in the library," recalled Pickard. "An inmate approached me one day with a note from Whitey, saying he was aware of my case and wanted

---

1. Kaczynski was one of twenty-two student volunteers in 1958 who participated in a governmbent-sponsored Harvard experiment to see if LSD could be used as a disorienting weapon of war—an experience he later described as "the worst experience of my life."
2. Not so, according to the Bureau of Prisons. Mitchell suffered no lingering injury from a running feud between him and a rival inmate. Nonetheless, a Bureau spokesman conceded, Mitchell was recently transferred to an Oklahoma penitentiary for his own safety.

to talk about his experience with LSD in 1957 at the Atlanta Penitentiary."

In those days, the federal government occasionally sought drug research volunteers among soldiers and prison inmates, noted Pickard. Whitey claimed to be among them.

"Generally, inmates volunteering for drug researchers were not told of the substance's identity," said Pickard. It didn't necessarily have to be LSD. Could have been mescaline or psilocybin or any of a dozen other psychedelics. "I told him to visit me in the library, but he never made it."

Instead, in 2018, Bulger was transferred to Hazleton Penitentiary in West Virginia where he was bludgeoned to death with a sock load of padlocks. He was eighty-nine.

"So, death can occur at any time, for any reason, even over some personal illusion or another," said Pickard. "Other than knives, 'locks and socks' are the preferred method. I've seen more attacks than I can count.

"Within the last six months, a schizophrenic inmate who thought people were always talking about him crept up behind another who was peacefully watching TV. After the first stunning blow, the next ten or so (full arm swings) were delivered on the unconscious victim. He's never been seen again, but the assailant returned to general population after a month or so in the hole."

Any exaggeration on Pickard's part about instant unprovoked terror can be forgiven. Tucson remains a somber place where gossip runs rampant. Whether eight or eighty, a blow to the skull or stab to the gut is never acceptable, even among the world's most notorious, many of whom wound up here for committing their own ghastly murders.

Arguably, William Leonard Pickard should never have been among them. A quick-witted chemist and con man with a passion for the good life, a talent for spinning the truth, and a dubious gift for mixing business, diplomacy, and neurochemistry—but a bloodthirsty criminal capable of gutting a fellow human being? Not in a million years.

Nonetheless, he has learned to adapt. With two life sentences, Leonard, as he prefers to be addressed, ranks high in the Tucson pecking order—an *éminence grise* among capos and rapists. At seventy-four, he's one of the oldest inmates. Most agree he is unlikely to ever walk free.

He helps his peers with their appeals when he isn't busy himself. He meditates, exercises, does some yoga. The rest of the time he plunges into reams of correspondence, reads voraciously, and revises his self-published 654-page fantasy/memoir, *The Rose of Paracelsus.*

His latest publishing project involves an inch-thick primer on fentanyl which argues that Leonard correctly predicted the current opioid crisis over twenty years ago, while he was still a research fellow at Harvard University. His attorney recently sent bound copies of his "Fentanyl Proposal" to all 535 members of Congress in support of his bid for freedom. He also asked Kim Kardashian to work the same clemency magic on President Trump that she did for convicted drug dealer Alice Marie Johnson[3].

To date, his appeals have failed, but Leonard is resilient. His network of friends and admirers on the outside has only mushroomed since his 2003 conviction as the world's biggest and best supplier of lysergic acid diethylamide-25.

"Just was thinking this week that, even in captivity, I've come to know so many more than when free," he said. "I say a nightly prayer for all the kind people."

None would know his shadier side if Pickard had his way. He

---

3. Sentenced to life in 1996, the sixty-four-year-old Memphis housewife and grandmother was convicted of trafficking in Colombian cocaine and money laundering. Like Pickard, she was one of 16,776 drug offenders who petitioned the Obama Administration for clemency in 2014. President Obama commuted 1,927 sentences; Johnson and Pickard were not among them. President Trump granted Johnson clemency in June of 2018 at the behest of Kardashian and son-in-law Jared Kushner.

stifles the negatives while maximizing pretensions. The "about the author" paragraph at the close of *The Rose of Paracelsus* tells all that he cares to share about himself:

William Leonard Pickard is a graduate of the Kennedy School of Government at Harvard, with degrees in chemistry and public policy. He was formerly a research associate in neurobiology at Harvard Medical School, a Fellow of the Interfaculty Initiative on Drugs and Addictions at Harvard, and Deputy Director of the Drug Policy Analysis Program at UCLA. His interests include Victorian-Edwardian literature, deincarceration technologies, the neuropolicy of cognitive enhancement, and the future of novel drugs.

He is, of course, so very much more.

Leonard Pickard is a rail-thin stretch of a man who resembles a beardless Gandalf in a khaki jumpsuit and size-twelve bath clogs. He might be mistaken for an underfed Zen monk, which, in fact, is precisely what he is. He accepted his vows in a Taos ashram nearly thirty years ago. Over the ensuing years, his frosty shock of hair has come to match his translucent complexion. Against all odds, laugh lines crinkle the sockets surrounding his eyes.

"I treat this place as a monastery, except that the other monks shout all day and are often violent," he quips. Even at this late date, there is no hard edge to his voice.

But Zen or no Zen, Leonard yearns for all that he has lost, beginning with family. He has at least three children by three different mothers, two of whom he never sees. Only one son and one of the mothers ever visit.

However eager he might be to leave this desolate concrete and steel oasis in the Arizona desert, at Pickard's core is ironic stoicism. A practicing Buddhist and vegan, he lays himself down to sleep each night with a Baptist prayer of gratitude that he learned at his Unitarian father's knee. His mantras are few but binding. The best strategy for survival is to blend in, make few waves, and stay busy. Were it not for the natural human compulsion to scheme, his would be a purely ascetic existence, stripped of pretense, powered by compassion.

And yet, hope does spring eternal. Pickard remains fit, vital, and ambitious—bent but not broken. He no longer fancies himself the lady killer he once was, though it seems he'll never get past his instinct for seduction. Taking acquaintances into his confidence comes so easily that he falls back into the routine like an aging do-dah man.

William Leonard Pickard remains the proverbial riddle wrapped in a mystery inside an enigma, only more so. He doesn't lie exactly—at least, not at first—but neither is he a slave to the facts.

Above all, Leonard is a voyager upon the high seas of brain chemistry. What Jason was to the Argo, Leonard is to the Psyche, and the oddball crew of lovers and confidants and chemists that joined him on his long strange trip were and are—like Leonard himself—psychonauts.

PART ONE
Logic and Proportion

I.

BOTH PRODIGY AND RENEGADE, LEONARD Pickard came of age at the very point in history when the Greatest Generation broke with their sons and daughters over Vietnam. Raised Southern Baptist[1] in the North Atlanta suburbs, Pickard was born two months after the end of World War II into Georgia's white-bread middle class.

"Suits on Sunday, no alcohol, learned to handle rifles at nine," he told *Rolling Stone* magazine. "Read endlessly. Azaleas, rhododendrons, lightning, fireflies. Many happy moments as a small boy observing paramecia under my great-grandfather's microscope. Visiting scientists from all over the world stayed with us. Much conversation."

He maintained that his father practiced corporate law and his biochemist mom took her doctorate from Columbia. She was a fungal disease specialist with the fledgling Centers for Disease Control, he said.

Public records imply a trickier and less romantic history, listing the elder William Pickard as a Southern Bell telephone switchman who worked his way through Oglethorpe University.

"He was a small-college All-American when they still wore

---

1. Governor Lestor Maddox's mother taught him and his older sister Sunday school. Later, when his father switched denominations, Leonard became a Unitarian.

leather helmets," Pickard recalled. "Boxed his way through law school as 'Kid Curly'."

William Pickard took his law degree in 1949, gaining admission to the Bar in 1951. By then, Leonard's mother Audrey Pickard had already divorced his father. Leonard never learned why.

"Audrey as a young woman was one of the southern belles with whom Gable danced at the opening of *Gone with the Wind* at the Loews Theater on Peachtree Street in, what, 1939?" said Pickard.

Audrey moved out of state and remarried three more times, working variously between husbands as a secretary, typist, cashier, and clerk. She outlived them all, but had no place in Leonard's upbringing.

"I received my healthy biology from Audrey whom I barely knew, but mind and spirit came from Lucille," said Pickard.

It was his stepmother, Lucille Georg Pickard, a University of Michigan biologist, who preached the gospel of science. She went to work for the early CDC at the end of World War II. At the time, the federal public health agency was little more than a collection of Quonset huts located adjacent to Emory University.

"Until CDC put in negative-pressure rooms to contain infectious diseases (air locks aimed only inward, not outward), I had free range," recalled Pickard. "I visited all the labs. The tanks where snails infected with schistosomiasis were raised, certain fishes and animals for leish-maniasis, and all the hosts for the world's great infectious killers."

Honored frequently over a thirty-year career for her insights into the biology of fungi, Dr. Lucille Georg kept her maiden name and her feminist identity. She was eight years older than her husband, and the dominant presence in the Pickard household.

"As a distinguished researcher with Public Health, she had a red diplomatic passport. My father tagged along when Lucille attended international conferences," said Pickard.

They traveled often to Europe in the grand old style, via luxury liner.

"Once my father brought home a complete espresso machine from Stockholm 'with all the fixins,' as he would say. But then he'd shake his head with each cup and add, 'It just doesn't taste the same.'

"I did ask Lucille in later years why she married him," he recalled. "She said, 'Because he's so full of life.' Sometimes they'd dance together, write poems. They loved each other greatly."

An early and outspoken champion of STEM[2] education in the public schools, Lucille Pickard's most important apprentice was her stepson.

"My stepmother was, and has been always, very much the primary woman figure in my life," said Pickard. "I spent most of my time with her, listened to her, learned from her. She was immensely gracious, and very much a lady."

A PhD trained in mycology at Columbia University's Vagelos College of Physicians and Surgeons, Lucille Georg Pickard explained the finer points of high culture to Leonard as well as the rudiments of the scientific method. She made him a reader. He devoured books about the Manhattan Project, biographies of J. Robert Oppenheimer and Albert Einstein.

"I remember the day Einstein died, and where I was standing," he said with hushed reverence. "It was 1955. April, wasn't it?"[3]

Lucille took him to the symphony, opera, concerts, museums, libraries, and her laboratory at CDC, which was well-stocked with biologic ephemera and a huge collection of prepared slides.

"She brought home irradiated fruit flies and showed me how to check for mutants; colorful agar slants of spores, molds and fungi; live samples of human placenta; and exotic glassware for measuring the number of red blood cells from a pin prick."

When other moms were teaching table manners, Lucille taught

---

2. Science, technology, engineering, and math.
3. Einstein died of an aortic aneurysm April 18, 1955. He was seventy-six.

Leonard how to tie silk knots in a matchbox using hemostats, mimicking the method med students use to practice suturing. On balmy summer afternoons while other youngsters waded into the woods in search of blackberries and crawdads, Leonard took Lucille's hand and learned to see the outdoors through a naturalist's eyes.

"Memories, some of my earliest, as a small boy hunting chestnuts with her by streams, and being told of the plant and animal kingdoms and that humans were animals made of cells. I learned my first scientific mouthful at her feet: 'Ontogeny recapitulates phylogeny,' which means 'the new life mimics the old life' . . ."

Lucille knew the Latin for wildflowers and chipmunks, mushrooms and songbirds. She gathered bog water, petals, feathers, and bark for closer scrutiny beneath the lens of her grandfather's ancient Carl Zeiss microscope, giving Leonard a glimpse into an unseen world.

"Lucille was friends with the world's great mycologists," recalled Pickard. "Her colleagues at CDC often came by the house, so that I was blessed with those influences. Researchers from around the world would stay; once, an entire Chinese family."

His father taught him discipline and the manly art of hunting.

"My father showed me how to shoot at an early age: .22s by seven, twelve-gauge by twelve. Packs of beagles with uncles, the works. I got very good with targets, as Southern boys tend to be, but put all weapons down at fifteen and never looked back."

Yet many of Pickard's classmates don't even remember him having parents, let alone shooting guns. They recall Leonard and his older sister Gala living with an aunt and uncle, Ed and Yogi Verner. Their upbringing was far more plebian than that which Leonard recalls. His cousin Dan Pickard knew a city nerd unaccustomed to the great outdoors.

"I remember taking him fishing once on Lake Allatoona," said Dan Pickard. "Lennie caught a catfish and went nuts, screaming and hollering as if he'd never seen a fish before."

The one point upon which Leonard's cousin and classmates do seem to agree is that he was brilliant.

"Lennie was *not dumb*, as you probably know," said Dan Pickard. "The boy was super smart and could have done wonders."

Pickard lettered in track, shot photos for the school newspaper, and was declared "most intellectual" in the 1963 Daniel O'Keefe High School yearbook. He played forward on the basketball team, ran cross country and rose to the rank of First Lieutenant in ROTC.

"Our drill team had chrome helmets, blue ascots, and white spats over our boots, with O'Keefe green and white shoulder braids," he recalled. "I marched at the head of the column right, sometimes backwards, and called the cadence. The uniform had multiple insignia and patches, and—get this!—I had a chrome saber drawn and held to shoulder while marching. I learned to salute with it."

He wasn't all discipline. He was also a storyteller with a wry sense of humor.

"Lennie Pikurd," chuckled classmate Mary Ann Haney, pronouncing his last name "Pik-urd," instead of the more elegant "Pick-*card*" that Leonard prefers. "Lennie liked to live on the edge. Tease the girls. Craved attention. Excitement! He had a great wit, but he always acted just a little bit superior."

That, he says, is because he *was* superior. Leonard Pickard led two lives, even when he was still in high school.

"O'Keefe[4] was an island on the Georgia Tech campus," he recalled.

His alma mater was undemanding, according to Pickard, but its proximity to Georgia Tech made it a mecca for the hyper-curious. He recalled Burroughs, Remington Rand, and IBM installing punch-card behemoths on campus—Univac forerunners of the

---

4. Named for the father of the Atlanta public school system, Daniel O'Keefe High closed in 1973.

PCs later developed by Apple and Microsoft. He spent as much time tinkering with early computers and browsing bound editions of *Scientific American* in the Price Gilbert Library ("a real pleasure dome for science students") as he did with the ROTC or O'Keefe's basketball team.

Which is not to say he had no social life. Moonlit hayrides past Stone Mountain[5], Sunday school socials, requisite high school hops—he wooed women in the woods or on the tennis courts. But "Lennie" spent just as much time exploring the mind—his and those of his peers.

"O'Keefe was a platform from which I circled into distant groups and activities unknown to my co-students, for I never talked about it," he said.

Influenced by his stepmother, he channeled his perceived superiority into an early and intense love of science. He tapped into youth programs at the National Science Foundation, International Science and Engineering Fair, Atomic Energy Commission, Westinghouse Science Talent Search . . .

Each year since the end of World War II, Westinghouse Electric had sponsored an annual competition to identify the forty best high school science students in the nation. On its face, the venerable prize appeared to be corporate America's token appreciation of the scientists of tomorrow. Its deeper significance, according to Pickard, was that it fostered a pool of geniuses that helped steer the nation past the nuclear hazards of the Cold War. He counted himself among their number.[6]

---

5. Pickard: "I got my first kiss on Stone Mountain."
6. In August 1963, the National Institute of Mental Health flew Leonard and two other Westinghouse winners to its Bethesda headquarters for a study of high IQ students, according to Pickard. "In Atlanta, I once was called to a building with no name, down a corridor with no signs, into a bare room and desk, with a besuited presumed physicist who just asked questions and otherwise disclosed nothing."

"In 1996, the Westinghouse Science Talent Search[7] did a fifty-year review of the prior 2000 student winners, listing their positions and achievements," he said. "Of the 2000, six had Nobels. Many were National Academy of Science members. The internet is replete with Westinghouse examples."

In the summer of 1962, as a high school junior, Pickard interned at the Argonne National Laboratory near the University of Chicago. He built two linear particle accelerators at a time when most teens thought accelerator meant gas pedal. By the time he was a senior, he'd won national science fair competitions two years running. One of those years included an all-expenses-paid trip to Seattle, where he got his picture in the paper, competed for $34,000 in scholarships, and delivered a lecture on "The Radiobiology of Pinocytosis."[8]

Back home in Atlanta, most of his classmates had no idea how big a deal Lennie Pickard had become. Recruited by twenty-two colleges and universities, he accepted a Princeton scholarship, where he planned to dig even deeper into cellular biophysics and eventually nail down his own Nobel. He meant to step into big shoes at Princeton.

"First thing I did after dropping my luggage off at Patton Hall was wander down Nassau Street, turn left on Mercer, and stand before Einstein's old place," he said. "It was a modest eighteenth-century white clapboard house with a tiny front yard, screen doors, and a loft overlooking a small back yard—very humble.

"I stood at the front door for half an hour, but didn't have the nerve to knock. He died just seven years earlier. Little did I know that the house was still occupied by his last wife and his secretary

---

7. Following near collapse in the 1990s, financially-strapped Westinghouse surrendered sponsorship to Scripps Research, then Intel Corporation. Today the competition is called the Regeneron Science Talent Search.

8. Greek for "cell drinking," pinocytosis tracks the formation of channels from a cell's surface membrane to its plasmatic center—a process that can only be observed through an electron microscope.

of fifty years, Helen Dukas. All his furnishings, books, files, and letters were still there. Likely they would have welcomed a young student like me."

Missing Einstein was the first of many lost opportunities. Leonard was an awkward fit at Princeton, still very much invested in his ROTC training, but appalled by Vietnam. He thought the university would be a refuge from politics, not a cauldron.

"I joined the Cliosophic Society[9], which invited Madame Nhu down to speak," he said. "She appeared in black *áo dài* and makeup. Handshakes all around inside Witherspoon Hall while outside, students were throwing eggs, shouting protests. I didn't know what to think. I'd just turned eighteen that week.

"As we left Witherspoon, a wizardly teen appeared in Buddhist robes and began shouting in Vietnamese. We didn't understand, but Madame Nhu did. Weeks earlier, several monks burned themselves to death protesting the Saigon government. Madame Nhu shrugged it off. She said all monks should be barbequed.

"So this student holds up a can labeled 'GASOLINE' then sits down in lotus posture and douses himself. Security began working their way in. Crowd ooohs and ahhs as the student strikes a match. The Princeton Marching Band played 'Smoke Gets In Your Eyes.'

"Madame Nhu and her entourage stood in horror. Student delivers his final prayer in Vietnamese, then slowly brings the match to his robe. It goes out. The gas can was filled with water. Student stands, then in his best Bronx accent shouts, 'Well, folks, that's show biz!' Then he flees into the crowd.

"The whole event created an alumni uproar. How *dare* students embarrass the school! Two weeks later President Diem and his brother, Madame Nhu's husband, were executed in Saigon while she was partying in Bel Air."

---

9. Founded in 1765 by Aaron Burr, James Madison, and other Founding Fathers, the American Whig-Cliosophic Society at Princeton is the oldest collegiate debate club in the US

Princeton was no political asylum. For Pickard, the contradictions persisted. While Mississippi governor Ross Barnett preached segregation to the Cliosophic Society, protesters dogged his steps and hounded him off campus. Leonard joined the chorus.

He lasted one semester at Princeton.

"Leonard thought he was such a genius that he could skip classes, do drugs, and *still* ace all his exams," recalled a fellow psychonaut who would get caught up decades later in Pickard's world.

In Leonard's version, his short-lived Princeton experience derailed after he discovered wine, women, and song in nearby Greenwich Village—an easy fifty-mile bus trip from the New Jersey campus.

"This was before drugs appeared, when marijuana was only something rumored to be used by Puerto Rican musicians, and was not remotely a topic of interest," he said. "No Beatles. No rock 'n' roll. MacDougal Street was some prescient omen of the future. The espresso houses, the Vanguard, Buddy Rich wailing away at the Metropole, Sun Ra and his Solar Arkestra. We'd follow Moondog[10] around Manhattan.

"I saw Richard Pryor in his youngest days! I recall the entirely white audience laughing uproariously every time he said 'motherfucker,' thinking it was outrageous or a joke, never realizing that it was just basic vernacular."

Despite his outward appearance of straitlaced Southern privilege, Leonard evolved rather quickly into a rebel with no visible cause.

"No one had quite seen anything like it," Pickard recalled. "So many people stepping out of line, discussing theology and philosophy, seeking explanations, exploring their place in life."

---

10. The blind "Viking of 6th Avenue," Lewis Thomas Hardin was an itinerant jazzman and Midtown Manhattan fixture through most of the twentieth century.

During Thanksgiving week, 1964, he was arrested twice in Alabama for forgery.

"Dim recollection," he said. "Something about a girl's over-draft near Auburn. It was dismissed. None of these early brushes with the law required more than a few hours' detention as matters cleared up."

He spurned the bourgeois lifestyle and vowed to quit the middle class. His new role model was less Einstein and more Dean Moriarty, the bipolar protagonist of Jack Kerouac's *On The Road*.

"He decided to steal a car for a joy ride—a Pontiac GTO, I think," said his fellow psychonaut.

Dan Pickard dimly recalls cousin Lennie phoning one day in January of 1965 with an offer he and his two older brothers couldn't refuse.

"He called to ask us if we wanted a car. Well, *yeah!* We were kids," said Dan. "But he never came through, and we never heard from him again."

Instead of delivering the stolen GTO, Leonard got arrested in Newark by US Marshals for transporting a stolen vehicle over state lines. He clams up about what happened next. Even fifty years after the fact, he remains elusive, ducks his head, changes the subject. He will not discuss it.

But his peers will. His father stepped in and persuaded the court to grant Leonard probation, the first two years of which he was to serve under professional observation at the Institute of Living in Connecticut.

Officially a "residential psychiatric facility" located near the state capital of Hartford, the sanctuary had a dicey history. Constructed in 1823 for $12,000 and situated on thirty-five pristine acres,[11] the Institute of Living was only the third psychiatric hospital ever

---

11. Landscaped during the 1860s by New York City's famed Central Park architect Frederick Law Olmsted.

built in the US. Originally dubbed the Connecticut Retreat for the Insane, the forty-bed facility underwent dozens of changes over the next two centuries. It became a lobotomy factory during the 1930s, a pioneer in electroshock therapy,[12] and a favored refuge for hundreds of Catholic priests identified by the Church as pedophiles.

During his intake interview, Leonard struck a sour note.

"Young Leonard was dressed in a Navy-blue blazer and a rep tie," recalled Pickard's associate. "And when asked why he believed he was there, Leonard said that he had decided to make his time at the Institute a learning experience. Then he asked the intake psychiatrist, 'How can I be of help to *you*?'"

Not true, protests Pickard.

"There's nothing in the records but a little discussion of my father versus my aunt," he said. "No typing or DSM[13] categories; no mention of sociopathy. And no one at the Institute of Living would remember an eighteen-year-old from fifty years ago. . . ."

Nonetheless, maintained his associate, impudence got Leonard labeled a troublemaker: a narcissist, incapable of introspection. Right or wrong, the label stuck. The funny, quirky, brilliant kid that Mary Haney and Dan Pickard recalled growing up did a slow fade.

Over the next twenty years, Pickard lived life on the periphery, dropping in and out of communes, spending time in jail, haunting college campuses and entering into loose-knit social networks dedicated to psychedelics. He made no pretense about depending upon the kindness of strangers. He soaked up altruism and neuropharmacology wherever he found it.

While he was still in Connecticut, he audited classes and worked at the hospital that eventually acquired the Institute of Living.

---

12. Actress Gene Tierney underwent twenty-six shock treatments, later claiming they erased significant portions of her memory.
13. Diagnostic and Statistical Manual of Mental Disorders, unofficial Bible of the American Psychiatric Association.

"My first job was male aide at Hartford Hospital, then moved to psychiatric aide, then to surgical tech at Laboratory for Experimental Surgery, all while at Trinity College in my spare time," he said.

From 1968 through 1988, Leonard Pickard cycled in and out of schools and universities, never actually matriculating, but learning all that he needed to know, then moving on.

"Note that public records and cross-talk are thin on two decades," he said.

What happened next remains hazy. There are few employment records, addresses, phones, cars, bank accounts, "or any threads whatsoever to exploit. Zero," he said proudly. "In the decades I went dark, the FBI would appear now and then and ask people 'Where is he?' One might argue, given the lack of records, that I labor under some secrecy agreement."

He insists he isn't being coy. If his story sounds a little too John le Carré, it isn't because he's given over to spy novels. Even now, festering inside a federal prison, he reveals precious little about those years between Princeton and his re-emergence at Harvard Square in 1994. To blab, he contends, would put lives at risk and violate a code of silence he accepted half a century ago, when he first became a psychonaut.

II.

PSYCHONAUTS BELIEVE IN BETTER LIVING through chemistry. They seek spirituality through magic mushrooms, mescaline, peyote, psilocybin, ayahuasca, ibogaine, DMT and, of course, LSD. Literally Greek for "sailor of the soul," the term came into broad usage during the 1960s, when Leonard Pickard first came aboard. But the sea upon which psychonauts sail is as old as humankind.

Dr. Albert Hofmann was arguably the first modern-day psychonaut. The Swiss-born biologist launched his revolution in April of 1943, two-and-a-half years before Leonard Pickard was born. Hofmann stumbled upon his most notorious discovery during a routine lab procedure. Now seared into psychonaut legend, Hofmann's tale has been told and retold thousands of times. Leonard Pickard knows the details by heart:

- How Hofmann synthesized the lysergic molecule from rye fungus in 1938 at Sandoz Pharmaceuticals while looking for a possible cure for post-partum bleeding;
- How he set the compound aside for five years until—quite by accident—he ingested a microdot and watched his lab morph into a wobbly kandy-kolored kaleidoscope;
- How he followed up three days later with an intentional dose,

then rode his bicycle home through the drab cobblestone streets of Basel;

- And how the alleyways began to sparkle then twist and roll into incandescent reptilian rivers, and cloud formations billowed into hot-pink cotton candy accompanied by full-blown symphonic orchestrations that ricocheted between Dr. Hofmann's ears.

Psychonauts commemorate April 19, 1943, as the first Bicycle Day, when acid officially left the lab and took to the streets. Pickard would not learn to commemorate Bicycle Day for another quarter century, but once he did, he too made LSD his life's work.

Near the turn of the twenty-first century, Pickard got to meet Dr. Hofmann in the flesh, during the 1996 European Conference on Consciousness. Just ten years shy of the legendary Swiss biochemist's hundredth birthday, Hofmann posed for a selfie with Pickard. The photo remains one of Leonard's great personal treasures.

"Albert and I spoke of the Harvard work," he recalls with hushed reverence.

Pickard was deep into his double life by then: studying drugs and diplomacy at Harvard's Kennedy School was behind him, but he still found time to tinker with theoretical chemistry in New Mexico while holding down a drug policy post at UCLA and schmoozing on the psychonaut circuit. He shared none of these details except on a need-to-know basis. Hofmann didn't need to know.

Weeks later, Hofmann surprised Leonard by sending him an autographed copy of his memoir. The frontispiece read, "With fond memories of our meeting in Heidelberg."

Unlike Leonard, Hofmann had never been arrested. By contrast, Pickard's rap sheet dated back decades. Hofmann would have been neither surprised nor offended that he'd been canoodling with a felon. Despite his spotless record, acid's premiere elder statesman understood full well the paradox of the Pandora's box he'd opened that spring day in 1943. He titled the memoir he published on the subject *LSD: My Problem Child*. It was the very book that he autographed for Leonard.

In *My Problem Child*, Hofmann detailed that first deliberate encounter with LSD, when he cycled home from his job at Sandoz. Even after he recovered, the strait-laced biochemist was never the same. Hofmann devoted the remainder of his very long life to the study of all things psychedelic.

So did Leonard Pickard, though his route was far more circuitous and involved detours into the darker recesses of the human psyche.

Hofmann suffered a fatal heart attack at his home in Basel in 2008. Dead at 102, he'd recently topped an international list of the world's 100 greatest living geniuses.[1]

Leonard read Hofmann's long, adoring obituary while sitting alone in his cell. He was seven years into a life sentence for manufacturing Hofmann's "problem child." The modern world's first psychonaut commanded universal veneration. Pickard's reward was jail, forever.

From Dr. Hofmann's Swiss laboratory to the corner of Haight & Ashbury, LSD-25 took a circuitous route over the two decades before its re-discovery during San Francisco's Summer of Love, and Leonard Pickard's induction into the acid underground. Before winding up a Flower Power staple, acid required the help of the US government to complete its 10,000-mile journey from Basel to the Bay.

While agreeing that Dr. Hofmann's discovery was indeed astonishing, his bosses at Sandoz Pharmaceuticals could find no practical

---

1. Published the previous year by the London Daily Telegraph, Hofmann shared the top spot with Tim Berners-Lee, inventor of the World Wide Web. Runners-up included philanthropist George Soros, *The Simpsons* creator Matt Groening, and South African statesman Nelson Mandela.

use for the substance. Nevertheless, they tried to market it in post-war America under the brand name Delysid. The best that Sandoz salesmen could tell their customers was that LSD-25 seemed to do a pretty good job of mimicking schizophrenia. Thus, initial consumers were mostly psychiatrists.

Freud and Jung were still the major role models for the new sciences of psychology during the late 1940s. Unlike the rest of human biology, brain chemistry hadn't advanced much beyond that of Mary Shelley's *Frankenstein*. By mid-twentieth century, surgeons understood quite well how a heart, liver, spleen or lung functioned, but they knew precious little about the central nervous system. Any mucking about in neuropharmacology was viewed by the general public as one step above voodoo.

Postwar spies, politicians, and the Pentagon held a different view about Delysid. Chartered in 1947 as the Cold War heir to World War II's Office of Strategic Services, the newly-created Central Intelligence Agency saw real promise in LSD.

"CIA had a mandate to monitor any advances in science, technology and medicine, as it does today," said Leonard Pickard.

The spy agency became Sandoz's biggest customer during the early 1950s. For the next 20 years, working hand in hand with the Department of Defense, the CIA oversaw scores of experiments. Under a half-dozen code-word operations ranging from MKDELTA to MKOFTEN, the agency dabbled in all sorts of neurotransmitter necromancy. The best-known was MKULTRA, and its star biologic was LSD.

The CIA theorized that Delysid, mescaline,[2] and similar hallucinatory drugs could disorient and/or disable US enemies. Failing that outcome, the early spymasters conceived of LSD as a truth

---

2. First developed from the peyote cactus in 1897 by German pharmacologist Arthur Heffter, mescaline became a staple of early psychiatry, along with psilocybin mushrooms. After discovering LSD, Dr. Hofmann synthesized both mescaline and psilocybin in the laboratory.

serum that might force spies to blab their secrets and/or act against their will.[3] Over the next twenty years, after dosing hundreds of test subjects, the agency jettisoned both theories . . . but not without collateral damage.

The most notorious early acid victim was believed to have been Frank Olson, a forty-three-year-old bacteriologist who worked on a clandestine germ warfare project for the Pentagon and the CIA. On the evening of Nov. 28, 1953, Olson supposedly leapt from a twelfth-story window of the Statler Hotel in New York City while loaded on LSD.

The first official story claimed a clinically depressed Frank Olson committed suicide. The second, offered up during a Congressional inquiry twenty years later, maintained that he flew out the window in an acid-induced trance. While admitting no culpability, the US government paid a $750,000 out-of-court settlement to Olson's heirs. President Gerald Ford publicly apologized to his widow and family.

The third and most recent claim, embraced by Olson's two surviving sons, is that the CIA permanently silenced their father after he threatened to expose the Pentagon's biological warfare program. In the 2017 documentary *Wormwood*, filmmaker Errol Morris[4] theorizes Olson was assassinated for his dissent, and that LSD's only role was that of convenient scapegoat.

While the CIA tried exploiting the worst effects of LSD, early psychonauts outside the government concentrated on the best. Humphrey Osmond and Abram Hoffer, a pair of Canadian

---

3. Both theories were exploited early and often by Hollywood. Alfred Hitchcock's *Spellbound* (1945) and Walt Disney's *Fantasia* (1940) brought hallucination to the big screen while *The Manchurian Candidate* (1962) exploited the truth serum fantasy. Delysid made its screen debut in Vincent Price's medicine cabinet in a mad scientist scene from *The Tingler* (1959).

4. His son Hamilton Morris is a psychonaut columnist for *Harper's* and producer of Hamilton's *Pharmacopeia*, a Vice TV documentary series about hallucinogens.

physicians, used Delysid to treat schizophrenic patients with limited success. When they switched to treating chronic alcoholism, however, they achieved an astounding 55 percent cure rate.[5] In dozens of studies that replicated their methods over the next decade, other clinicians reported similar results. For the first time, it appeared Western medicine had a potential weapon with which to battle addiction.

Popularizing their findings was another matter. The medical establishment refused to listen.

One of acid's earliest champions wasn't a doctor at all but, rather, the celebrated novelist Aldous Huxley. The British-born Huxley's popularity peaked in 1932 with the publication of his dystopian classic, *Brave New World.* The book made him famous but, as with so many celebrated authors before and after, Hollywood promised to make him rich. He moved to California in 1937 to cash in as a screenwriter.[6] Over the next fifteen years, Hollywood disillusioned Huxley. The money was great, but the lifestyle was vapid. He was nearing sixty before he first treated ennui with hallucinogens.

In 1953, Huxley met Dr. Osmond at a scientific conference in LA. A lifetime of literary pursuit had left the author with few answers about the meaning of life. Osmond suggested mescaline. Following his experience, Huxley famously maintained that "the doors of perception"[7] had opened for him. His account of that first

---

5. One of Osmond's patients was Bill Wilson (Bill W.), cofounder of Alcoholics Anonymous, who later declared that acid was the only drug he'd ever encountered that appeared to curb alcohol addiction.

6. *Pride and Prejudice* (1940), *Jane Eyre* (1943) and *A Woman's Vengeance* (1945) were among the screenplays he adapted that allowed him to purchase a home at the foot of the Hollywood sign. One of his unproduced scripts was an adaptation of *Alice in Wonderland* that Walt Disney commissioned in 1945. When the studio released its 1951 feature-length cartoon to a tepid box office, thirteen different writers were credited, but Huxley was not among them.

7. From William Blake's eighteenth-century book of poetry, *The Marriage of Heaven and Hell*: "If the doors of perception were cleansed everything would appear to man as it is, Infinite."

trip bore the same name: *The Doors of Perception* (1954)[8] quickly became a seminal psychonaut text.

In a subsequent exchange of letters, Huxley tried to articulate for Osmond what mescaline had revealed for him. He coined a description in rhyming couplet:

> *To make this trivial world sublime, take half a gram of phanerothyme.*[9]

Osmond responded with a couplet of his own:

> *To fathom Hell or soar angelic, just take a pinch of psychedelic.*

Osmond's description stuck. For the remainder of the Eisenhower era, Osmond and Huxley were twin beacons of the psychedelic vanguard, but a third psychonaut soon joined their ranks, spreading the gospel further and more effectively than either the Canadian psychiatrist or the British novelist.

With colorful flimflam roots uncannily similar to those of William Leonard Pickard, Alfred Matthew Hubbard—boy scientist, rum runner, soldier of fortune, and international man of mystery—made the propagation of psychedelics his life's work. His efforts earned him the titles "Johnny Acidseed" and "Captain Trips," and established his place forever in the pantheon of psychonauts.

Like Pickard, Hubbard started out as prodigy, barely out of high school before he patented a contraption that purported to power everything from vehicles to light bulbs by extracting energy out of thin air.

---

8. The book also became namesake and inspiration for the classic '60s LA acid rock group, The Doors.
9. From the Greek phanein, "to reveal," and *thymos*, "mind-soul."

The year was 1920. Though only nineteen at the time, the Kentucky wunderkind persuaded gullible newspaper reporters from coast to coast to print article after article about his discovery. "Boy Inventor Drives Boat with Mysterious Electric Air Engine—Experts Scoff," read a headline in the *Washington* (DC) *Herald*; "Boy Inventor Heads $5 million Company," proclaimed the *Oregon Daily Journal*.

A decade later, the millions had vanished, as did Hubbard Universal Generator Inc. The now-penniless boy genius apprenticed himself to a Seattle bootlegger. In a sensational federal bribery scandal that involved a boatload of booze and a US senator, Hubbard became the prosecution's star witness. His testimony sank the Senator but saved Hubbard from jail. Alas, the lure of easy bootleg money lingered. Six years later, a California jury convicted Hubbard of smuggling $1 million in Mexican liquor into the US. He got two years in federal prison.

Upon his release, Hubbard reinvented himself. Approaching middle age, he bought part ownership in a San Pedro fishing vessel, called himself Captain Al Hubbard and adopted the self-proclaimed rank of Master Mariner. He moved to British Columbia, invested in a Canadian uranium mine, and earned enough to lease a small island off the coast of Vancouver where he chartered yachts and lived like a millionaire.

And yet, like the very successful Aldous Huxley, Captain Al felt empty inside. What exactly *was* the meaning of life? His chance meeting with Humphrey Osmond changed everything, just as it had for Huxley. Hubbard took Humphrey's mescaline and became an evangelist.

In 1955, Captain Hubbard bought a PhD from a Chattanooga diploma mill and reinvented himself again, this time as Dr. Al Hubbard. He began crisscrossing the country, proselytizing like Professor Harold Hill. He wore a buzz cut, a tight-fitting khaki outfit akin to a Boy Scout uniform, and carried with him a pistol and omnipresent brown leather satchel that became the stuff of psychonaut legend: Captain Al's pharmacy-in-a-briefcase.

Exactly how he acquired his endless supply of psychedelics remained a mystery. Some believed he had CIA connections; others thought his Boy Scout uniform got him past the Marine Guard at the Pentagon and into the Defense Department's secret stash. But regardless of his sources, most subsequent psychonauts credit Captain Al with turning on America.

"We waited for him like a little old lady for the Sears Roebuck catalog," recalled Dr. Oscar Janiger, the Beverly Hills psychiatrist who was responsible for dosing Cary Grant, Jack Nicholson, Otto Preminger, Rita Moreno, and dozens of other celebrities during the 1960s.

Before his death in 1982, Hubbard allegedly introduced more than six thousand psychiatrists, politicians, actors, and artists to LSD, including such notables as Mrs. Robert F. Kennedy, *Time* magazine publisher Henry Luce, his playwright wife Claire Booth Luce, crooner Andy Williams, and Dr. Timothy Leary himself.

"He blew in with that uniform laying down the most *incredible* atmosphere of mystery and flamboyance, and *really* impressive bullshit!" Leary effused.

Claiming to know everyone from the Pope to the President, Captain Al disarmed all he met, preaching the acid gospel like an overcaffeinated used-car salesman.

"On the one hand he looked like a carpetbagger con man," said Leary, "and on the other, he had the most impressive people in the world in his lap."

While there were other voices[10] joining Captain Al's crusade, Dr. Timothy Leary clearly succeeded Hubbard as psychonaut-in-chief.

---

10. Chief among them, R. Gordon Wasson, a J.P. Morgan executive and amateur ethnomycologist who published a *Life* magazine article in 1958 about Mexican magic mushrooms, which is now credited with launching the psychedelic experience into America's cultural mainstream.

A dozen years before Richard Nixon canonized him "the most dangerous man in America," Leary was an unexceptional psychology professor who'd been bounced from his untenured post at Harvard along with Dr. Richard Alpert, another tweedy academic seduced by psychedelics. Both dropped Hubbard's acid, expanded their minds, tie-dyed their wardrobes, and set out to change the world.

Harvard president Nathan Pusey deemed them both expendable. Getting their graduate TA's high was tolerated in 1963; dosing undergrads was not. Following their extensive experimentation with students, Pusey showed them the door.

After they were banished, Leary and Alpert moved to the Hudson Valley estate of Bill and Peggy Hitchcock, the freewheeling brother and sister heirs to a fortune amassed by Gulf Oil founder William Larimer Hitchcock and multimillionaire financier Andrew Mellon. Leary and Alpert turned the Hitchcocks' sixty-four-room Millbrook mansion into an upscale ashram, then proceeded to amplify Al Hubbard's acid gospel a thousand-fold. The Hitchcocks charged rent of $1 a year. From their new digs, Leary and Alpert launched a revolution.

As famously chronicled in Tom Wolfe's *The Electric Kool-Aid Acid Test*, novelist Ken Kesey[11] paid Millbrook a visit in 1964 that was meant to link West Coast psychonauts with the East. The acid summit fizzled when Leary was too busy tripping with his girlfriend to meet the author and his busload of Merry Pranksters.

But Leary and Alpert more than made up for the faux pas. They subsequently welcomed Humphrey Osmond, psychologist/author R. D. Laing, Beat laureate Allen Ginsberg, jazz trumpeter Maynard Ferguson, and a host of other dignitaries. All made the pilgrimage; all spread the gospel.

"Jet setters, celebrities, curious aristocrats," Leary recalled. "A

---

11. The author of *One Flew Over the Cuckoo's Nest* became a psychonaut in 1958 at the V.A. hospital in Menlo Park, where the CIA paid volunteers like Kesey $75 a day to take LSD.

weekend at Millbrook was the chic thing for the hip young rich of New York. At the same time, we entertained biologists from Yale, Oxford psychologists, Hindu holy men.'"

By 1967, the Hitchcocks wearied of notoriety. Lawmen came snooping,[12] house guests got busted (including Leary), and the blue-blood brother and sister finally invited Leary and Alpert to leave—but by then, the two ex-professors had become undisputed standard bearers of the psychedelic movement.

Alpert moved to India, changed his name to Ram Dass, and wrote a 416-page *New York Times* bestseller that summed up his life's work in its title: *Be Here Now*. He came to favor navel-gazing over neuropharmacology.

Leary went the opposite direction, following fame, chemistry, and Kesey's Pranksters back to California.

"I had become a nationally recognized symbol of change," he announced with characteristic modesty.

Leary arrived in San Francisco just in time for the Summer of Love. He became the High Priest of Haight-Ashbury and his newly-minted mantra ("Turn on, tune in, and drop out"[13]) became a Boomer meme along with his bumper-sticker refrain, "Question Authority!"

On Aug. 24, 1967, Captain Al Hubbard tried to leave Bern, Switzerland, with a suitcase full of LSD. Swiss customs stopped him at the border and confiscated 4,500 ampules. They did not arrest him. European laws forbidding acid were brand new and untested at the time.

Besides, Captain Al—who insisted on being addressed as

---

12. Notably, future Watergate burglar G. Gordon Liddy, who participated in a 1966 Millbrook raid that resulted in no conviction.

13. Leary's notorious catch phrase, inspired by media guru Marshall McLuhan, became a clarion call during the first Human Be-In held on Jan. 14, 1967, at San Francisco's Golden Gate Park, where over 30,000 flower children launched the counterculture movement.

"Doctor Hubbard"—had the solemn air of a mental health professional. He told Swiss authorities he represented the International Foundation for Advanced Studies, a California medical non-profit that purported to research the effects of psychedelics on human behavior. Purely medicinal. Everything on the up and up.

No dice, said the Swiss. They sent Hubbard back home empty-handed. He'd made the trip many times before, but the halcyon days of Delysid were officially over. Under increasing international pressure, Sandoz quit making LSD in August of 1965. Hubbard's intercepted cache was among the last of the pharmaceutical company's dwindling supply.

The previous year, Dr. Hubbard testified before the California state Senate Judiciary Committee, praising the salutary effects of psychedelics. In a final desperate attempt to curb legislation that would outlaw LSD, he pointed to the work of Dr. Humphrey Osmond, Dr. Oscar Janiger, Dr. Sidney Cohen, and dozens of other legitimate physicians who'd shown how LSD could improve mental health.

Hubbard wasn't alone. No less a national icon than CBS correspondent Charles Kuralt aired an hourlong *CBS Reports* seen by millions about an alcoholic accountant who took LSD twice at a Maryland mental hospital, then never drank again.[14]

But televised testimonials, as well as the voices of Hubbard and other acid proponents, drowned beneath the scare headlines of the day: "LSD Happiness Declared Hokum";[15] "Lack of LSD Laws Hinders Police";[16] "Expert Fears LSD Ban—May Prompt Deadly Drug Use."[17]

---

14. In 2009, Arthur King and his bride of more than fifty years told the author that he'd never touched alcohol since CBS televised his LSD treatments at Maryland's Spring Grove Hospital in 1966.

15. *Los Angeles Times*, July 12, 1966

16. *Long Beach Independent Press-Telegram*, February 6, 1966

17. *San Francisco Examiner*, June 6, 1966

In its March 11, 1966, edition, *Time* warned of "An Epidemic of 'Acid Heads'":

> The disease is striking in beachside beatnik pads and in the dormitories of expensive prep schools; it has grown into an alarming problem at UCLA and on the UC campus at Berkeley. And everywhere the diagnosis is the same: psychotic illness resulting from unauthorized, nonmedical use of the drug LSD-25.
>
> Patients with post-LSD symptoms are providing the UCLA Neuropsychiatric Institute with 10% to 15% of its cases; more are flocking to the university's general medical center and the County General Hospital. By best estimates, 10,000 students in the University of California system have tried LSD (though not all have suffered detectable ill effects). No one can even guess how many more self-styled 'acid heads' there are among oddball cult groups.

Leary's public antics didn't help. He stoked growing alarm among the so-called Silent Majority with his "drop out" drumbeat. Pop culture joined the chorus. "Lucy in the Sky with Diamonds" intoned a Beatlific endorsement. When Bob Dylan sang of sons and daughters beyond their parents' command, those same mothers and fathers blamed Leary's LSD for wrecking the American Dream.

On Oct. 3, 1966, California and Nevada became the first two states to outlaw LSD. The remaining forty-eight states followed in short order, as did the federal Bureau of Narcotics and Dangerous Drugs and the Food and Drug Administration. Almost overnight, acid became a global pariah. As Al Hubbard learned when he returned from Switzerland with his empty briefcase, Delysid could no longer be had at any price.

Just as Leary, Ram Dass, and their psychonaut tsunami washed over America, the drug that launched it all seemed to have virtually disappeared. Thus began the rise of underground chemistry.

The closest any unauthorized civilian had come to duplicating the Sandoz elixir was the cookbook efforts of an oddball pair both named Bernard and both busted by the FDA on April 3, 1963. Amateur chemist Bernard Roseman met amateur hypnotist Bernard Copley six years earlier while they were hiking the desolate Joshua Tree barrens east of Palm Springs. They struck it off, tried peyote together under the stars, and became psychonaut evangelists. Like Huxley and Hubbard or Leary and Alpert before them, the Bernards sought the meaning of life from a test tube.

While Roseman struggled to master an American version of Dr. Hofmann's original formula,[18] Copley raised capital and consciousness through his Hypnosophic Institute. In 1962, he published "Hallucinogenic Drugs and Their Application to Extrasensory Perception."

Meanwhile, Roseman played trial and error with the recipe, missing a step or two in the refining process, but still came up with a crude Delysid facsimile that was sufficiently potent to attract government attention.[19] While possessing LSD was not yet a felony, it still fell under Food and Drug Administration regulation. When the Bernards began selling their wares, the FDA took notice.

Roseman and Copley were arrested and put on trial in San

---

18. Underwritten by the Pentagon, a salaried chemist for Eli Lilly and Co. named William Garbrecht refined the Sandoz process in 1954, then later patented the procedure and published the formula in the *Journal of Organic Chemistry*. The cumbersome twelve to fifteen step Garbrecht method yielded small batches of a few hundred milligrams and became a blueprint for early underground chemists, but was considered "antique" by the time LSD was outlawed in 1966.

19. At the same time the two Bernards were distributing their LSD, Aerojet General physicist Douglas George was synthesizing his own poor-quality "green goo" acid. Unlike Roseman and Copley, George never ran afoul of the FDA. He stopped his alchemy before it was outlawed.

Francisco. In the first of a long series of such prosecutions, both were found guilty in what became known as the "LSD Home Brew Case."[20] They appealed, jumped bail and eluded capture for four more years.[21]

By then, their crimes were small potatoes. Their extradition, re-arrest, and jail time barely made a media ripple. The primitive efforts of the two Bernards had been superseded many times over by acid's first master craftsman.

While Augustus Owsley Stanley III, a.k.a. Bear, is credited as America's first great LSD entrepreneur, it was his lesser-known girlfriend Melissa Cargill who actually picked up Albert Hofmann's torch. Cargill made the elixir; Bear took the credit.

"Melissa studied organic chemistry at Cal and taught Owsley a few rudiments," recalled Leonard Pickard. "But he didn't really know any chemistry. He just followed a cookbook recipe and used an antique method."

Described in an early *Los Angeles Times* profile as "a drifter, a dapper ladies' man and a professional student," Owsley found both his calling and partner at UC Berkeley in 1963. He was twenty-eight. Cargill was twenty-four.

By then, Owsley had married twice, fathered two children, spent time in a Washington DC psych ward, had been honorably discharged from the Air Force, and dropped in and out of engineering courses at the University of Virginia, Los Angeles City College, and Berkeley, where he lasted a single semester.

He wasn't dumb. Like Pickard and Hubbard, Owsley had been identified early by teachers and his patrician parents as a scientific prodigy. His father, a District of Columbia apparatchik, described

---

20. *San Francisco Examiner*, May 21, 1964.
21. Roseman fled to Mexico, Copley to Brazil. They were extradited in 1968, all but forgotten in the press.

Owsley as "emotionally unbalanced, but has a brilliant mind." His boy just couldn't seem to get on with authority. When challenged, Bear would go silent, become elusive, and, if pushed, snarl, brood, and withdraw—hence his nickname. The tips of two fingers lost in a childhood accident added to the illusion. Bear had no sense of humor, a hairy chest, and a claw for a right hand.

Owsley followed closely the trial of the two Bernards and got his first taste of acid from a friend of a friend of Douglas George. The Aerojet physicist's grody green goo might be impure, but it had enough Technicolor kick to turn Owsley on before Tim Leary ever uttered his infamous slogan. He and Cargill shared Leary's calling: they tuned in and dropped out of Berkeley together. The couple quietly plotted to enlighten Boomers with their own version of Delysid.

They set up a lab in the bathroom of their Berkeley rental and tinkered with Dr. Hofmann's original formula. Owsley scouted chemical supply houses for the raw ingredients while he networked with Ken Kesey, the Pranksters, and an emerging Berkeley blues band called the Warlocks.[22] For her part, Cargill—misidentified ever after as Owsley's "female lab assistant"—perfected their alchemy.

Berkeley cops first busted the couple's bathroom lab in 1965.[23] They were charged with making methamphetamine. Chemical analysis proved they weren't speeding at all, and LSD was still a year away from being outlawed. The court forced police to return their labware, after which they decamped to Southern California.

There, Owsley set Cargill up in another bathroom in another rental near Cal State University, Los Angeles. They began

---

22. Kesey staged his first "acid test" with Owsley tabs in November 1965, the Warlocks supplying the soundtrack. "The whole world just went kablooey," recalled Jerry Garcia. "My little attempt at having a straight life was really a fiction." Months later, he changed the band's name to the Grateful Dead.

23. The Dead commemorated Owsley's first bust in their song "Alice D. Millionaire."

stockpiling raw ingredients under the name "Bear Research Group" and sold the finished product by mail order. A blue Owsley tab the size of an aspirin was imprinted with a Batman caricature and cost $5 a hit.

"Owsley saw his role as a psychedelic Prometheus," recalled Rhoney Gissen.

His standby "old lady" in a three-way with Cargill, Gissen joined the family business after Bear dosed her with a drop of liquid LSD. He carried a Murine squeeze bottle with him at all times, wielding it like a wand among the uninitiated. Like the two wives he'd divorced before LSD, both Gissen and Cargill would each bear him a child. They remained close long after Bear left the country and the planet.

Following the example of Leary's hubris, Owsley advertised himself and his wonderful acid through word of mouth from his home base in LA, and made a fortune in the process. By the time Owsley moved back to Berkeley, the LAPD estimated Bear Research had sold or given away ten million tabs—an exaggeration very much in tune with the times.

Bear and Cargill didn't explode onto the national stage until 1967, the same year *Bonnie and Clyde* was nominated for an Academy Award. By then, the Bonnie and Clyde of acid had been transubstantiating rye fungus for over three years. Though few outside their circle of Grateful Deadheads knew their names, many knew their brand. Owsley acid was of such purity that connoisseurs still enunciate the most famous batches in hushed tones: Purple Dragon, Blue Cheer, White Lightning. . . .

Once the substance was outlawed, however, Owsley fell silent and never posed for pictures again. One of his final photos, shot in late 1967 in the hallway outside an Oakland federal courtroom, depicts a muscular, mustachioed middleweight in buckskins and ponytail rushing away from photographers. Three months earlier, he gave his name as Robert Thompson to an inquisitive reporter from the *San Francisco Examiner*. Owsley "is as elusive as a seal," reporter Mary Crawford wrote in a breathless account headlined "Exclusive Chat with Acid King":

> He has an unlisted phone number and he frequently moves to keep his address unknown. But the *Examiner* has found that he is living in "retirement" in a charming brick cottage in Berkeley, a pad he shares with his "old lady" Melissa Cargill, an attractive, plump brunette who wears thick lensed owlish glasses. . . .
>
> The barefooted, bare chested man who answered the door at Owsley's house (said), "Owsley is out of the country and he won't be back. Owsley moved out of here last spring."

Owsley's switch from Acid King to acid phantom reflected a fearful era. LSD was only one symbol of an ever-widening generation gap, but the drug's mind-blowing, myth-exploding properties made acid a most convenient scapegoat.

The times were indeed a-changing, but more so for psychonauts, it seemed, than for obedient heirs of the middle class—and not necessarily in a good way.

III.

LEONARD PICKARD LIKED TO BELIEVE he was Old School, descended from a finer tradition of psychedelic exploration dedicated to altruism and universal enlightenment. He never was, nor ever could be, a Yuppie.

He first read about LSD in junior high. He remembered *Time*, *Life*, *Look*, and the *Saturday Evening Post* alternately praising, then condemning LSD.

"I was reading a magazine in a barber shop once when I was twelve. I noticed mention of a drug that had philosophical implications," he said.

The hallucinogenic stories intrigued him, but he didn't enter the acid fraternity until years later, at the dawning of the Age of Aquarius.

After his release from the Institute of Living, he returned home to Atlanta, where not a lot had changed. His mother had divorced and remarried for a third time. His older sister wed a nascent alcoholic. His father retired from Southern Bell as a systems analyst. He and Leonard's stepmother moved to the tony suburb of Decatur. The elder Pickard became a gentleman farmer. He eventually purchased his own herd of Angus beef and joined the Georgia Cattlemen's Association.

Meanwhile Leonard floundered. His time in rehab had little

impact on his respect for the law. If anything, it killed his passion for formal education.

"I sought a greater breadth of the human condition than tenure-track would allow," he said, tongue planted firmly in cheek.

Even if Princeton had let him return, he would probably have refused to go. He settled instead near Harvard, seeking out rebel heirs of the Leary/Alpert tradition.

"Harvard Square was lively in those days," said Leonard. "I was always fond of Tim Leary's attempts to describe the ineffable. There were no elders to ask, or vast online feedback the way there is now, so people were often alone or in small groups as they encountered transcendent phenomena.

"My circles tended to be very circumscribed—just a handful of friends, but close ones. I worked in '66 and '67 at the Retina Foundation for Experimental Biology in Boston, preparing mitochondria from beef hearts for biochemists."

Pickard built a reputation as a reliable, efficient second-tier lab rat who could be depended upon to perform routine research. Soft-spoken yet uncommonly skilled, his arrest record and the time he'd spent at the Institute of Living never came up. During off hours, he dabbled in his own experiments.

"Joan Baez played Cambridge sometimes. Loved her ethereal voice," he said. "My hangout in the Square was the Blue Parrot in the basement of the Brattle Theater. I recall hearing *Sergeant Pepper* there for the first time, like no music there ever was before. Young people on Beacon Hill were dancing in the snow and giving away LSD—from whom, I wonder?"

Later that same year, Pickard headed west. California was a revelation: a land of "naked moonlight swimming, endless campfires and theology in the High Sierra, refinement of the soul in the vast deserts, finding what was of true value in the world and what was proper conduct among others."

He fondly recalled his first trip to Berkeley in '67. "I was amazed by all the long hair on Telegraph, and the obvious social movement of the times. The first large gatherings for music and be-ins. I was tear-gassed at anti-war demonstrations as barricades burned."

His dismal record at Princeton ruled out admission to Berkeley, but not employment. His experience with Boston's Retina Foundation helped him land a job with Berkeley's Department of Bacteriology & Immunology, where he worked his way up the research ladder.

"It was an extraordinary time," recalled Talitha Stills, younger sister of rock star Stephen Stills, and one of Pickard's first California companions. "Everybody was hanging around Berkeley and Stanford, whether they were enrolled or not, because they were involved in the protests."

A twenty-two-year-old college dropout, Pickard was ripe for the draft, but he'd always been on the move and never bothered to re-register. He retained his student deferment throughout the Vietnam War.

"There was no draft avoidance," he said. "I lost a cousin in Vietnam. If called, I would have gone. I thought carefully about enlisting in the Navy twice, possibly as a Corpsman. Maybe I would have been more useful that way."

Instead, he hunkered down in Berkeley's Latimer Hall and took up organic chemistry alongside a future Nobel laureate.

"While I was managing Bacteriology at Berkeley, Kary Mullis was a young PhD candidate in biochemistry, fresh from Georgia Tech," said Pickard. "As he noted in his autobiography *Dancing Naked in the Mind Fields*, Kary managed to synthesize a gram of LSD, which lit up the Biochem building most thoroughly."

Pickard speculated that Mullis made his acid using *Claviceps purpurea* (ergot) grown in Biochem's vast subterranean culture rooms. Leonard coyly suggested that a research associate such as himself would have had unfettered access to those essential ingredients.

Indeed, without mentioning Leonard by name, Mullis conceded

he was not the only impatient, impulsive Berkeley researcher tinkering with acid during the late sixties:

> As we learned very quickly, LSD was not the only mind-altering chemical. When it became illegal, we started synthesizing other chemical compounds. It usually took the government about two years from the time the formula for a new psychoactive compound was published to make it illegal. Numerous derivatives of methoxylated amphetamines were created, for example, and every one of them had a different effect on the brain.
>
> I was very careful to make only legal compounds. Other people were not. And the authorities were serious about this business. People were going to jail for chemistry.[1]

Mullis was not among them. When cops busted a fellow researcher, his biochem professor Dr. Joe Neilands took Mullis aside and warned, "If there's anything in the freezer that shouldn't be there, maybe now would be a good time to clean it out."

Paranoia infected Mullis and Pickard at the same time and for the same reasons:

> LSD somehow got connected with the anti-Vietnam War movement. Drugs had to be the reason that the youth of America had long hair, wore beads, enjoyed sex, and didn't think it was a good idea to go to a foreign country and kill the locals. Psychedelic drugs were made illegal.
>
> The one serious side effect it had, besides putting a lot of people in overcrowded jails, was to bring to an end serious research by people who knew what to look for. The only

---

1. From *Dancing Naked in the Mind Field* (Vintage, 1998), in which Mullis also extolled his belief in astrology and described an encounter with an extra-terrestrial fluorescent raccoon.

scientists permitted to work with psychoactive chemicals now were people who never used them and knew nothing about them. For the first time, science reference books were censored. Standard chemical reference books like the *Dictionary of Organic Chemicals* eliminated all mention of LSD and methamphetamine. How dare they censor reference books? It was as if an entire class of chemicals no longer existed. It was getting darker in America.[2]

Tim Scully was a tall, geeky prodigy from the East Bay headed for the same precocious glory as Kary Mullis and Leonard Pickard. Born within a year of each other, Scully mirrored Pickard's early schooling: both excelled at science and gravitated toward post-Sputnik STEM programs; both interned at nuclear think tanks;[3] both created model linear accelerators while still in their teens, and both were unmitigated nerds.

"I think I have a touch of Asperger's, although no one's ever formally diagnosed me," said Scully.

Scully and Pickard each won easy admission to prestigious universities. In Scully's case, the school was UC Berkeley. Unlike Pickard, Scully stuck it out for two years.

But once he and childhood pal Don Douglas dropped acid on April 15, 1965, all bets were off.

"We agreed that we wanted to try to make a lot of LSD and make it available to everyone," he recalled.

Scully spent weeks at the library boning up on Dr. Hofmann's problem child. He scoured the East Bay for ingredients. Eventually Owsley Stanley heard about him and came knocking at his door, but not because he wanted his help.

---

2. Ibid.
3. Lawrence Berkeley Laboratory for Scully; Argonne National Laboratory for Pickard.

Scully was twenty-one, Owsley was thirty, but they shared a passion for the Grateful Dead. Warily, Owsley got the younger man and his friend Don Douglas hired as Dead roadies. When finally satisfied they weren't narcs, he brought them on as trainees at a new lab in Point Richmond. Just weeks before California declared LSD illegal, the new Bear Research crew cranked out 300,000 doses.

The first thing Scully and Douglas learned was that making LSD is not like cooking mac and cheese. The finesse, care, and attention to detail rivaled requirements for a perfect soufflé.

"Lysergic acid compounds are very fragile, and they have to be handled with much more care than many chemists would believe," said Scully. "So someone who hasn't had experience working with those compounds is likely to not have very high yields and not get very good purity."

The Bear Research Group was all about high yield and purity. Owsley was equal parts perfectionist, huckster, and sorcerer. When standard flasks and beakers weren't sufficient, he hired a scientific glassblower to customize. He applied new coolant processes to pinpoint temperatures. He anguished over each batch like an expectant father.

Simultaneously, he consulted fortunetellers for guidance on where and when to harvest the goods. Some believed Stanley dispatched Scully and Douglas to Colorado in the winter of 1966 because newly-elected Governor Ronald Reagan swore he'd rid California of LSD. Not so, according to Bear's widow Rhoney Gissen Stanley. In her 2012 memoir, she said Bear Research secretly moved to Denver because the purest acid in the highest yields could only be produced on the east side of the Rockies during Aquarius (Jan. 20—Feb. 18).

"It is true that we often used the *I Ching* as an Oracle and that we sometimes had horoscopes drawn up," conceded Scully, though he held that the Denver move was precipitated by Reagan, not Aquarius.

Scully and Douglas started scouting a new location in Seattle, then Idaho and Wyoming, before finally leasing a house a few blocks from the Denver Zoo. They set up a sterile, dim-lit lab in the basement, per Owsley and Cargill's specifications: vacuum pumps, goosenecked flasks, yellow "bug lights" to minimize ultraviolet rays, dry-ice deep freeze, glass encased precision scales, chromatography column. . . .

The result of their painstaking efforts was 14,000 tabs of Monterey Purple, an Owsley commemorative readied just in time for the Monterey Pop Festival, officially kicking off the Summer of Love.

When Owsley and his growing entourage returned in lysergic triumph to California, Scully and Douglas stayed behind. During their time alone in Denver, Scully worked up a batch of STP, a psychoactive first created in 1963 by Dow Chemical alumnus Alexander Shulgin. Combined with further shipments of acid, the Denver deliveries kept San Francisco loaded through the Summer of Love and well into the fall.

But by December, Bear's remarkable run hit a wall. Undercover state and federal narcs descended upon Owsley's East Bay pill factory. It was there that Bear's troops converted the Scully/Douglas concoctions into tablets: 350,000 hits of acid and 1,500 doses of STP. Melissa Cargill and Rhoney Gissen were among the Bear Research associates caught in the dragnet. Buck naked except for his walrus mustache, Owsley himself was hauled away in handcuffs on Christmas Eve.

Though the Colorado contingent remained at large, Bear's bust spooked Douglas. He left Scully to break down and store the Denver lab. Soldiering on, Scully looked for a new backer. He found his angel in Billy Hitchcock. Leary's ex-landlord put up $12,000 and Scully was back in business. No longer Bear's apprentice or Douglas's partner, he needed a new sidekick. He would find him in Nick Sand.

The Brooklyn-born son of a Soviet spy, Nicholas Sand[4] took his first lysergic journey in August of 1964 at an ashram in upstate New York. Staring at heaven, he sat in a nude lotus position, perspiring before an open bonfire.

"I was floating in this immense black space," he recalled. "I said, 'What am I doing here?' And suddenly a voice came through my body, and it said, 'Your job on the planet is to make psychedelics and turn on the world.'"

Obeying the bonfire, Sand returned to Brooklyn, divorced his wife, set up a pharmacy in the attic of his mother's brownstone, and named his brave new enterprise Bell Perfume Labs.

Like Scully, Sand was self-taught. Besides mescaline, he isolated DMT in his bathtub and found it jolted into a richer euphoria if smoked, not injected—his first major contribution to psychonaut lore.

Three years older than Scully, Sand graduated from Brooklyn College in 1966 with a degree in sociology and anthropology. Several pilgrimages to Millbrook ended that career path. After consulting Alpert and Leary, Sand adopted a new goal: commando in the psychedelic army.

Before his own reincarnation as Ram Dass, Alpert named Nick official alchemist of the Original Kleptonian Neo-American Church, whose priests—known as Boo Hoos—celebrated psychedelic mass.[5] Not to be outdone, Leary created his own church and

---

4. Née Nicholas Francis Hiskey on May 10, 1941, Nick's parents Clarence and Marcia Hiskey divorced after Clarence, a chemist, was expelled from the Manhattan Project. Marcia gave her son her maiden name: Sand.

5. Psychonaut Arthur Kleps adopted the title Chief Boo Hoo in his 1966 testimony in support of psychedelics before the Senate Subcommittee on Juvenile Delinquency: "It is our belief that the sacred biochemicals such as peyote, mescaline, LSD, and cannabis are the true host of God and not drugs at all as the term is commonly understood. We do not feel that the Government has the right to interfere in our religious practice, and that the present persecution of our coreligionists is not only constitutionally illegal but a crude and savage repression of our basic and inalienable rights as human beings."

called it the League for Spiritual Discovery. Again, Sand was official alchemist.

Meanwhile back in Brooklyn, complaints rolled in from the neighbors about the smell emanating from Marcia Sand's attic. At his mother's urging, Nick moved to a dental supply building across the street from the Brooklyn Hall of Justice.

Throughout acid's peak year of 1967, Owsley remained the bodhisattva of LSD. Inevitably, Nick set out to pay his respects. He put Bell Perfume on wheels. Disguised as a meat-delivery van, his tricked-out camper featured a pot-bellied stove, a rooftop exhaust, and a half-million dollars' worth of glass tubing, chemicals, gizmos, and flasks.

On April Fool's Day, Sand and David Mantell, another budding psychonaut, blew past a border check point as they entered Colorado on their way to the West Coast. Sheriff J. J. Johnson chased them down and fined them $50 each. On principle, Sand objected. He and Mantell were rewarded with ten days in the Moffat County Jail. While they cooled their heels, the sheriff searched their van. He later claimed he'd found enough psychedelics to dose every man, woman, and child in Wyoming, Colorado, and Utah.

By the time the feds got wind, Sand and Mantell had vanished with no forwarding address. They continued on to California, where Sand turned Bell Perfume into D&H Custom Research and opened for business in an industrial zone south of San Francisco.

Mantell rented a ranch in Cloverdale, two hours north. Over the next several months, Nick honed his skills, creating STP, MDA and further batches of his eminently smokable DMT, which he sold through D&H. He still had neither the expertise, glassware, nor the ingredients to tackle LSD.

But Tim Scully did. He'd heard plenty about Nick. Though younger, Scully was far more experienced. Nick understood and accepted his junior role. Master and student. Mentor and tenderfoot.

Abbott and Costello. Over time, their roles reversed, but Scully and Sand were destined to be the dynamic duo of LSD.

Despite Billy Hitchcock's cash infusion, Colorado got too hot at the beginning of 1968. Citing illegal search and seizure, the courts ordered the return of Sand's truck, but the feds had taken notice and were closing in.

In February, Scully rented a house a few miles southeast of his first lab. While he scrounged for ingredients in Europe, Scully left his girlfriend in charge. On June 23, 1968, the landlord stopped by. The lawn was brown. No one answered the door. When he let himself in, the stench nearly flattened him. Assuming the worst, he reported a rotting corpse to the cops.

Scully's girlfriend had been in California. Upon her return, police arrested her, confiscated $25,000 in lab equipment, and demanded to know where Scully was. Now officially a fugitive, Tim laid low after he returned from Europe.

In the fall, he and Sand joined forces in California wine country. There, they cooked themselves into the history books in the basement of a remote farmhouse near the Napa Valley town of Windsor.

"Nick had been distributing the STP he made at D&H Custom Research through the Hells Angels," said Scully.

No more Angels, he told his new partner. Hard drugs and violence did not mix with acid. Sand agreed and the Damon and Pythias of LSD began baking their first batch in March of 1969: four million doses. Their eventual goal was 750 million—enough acid to foment an insurrection. They called their newest brew Orange Sunshine. All they needed was a peaceful method for getting it to the masses.

Between 1966 and 1970, the number of psychonauts in the US rose sixfold, from 168,000 to 956,000.[6]

---

6. 2002 report on psychedelic use from the federal Substance Abuse and Mental Health Services Administration.

"A great breakthrough in evolution is underway, a drastic change in the way men think,"Tim Leary preached on Valentine's Day, 1968. "With psychedelic drugs, we are learning to use all of our brain, not just the cortical fraction in which our consciousness is centered."

Furthermore, he boasted, "We have dedicated men who manufacture LSD and other psychedelics, and release them under controlled circumstances in given areas to see what will happen. One million doses were released recently in the Haight Ashbury district of San Francisco—the most ever released in one place at one time so far, but there are men now who can release up to ten million doses at a time."[7]

These unidentified Samaritans were members of the Brotherhood of Eternal Love, a cheeky title that evolved out of Leary's smug love of irony. Like his League for Spiritual Discovery, the Brotherhood was a New Age religious order that laid claim to First Amendment protection. As such, not only did the loose-knit cabal of beach bums and bikers claim psychedelics as sacraments; their organization was also tax exempt.[8]

The Brotherhood operated out of a Laguna Beach bong shop under the leadership of a charismatic ex-con named John Griggs.[9] Over time, the hemp denizens of Laguna's Mystic Arts World emporium became an affluent cult that funded itself chiefly through acid sales. By 1968, the Brotherhood was rich enough to afford its own mountain retreat near the Southern California resort community of Idyllwild. Around the same time, despite Leary's boasts of a limitless supply, its primary source of LSD dried up.

---

7. From "Leary Seeks 'Wise Man of Century' Title," *Long Beach Independent*, Feb. 15, 1968.

8. In 1966, the California Franchise Tax Board granted the Brotherhood exempt status.

9. Griggs, a.k.a. The Farmer, a.k.a. The Hippie Messiah, was a small-time motorcycle gangster until he dropped acid and evolved into the enlightened godfather and CEO of the Brotherhood of Eternal Love. He died aspirating his own vomit following an overdose of Swiss psilocybin crystals on Aug. 3, 1969.

"(Leary)'s living in a different world than we do," said Lt. Norman H. Currie, narcotics chief of the San Francisco Police Department. "There has been no indication of an upsurge in LSD. In fact, we're not turning up much more than six months ago, and a lot less than a year ago."

Following his Christmas Eve bust in 1967, Augustus Owsley Stanley III had been effectively neutralized. He continued fighting the good fight, but it was ultimately a losing battle. While legal fees drained his coffers, narcs followed him everywhere. Cooking acid became impossible.

"To Bear, the manufacture of LSD was the right of personal domain and a victimless crime," said his newest old lady, Rhoney Gissen Stanley.[10] "It was only after he was in prison that his viewpoint changed. It was sad to see him let it go. Prison made him a bona fide outlaw and an enemy of his country."

Owsley was not suited for confinement. During his first week in jail, another prisoner broke his nose. He could disguise himself all he wanted, but with each court appearance he was fast becoming as notorious as Tim Leary. Owsley envied the anonymity of Scully and Sand. The slow defanging of the Bear left an acid vacuum that his two apprentices were more than happy to fill. The Brotherhood needed product; Tim and Nick gave them Sunshine.

At the end of the sixties, LSD resurged not only in Lt. Currie's territory, but all across the globe. Before the feds figured it out, the Brotherhood created an international network that stretched from Maui to Marseilles, and the Sunshine twins—Tim and Nick—fed the pipeline with the finest acid ever made. The Brotherhood augmented its acid exports with a flourishing marijuana and hashish import business, inventing new and creative ways to dodge customs: packing hollowed-out surfboards; loading tire wells, mufflers and gas tanks with product; flying drugs in with Cessnas; swallowing loaded balloons to be harvested later from the toilet bowl.

---

10. Gissen took Owsley's last name after bearing his son, Starfinder.

But the tide slowly turned in the government's favor. Richard Nixon followed Ronald Reagan's law and order example when he entered the White House. Like California's antidrug crusader (who'd been instrumental in bringing down Owsley), Nixon declared war on drugs[11] in general, and Tim Leary in particular.

The day after Christmas, 1968, Laguna Beach police busted Leary, wife Rosemary, daughter Susan, and son Jack as they cruised past Brotherhood headquarters. By his own count, Leary had been previously arrested a dozen times: "My daughter has been arrested eight times, my son six, my wife twice...."

Cops found two roaches that Leary swore were planted. They impounded his car and arrested the entire family.

Three years earlier, the Learys had been similarly rousted crossing the border at Laredo, Texas. Susan, then a minor, hid Rosemary's cannabis in her underwear. During that first encounter with the law, Leary gallantly took the rap, for which he was rewarded with a thirty-year prison sentence, subsequently overturned on appeal.

As charges mounted and appeals continued, the Learys managed to remain out on bail, but Dr. Tim's defense strategy was the exact opposite of the now-silent Owsley.

"I cannot abide his lust for publicity," said Bear. "He is a magnet for attention."

Leary amplified his crusade, babbling to anyone with a press pass. He ratcheted up defiance with a run for California Governor in 1970:[12] a mock campaign that ended with his long-delayed imprisonment for the Laguna Beach bust.

Leary and the Bear both went off to prison in 1970. Owsley kept

---

11. At a June 18, 1971, press conference, Nixon declared drug abuse "public enemy number one."

12. His campaign slogan "Come together, join the party," inspired John Lennon's "Come Together" which became Leary's campaign song. His war with Reagan extended into his Presidency when Leary mocked Nancy Reagan's "Just say no" anti-drug slogan with a bumper sticker that advised, "Just say know."

his profile low; Leary mugged for the camera at every opportunity. America's first two acid outlaws would continue muted protest for decades to come, but their dream of dosing humanity into mass epiphany ended with the clang of a jail cell door.

That left the Brotherhood and its Sunshine boys to carry on.

In the spring of 1969, federal agents arrested Tim Scully in California on a fugitive warrant based on the previous year's Denver raid. He made bail, but faced fifty-six years. Over the next several months, Scully commuted to Colorado for court dates, paranoia his constant companion.

When Scully picked up a tablet machine in Chicago one day during the summer of 1970, he noticed a vaguely familiar profile passing him on the street. Couldn't quite place it, but the face stayed with him. After he rented a truck to cart the machine back to the West Coast, he saw another vehicle parked nearby with another familiar face behind its wheel. The driver ducked, trying to look inconspicuous.

Scully wrinkled his brow. He wasn't hallucinating.

"I'd always been able to lose them in the past, but not this time," he recalled.

Scully wound up abandoning the incriminating machine in Pocatello, Idaho. His attorney later re-sold it to a candy company.

When he finally did return home, the paranoia didn't dissipate. During a lab accident one day, he caught a whiff of acid fumes, later glanced out a kitchen window and saw ghostly feds lurking behind every bush.

"A clear message from my unconscious that it was time for me to quit," he said.

Scully put the brakes on, but Nick Sand didn't—nor would he. Ever.

Cozying up to Billy Hitchcock, Scully's far more defiant junior partner learned to love the money associated with LSD as much as or more than he did the evangelism. Hitchcock was his man.

During an acid séance once at Millbrook, Leary had asked Billy what enlightenment meant to him. Hitchcock answered, "Being better able to predict the stock market." Despite a hefty trust fund that yielded $15,000 a month, Hitchcock never gave up arbitrage. He loved the trading floor as much as he did Leary's pharmaceuticals. Nick began to model himself after Hitchcock.

After evicting Leary and Alpert from Millbrook, Hitchcock relocated to Sausalito in '68. There he brokered the first summit meeting between Brotherhood leaders and the Sunshine twins. He laundered Bear's cash reserves[13] and bankrolled Leary. According to the government, Hitchcock kept both Scully and Sand on $12,000 annual retainers—an allegation Scully disputed.

"Billy Hitchcock did not pay Nick or me to do any chemistry," he said. He did loan Scully money, however, at three-to-one interest.

Hitchcock seemed to favor Nick over Scully. He helped Sand open an account at the Nassau branch of Fiduciary Trust[14] under the alias Alan Bell. It was Nick, too, whom Hitchcock hooked up with a spooky expat named Ronald Hadley Stark[15] who operated

---

13. "Billy Hitchcock knew a friendly Bahamian banker who was willing to fly to Manhattan and pick up Bear's cash, open an account for him under the name of Robin Goodfellow and fly back to the Bahamas to deposit the cash for him," said Scully.

14. A wholly-owned subsidiary of Investors Overseas Services, a global money laundromat founded by con man Bernard Cornfeld to aid US expatriates in avoiding income tax.

15. Credited with being the first psychonaut to extract oil from hashish, Stark ran the Belgian lab with the same attention to the bottom line as Hitchcock. With a net worth of $1,400 in 1964, Stark's income purportedly rose to $1.2 million four years later when he vanished permanently into the acid underground. For decades, Leonard Pickard operated on the false assumption that Stark was a CIA plant, working both sides of the LSD revolution. According to Scully, he was nothing more than a very clever con man. He wasn't even a chemist. Psychonaut Tord Svenson made the Belgian acid. Stark just sold it.

   In 2011, Pickard obtained Stark's DEA file through a Freedom of Information request and debunked any romance surrounding the Brotherhood renegade. Italian police arrested him in 1975 for conspiring with fascists. According to Italian court records, he entered the Middle East drug world in order to infiltrate and inform upon European terrorist groups. Sentenced to fourteen years, he continued to associate with the Red Brigades in prison while maintaining his CIA contacts. Released on appeal in 1979, he fled Italy and died in San Francisco of heart disease on May 8, 1984.

the Brotherhood's Belgian LSD lab, far from the prying eyes of US authorities.

Nick returned from the Bahamas with big ideas. He closed the Windsor lab, pooled his money with David Mantell, and moved into the Cloverdale ranch where he rebooted the acid operation. In the fall of '69, Nick started yet another company: Tekton Development, dedicated to the manufacture and/or acquisition of LSD labware.

As Scully's fervor waned, Sand's big ideas ballooned. The Belgian lab produced a pound of second-rate "brown" acid that needed purification, but Scully refused the task. Sand rented another lab house near Palm Springs and undertook the process on his own. He scoffed at Scully's paranoia as both unfounded and irritating.

Except that it wasn't.

After bagging Leary and the Bear, Nixon's Justice Department ratcheted up its dragnet. A flood of frightening headlines fueled the emerging War on Drugs: mostly made-up accounts of teens leaping from fire escapes or wandering into freeway traffic. Government propaganda also spread unfounded rumors that LSD could warp the DNA of the unborn.

When the twenty-one-year-old daughter of right-wing TV personality Art Linkletter leapt to her death from a Hollywood highrise in October of 1969, Linkletter used his celebrity to condemn LSD.[16] He repeatedly testified that Diane Linkletter's suicide happened while she was tripping, even though investigators found no supporting evidence.

Further alarmed by the notorious crimes Charles Manson's family committed while allegedly under acid's influence,[17] Congress

---

16. Linkletter held a press conference the day after his daughter died, declaring she "wasn't a suicide. She was not herself. She was murdered by the people who manufacture and distribute LSD."

17. Patty Hearst and Dr. Jeffrey MacDonald also invoked acid as the underlying demon in their notorious crimes.

rushed to judgment. Determined to ban LSD just as they had banned booze during the Roaring Twenties, lawmakers made mere possession a federal crime. Thousands would go to jail, some for decades.

Scully's fear was not imagined. Like Owsley, he got the government's message. Nick Sand remained oblivious.

To his everlasting regret, Leonard Pickard never met Captain Al or Tim Leary. Same with Humphrey Osmond and Huxley, and the whole inaugural generation of psychonauts.

He began writing to Owsley, but not until decades after the elusive Bear really *did* leave the country. In 1996, Owsley settled permanently in the Australian outback with yet another new "old lady," far from the prying eyes of The Man. He and Pickard struck up a correspondence in 2006 when Leonard asked his participation in a "Future Drugs" book project, but it withered once Pickard discovered the role model of his youth had devolved into an obsessive crank with scant interest in chemistry or medicine.

"He was emphatic about 'cyclonic storms' ravaging the hemispheres. Hence, his move to Australia," said Pickard.

By then, Owsley had become a recluse. He survived on red meat, a Murine squeeze bottle of liquid LSD, and sales of Grateful Dead wearable art that he sold over the Internet. If he'd ever actually earned millions from his acid days, the money was long gone. So was enlightenment. He combined astrology with climate change and concluded the world would end sooner rather than later. A hovel in the Aussie bush, he advised Pickard, was the only safe place to ride out the apocalypse.

"I discontinued writing to him," said Pickard.

Watching Bear degenerate from fearless hippie to carnivorous survivalist was a bitter pill to swallow. Leonard had picked up the psychonaut baton where Owsley left off. He'd expected more from the original Acid King, but Bear quit making LSD long before Tim Leary went to jail and Congress declared acid a Schedule One drug. It was 1970, when the "Me" decade began, and enlightened revolution regressed to narcissism.

IV.

By October of 1971, a federal task force secretly targeted Nick Sand and Tim Scully for tax evasion, drug sales, and acid manufacture. They became part of a larger probe aimed at taking down the entire Brotherhood of Eternal Love.

But Nick and Tim were no longer a team. Scully had given up chemistry for psychology, devoting his share of the Sunshine profits to researching the emerging field of biofeedback.

Sand remained devoted to the psychedelic cause. In April of 1972, he moved to St. Louis. Under the alias Leland H. Jordan, he bought a building in which he founded Signet Research and Development. In addition, Nick and his new partner, girlfriend/chemist Judy Shaughnessy, rented an aging manse in the nearby suburb of Fenton, where they set up a small lab in the basement to augment the larger one at Signet.

That summer, investigators drilled into Nick's safety deposit box at his bank back in San Francisco. They found a stash of STP. They also subpoenaed his tax attorney to testify before a grand jury investigating the Brotherhood. The attorney, Peter Buchanan, tipped off Scully, Hitchcock and Sand, but only Tim and Billy fled the country.

"We left to avoid the possibility of being subpoenaed and forcibly immunized, thus giving us a choice between prison or testifying against our friends," said Scully.

On August 5, 1972, the task force[1] indicted twenty-nine members of the Brotherhood, including Nick Sand. Scully was named an unindicted co-conspirator. In coordinated raids across the state, as well as in Hawaii and Oregon, sixteen were arrested. Police confiscated one-and-a-half million tabs of LSD, thirty gallons of hashish oil, and two-and-a-half tons of hash. Sand and Scully were not among those arrested.

Four months later, the total number of indictments expanded to forty-six. The Sunshine boys remained in the wind, but Operation BEL was well underway, and closing in fast.

Leonard Pickard read each dispatch, digested each rumor, mapped out each strategy that the renegade chemists had at their disposal. When Brotherhood of Eternal Love "wanted" posters went up in post offices across the land, Pickard memorized the name and face of every outlaw.

"I saw the actual DEA[2] flyer, with about eighty[3] photos," he recalled. "San Francisco, '73. That would be quite the collector's item these days."

The twenty-eight-year-old Berkeley lab manager mined newspaper articles as if they were treasure maps. He savored the details: Nick Sand's smokable DMT; Ronald Stark's Belgian hash oil distillery; the murky Czech origins of lysergic essentials like ergotamine tartrate. The personalities were never enough; Leonard lusted after the alchemy.

Since he first arrived in California, Pickard had tracked every phase of the government's cat-and-mouse game, beginning with the Bear, segueing to Tim Leary, and now, the Brotherhood itself.

---

1. Members included US Customs, the State Department, Bureau of Narcotics and Dangerous Drugs, and the California and US Departments of Justice, among others.
2. California Bureau of Narcotic Enforcement; DEA did not yet exist.
3. A gallery of twenty-six photos.

The chase became an obsession—a primer on how to keep on cooking while dodging narcs.

"Please keep in mind that I am not putting down Owsley, Nick, or Tim," he said. "Quite the opposite. As I began to study carefully these systems, I was honored to know them."

But only vicariously. Meeting his heroes in the flesh would come later, and would be a one-sided triumph, like that of a fan securing celebrity selfies.

Pickard had been following the Brotherhood's exploits long before the organization bankrolled Tim Leary's notorious 1972 escape from a California prison camp. Leonard devoured every episode of the fugitive professor's globetrotting misadventures:

- How the Weather Underground spirited Leary and wife Rosemary out of the country on false passports, securing them asylum in Algeria;
- How they were literally held prisoner by Eldridge Cleaver, the self-exiled Black Panthers' Minister of Defense;
- How they escaped to Switzerland, where the Learys split up;
- How Tim was once again imprisoned, this time by a Swiss arms dealer who wanted to force him to write his memoirs from jail;
- How Tim again escaped, hooked up with jet-setting girlfriend Joanna Harcourt-Smith, fled to Austria, then flew on to Afghanistan;
- And how his turncoat son-in-law finally tricked him into the custody of a CIA agent, who returned Leary to the US, and to prison.

Nick Sand's odyssey was neither so dramatic nor far-reaching as Leary's, but just as fraught with missteps. While the Learys navigated Algeria and Switzerland, Nick and Judy Shaughnessy left their new Missouri home for a long vacation.

In their absence, their mailbox spilled over with unopened mail, leading their postal carrier to alert police. The cops found water leaking from beneath the front door: a water line had burst. When they entered to stop the leak, officers discovered a lab in the basement and what appeared to be opium in an upstairs bedroom.

On January 19, 1973, Nick and Judy returned home to arrest warrants and possession charges.

That same day on the other side of the country, Leary landed at LAX in irons. His CIA handler handed him over to California authorities to serve out a ten-year sentence for marijuana possession.

And the following day, Richard Nixon began his second term as President, announcing dramatic progress in his ongoing War on Drugs.[4] The Nixon Administration was making good on its vow to wipe Leary's LSD legacy off the map.

On July 1, 1973, the federal Bureau of Narcotics and Dangerous Drugs officially merged with the Office of Drug Abuse Law Enforcement to create the new Drug Enforcement Administration. The agency's first mandate: obliterate the Brotherhood of Eternal Love.

When the Senate Judiciary Committee held hearings on the Brotherhood in October of 1973, tales of the so-called "hippie mafia" brought out Pickard's antiauthoritarian thrill junkie. Each

---

4. Shortly before his death in 1999, Nixon aide John Ehrlichman told author Dan Baum that the War on Drugs had been nothing more than a re-election political ploy:

"The Nixon campaign in 1968, and the Nixon White House after that, had two enemies: the antiwar left and black people. You understand what I'm saying? We knew we couldn't make it illegal to be either against the war or black, but by getting the public to associate the hippies with marijuana and blacks with heroin, and then criminalizing both heavily, we could disrupt those communities. We could arrest their leaders, raid their homes, break up their meetings, and vilify them night after night on the evening news. Did we know we were lying about drugs? Of course we did."

day's news produced another chapter: the clandestine labs, the exotic drug smuggling, the hiding in plain sight. The Man had a new acronym: DEA. Nick Sand and Tim Scully stood out as heroes and martyrs.

By then, Scully and Billy Hitchcock had returned to the US. No longer in the Sunshine business at all, Scully went legitimate with Aquarius Electronics, an acoustic and biofeedback specialty firm. Nonetheless, he and Sand were both indicted. Nick was held without bail in a St. Louis jail, but Scully turned himself in and was granted freedom pending trial. Of the three original Orange Sunshine creators, only Billy snitched.

As a trust fund heir and stock market speculator, Hitchcock was correctly singled out as the weak link. With steady pressure from prosecutors, he turned on the Brotherhood, naming names and delivering damning testimony in exchange for immunity. He encouraged Scully to do the same, and when Tim declined, Hitchcock loaned Scully $10,000 to hire an attorney.

When the trial of Scully and Sand[5] began in San Francisco's US District Court on November 12, 1973, Billy Hitchcock was the prosecution's star witness. Judy Shaugnessy stood outside the door, handing out buttons to all who entered. They read, "We're all in this together."

Inside, Leonard Pickard offered long-stemmed roses to the defendants' supporters.

"I later learned the prosecution thought I was some musician celebrity," he said. "Perhaps it was the dark blue velvet jacket, or the necklace of stars and moons."

He secured an introduction to Judy Shaugnessy and they sat

---

5. Dr. Lester Friedman, a forty-four-year-old chemistry professor at Cleveland's Case Western Reserve University, was also tried, but on a lesser charge of advising Sand and Scully on the making of LSD. He was acquitted, but subsequently convicted of perjury and did six months in prison.

through the entire trial together, making notes, trading comments, and taking names.

"I watched Billy testify, from his first word to his last," said Pickard. "He was responsible for bringing down the Brotherhood of Eternal Love. As *the* fundamental co-conspirator, he had some tax problems in Switzerland, and his father told him he would be disinherited if he didn't cooperate. He stood to lose $500 million."

The Sunshine boys, however, stood to lose their freedom. Regardless, they remained unrepentant. Sand declined to testify. When Scully took the stand, he bluntly told federal Judge Samuel Conti that the only thing he was guilty of was wanting to "turn on the world."

He also maintained he and Sand hadn't even been making LSD. The Orange Sunshine confiscated by the DEA, he said, was actually an analog called ALD-52. Although ALD-52 induced hallucinations similar to acid, it had not yet been classified illegal under federal law. He and Sand always tried to stay "one step ahead of the government," he proudly told the jury.

Pickard had to know more.

"There was a break," Scully recalled, "and I walked out into the hall, and Leonard introduced himself as a fellow chemist."

The tall, clean-shaven golden boy with the winning grin and haystack head of hair bore no resemblance at all to Scully's typical Haight Asbury hippie fan. Scully shook Pickard's hand, then gave him his full attention. Within moments, it was clear that they spoke the same language. Scully introduced Pickard to Sand and another friendship was born. Speaking in the oblique manner he'd developed since he first stormed the psychonaut fraternity, Pickard offered his services.

"From my notes of the era," he said, "people were going undercover, so to speak, to tease out the government's intent on Nicky and Tim, playing whatever game would yield useful data, including identifying the friendly opposition, their cars, surveillance methods, the questions they asked. A kind of reverse investigation."

Eternally fond of psychonaut subterfuge, Pickard made up code to throw off eavesdroppers. Counterintelligence was known as pulling an "Ivy Mike." The Sunshine boys shared his paranoia: the DEA lurked everywhere.

"I recall Tim got into a jam once because he popped out of a car, knowing the opposition would be following him," said Pickard. "He snapped their photo down a one-way street, then circulated the images."

Under the headline "Hunting the Nark Can Be Quite a Lark," the *Berkeley Barb* published Scully's embarrassing photos of fumbling narcs.

"Judge Conti was not amused," said Scully.

Aiming for irony, Pickard handed Scully a lapel pin worn by soldiers of the US Army Chemical Warfare Group.[6] To the uninitiated, the emblem seemed to be a crossed set of Florence flasks that resembled bronzed testicles.

"The golden insignia was not a flask and test tube design, but crossed retorts: an ancient alchemical distillation glassware," explained Pickard. "I owned several in my early teens."

Scully understood the subtext immediately.

"He was trying to express some brotherhood of underground chemists," he said.

For psychonauts, the irony went even deeper.

"In the insignia, the retorts cross over a hexagon representing the basic organic chemical structure of benzene, from which most organics are built," Pickard explained. "That includes LSD, mescaline, phenethylamines, and thousands of other medicines."

---

6. From 1955 through 1975, the Army tested a wide range of psychedelics on soldiers at its Edgewood Arsenal Medical Laboratories in Maryland. Dosing hundreds of enlisted volunteers in top-secret studies, Chemical Corps physicians recorded the effects of LSD and its incapacitating cousin, benzilate (BZ), which induced hallucinations and was weaponized during Vietnam.

Months later, Pickard similarly cemented his kinship with Sand.

"Nick and I spent quite a few days together after his trial," he said. "Nicky saw a ring I was wearing and asked to have it. It was heavy gold and bore an inscription of the Egyptian god of medicine. I gave it to him as a talisman."

A talisman, as it happens, that didn't work very well. The trial ended in February with guilty verdicts. Judge Conti sentenced the pair on March 8, 1974.

"Call it what you will: the psychedelic movement, the Brotherhood of Eternal Love, which sold some of this LSD, or the Hells Angels," raged Judge Conti. "It all ends in the degradation of mankind and society. I think deterrence should be given preference in determining sentences, or else you are going to see anarchy in this country."

The judge made examples of the Sunshine boys. Despite, or perhaps *because* of his righteous indignity in the courtroom, Scully got twenty years.

"I can say with 20/20 hindsight that if you're guilty you should never get on the witness stand," he said.

Nick Sand's apparent reward for keeping silent was a lesser sentence of fifteen years. For cooperating with the government, Hitchcock was fined a mere $20,000 and his five-year sentence was suspended.

Sand and Scully spent much of 1974 behind bars at McNeil Island penitentiary in Washington. They eventually made bail while their attorneys pursued appeals.

Sand married Judy Shaughnessy in the meantime, moved to a houseboat in Sausalito, and began studying to become an operating-room assistant. Scully resumed his biofeedback/computer business at his new home near Mendocino. Neither risked a return to underground chemistry.

To demonstrate his continuing support, Pickard put $5,000 on his American Express card for a rare lithograph by the Dutch artist

M.C. Escher. He gave it to Scully, who sold it to defray his legal expenses.

"American Express appeared later on and cut my card in half with a big pair of shears," said Pickard.

Sand ran low on legal funds too. As partial payment to his attorney, Michael Kennedy, Nick asked Leonard to help him move an 800-pound red agate Nepalese Buddha to Kennedy's San Francisco office.

Neither Buddha nor the Escher lithograph helped. They still lost.

In rejecting the Sunshine boys' 1976 appeal, the Ninth Circuit excused the fledgling DEA's missteps:

> The drug case involved laboratories in California, Missouri, and possibly in Europe. The tax case involved the transfer of cash from the United States through secret accounts in the Bahamas to other secret accounts in Switzerland. That government agents failed to grasp quickly the existence or scope of the enterprise is hardly surprising.

Tim Scully returned to McNeil Island on March 15, 1977, intent on making the best of a bad deal. While a public defender continued his appeals, Scully's interests switched permanently to biofeedback. He earned a PhD in psychology behind prison walls and entered the Internet Age well-grounded in computer technology.

"One of the least productive things a person can do is assume the victim stance," he said recently. "At the time, when my friend Don Douglas and I chose to make LSD, we were keenly aware of the fact that we were likely to end up spending a significant amount of time in prison. Almost everyone who's been busted for making LSD was well aware of the likely penalties. As they say in the big house, if you can't do the time, don't do the crime."

Nick Sand followed a different path. He posted, then jumped, his $50,000 bail.

"Nicky learned that he would be gathered up early to preclude flight," said Pickard. "They came into the houseboat in Sausalito two weeks before he was to surrender. Alas, he and his wife had already departed. Imagine that."

Pickard visited the houseboat shortly after the couple vanished.

"Just an empty one room, drifting afloat in the water," he recalled. "Mattress on the floor, Gods-eye on the wall . . . all the spirits had fled. I turned and left with a certain sadness, and happiness."

The only thing Sand left behind of any value was a canary-yellow Mercedes that his attorney drove for years thereafter. Kennedy called it his "Yellow Submarine."

Despite their clumsy debut, DEA agents could claim victory on several fronts in the War on Drugs. Before Watergate ushered President Nixon from office, Timothy Leary settled in at Folsom State Prison in a cell right next to Charles Manson. He was transferred to a federal facility, but served only two years before his 1976 parole, prompting many to suspect Tim was a DEA snitch—a charge that tarred him for the rest of his life.

Ram Dass and Allen Ginsberg turned on him. His son Jack told reporters "he'd inform on anybody if he could get out of jail."

He did indeed inform on friends, including his own lawyers and ex-wife Rosemary. When he walked out of prison, Leary walked into the Witness Protection Program.

Augustus Owsley Stanley III served two years behind bars, swearing he'd never cook another batch of acid. Indeed, upon his release, he resumed his side career as chief acoustics engineer for the Grateful Dead and remained as far backstage as possible. He perfected the band's legendary wall of sound, but publicly eschewed LSD.

The remaining members of the Brotherhood of Eternal Love either overdosed, did their time[7], or went so deep underground that the DEA never found them.

---

7. Sand's confederate David Mantell was captured and convicted after the Scully-Sand trial. He served two years.

Back inside McNeil Island, Tim Scully bore down on his computer/biofeedback research. Credited with a breakthrough in quadriplegic cyber communication that unlocked crippled voices, Scully achieved success after success. The Washington State Junior Chamber of Commerce honored him as its 1978 man of the year. Headlines underscored his feats. "He's a Genius!" read one; "Scully's Brilliant Past," read another.

His nemesis, Judge Samuel Conti, was reluctantly persuaded to halve Scully's sentence, but insisted he serve all ten years.

"Before you start considering rehabilitation and probation, which so many bleeding hearts advocate today, you have to punish the offender," he said. "What happens to the victims of this very brilliant individual . . . those thousands and thousands of pills ingested by humanity?"

Over the judge's objections, Scully was released early to a San Francisco halfway house in August of 1979. He returned to Mendocino where he continued his career as a computer engineer. He wrote and lectured on software, parapsychology and a range of other New Age topics, but never LSD.

Sometime later, Leonard Pickard stopped in for a visit. Eager to discuss the Brotherhood's glory days, he pressed and prodded.

"He wanted to compare and contrast methods of making acid," said Scully. "All I could do is be friendly and offer him a cup of tea."

The September day in '76 when he abandoned his name, his Mercedes, and his Sausalito houseboat, Nick Sand disguised himself as a vacationing angler intent on catching the last Canadian salmon of the season. A girlfriend drove him to the British Columbian border where he entered under the alias Ted Parody (Theodore Edward Parody III), and settled in the rural hamlet of Lumby (pop. 1,731). Judy joined him in November. They took up the cultivation of psilocybe mushrooms as a cash crop.

A veteran of subterfuge, Sand spent a few days each year in a

Vancouver office building researching the names and birth dates of dead infants who'd expired around the time of Nick's own birthday. He made copies of birth certificates and kept them tucked away. Ted Parody was an apt, if tongue-in-cheek alias, but he had several faux IDs in reserve just in case anyone got nosy and he needed to switch up in a hurry.

On a grocery resupply trip to Vancouver in the spring of 1978, a friend recommended a book by the Indian mystic Bhagwan Shree Rajneesh.[8] Nick read it and then another and another. Rajneesh meditated with the best of them, but he had no time for the poor and downtrodden. Here was a hedonist with a taste for the good life—right up Nick's alley.

He and Judy agreed: they had to make a pilgrimage to the Bhagwan's ashram in the Indian city of Pune. It took the better part of a year, but they saved enough from mushroom sales for airline tickets for themselves and Nick's infant daughter, Sorrel.

Once they established themselves at the ashram, Nick traded in the name Ted Parody for Pravasi. He and Judy endeared themselves to Rajneesh and his "sannyasins"[9] (followers) by creating a hydroponic garden, supplying the cult with fresh produce.

The Pravasi/Sand family did well enough with vegetable sales

---

8. In his autobiography, Rajneesh Chandra Mohan maintained he was born in his first incarnation seven hundred years ago in the mountains of western India and lived to be 106 years old. In his most recent incarnation, he was born Dec. 11, 1932, to a family of cloth merchants in the town of Kuchwada. He was born again on March 21, 1953, when the University of Jabalpur undergrad became Bhagwan (the Blessed One) Shree Rajneesh. He grew a waist-length beard and kept his unruly hair in place with a knit stocking cap. His robes were white and his eyes either enchanting or Rasputin, depending upon who beheld them. Even through his thick Indian accent, his English bore a strong lisp. The "enlightened master" had asthma and a bad back most of his life. He died Jan. 19, 1990, of heart disease, having been reborn once again the previous year—this time as a Buddhist named Osho. He was fifty-eight.

9. Each follower carried a "mala" with them at all times: a wooden necklace of 108 beads and a portrait of Rajneesh.

to purchase a two-story home fifteen minutes away from the ashram. Nick and Judy lived on the ground floor and built an LSD lab on the second. Once he located a reliable source of ergotamine tartrate, Nick was back in business. For the next two years, he and Judy satisfied the acid needs not just of Rajneesh but much of the Middle East.

In 1981, the Pravasi/Sand family returned to the US, accompanied by Rajneesh himself. The guru aimed to bring his affluent teachings to the West Coast. He began by buying a 125-square-mile ranch near Antelope, Oregon, about 120 miles southeast of Portland. He paid $6 million for the spread he called Rajneeshpuram. How much Nick's chemistry may have contributed to the $1.5 million cash down payment was never established.

The Bhagwan's first order of business was to upgrade the ranch's rolling stock. The first year alone, he acquired a fleet of twenty-one Rolls Royces for the use of his 540 closest disciples who, like the Pravasi family, lived rent-free on the ranch. From his brand-new Rajneesh Neo-Sanyas International Commune headquarters, the serene soothsayer spread good life gospel through more than four hundred meditation centers[10] that he established in store fronts and shopping malls around the world.

The good life didn't last. Rajneeshpuram imploded about the same time as Nick's marriage. In 1985, both the media and IRS auditors questioned the religious exemption Rajneesh claimed in his failure to pay taxes. At the same time, Judy questioned Nick's ongoing affair with a German sannyasin named Varuni. Neither the cult nor the marriage survived.

---

10. Meditation and growth programs such as "Rajneesh Tai Chi Intensive" and "Rajneesh Dynamic Bodywork" ran from $90 to $130 per session. Books, tapes, posters, ashtrays, cigarette lighters, bottle openers, and other items were priced more economically. Nearly thirty years after his death, Rajneesh's meditation centers have increased to over 750 in sixty countries.

Judy and Sorrel remained in Oregon. Nick and Varuni high-tailed it once more across the Canadian border. Facing arson, attempted murder, tax evasion, and drug smuggling charges, the Bhagwan sought asylum in twenty-one countries, was refused, and reluctantly returned to finish out his days at his ashram in Pune.

Nick may have lost faith in Judy and Rajneesh, but not in neuro-pharmacology. He and his newest consort resumed farming magic mushrooms, branched out into hydroponic weed and eventually shucked it all for gold mining. A legal skirmish involving the latter nearly exposed Ted Parody to be Nick Sand, so he changed names once more and left Canada.

For two years in the late 1980s, Nick was a man without a coun-try or a woman. After Varuni left him, he began an odyssey that took him through Mexico, Belize, and parts south. He returned to Canada as David Roy Shepard and resumed cannabis cultivation, working out a process to extract THC oil.

From there, he moved on to manufacture virtually every other known psychedelic as well as a few unknowns. He settled down with Gina "Usha" Raetze, his newest new old lady, and they set up a newer, bigger, better lab in the Vancouver suburb of Port Coquitlam. It quickly became a factory, grinding out more and better LSD, DMT, MDA, and MDMA than Leary or the Brotherhood ever could have hallucinated.

When the Royal Canadian Mounted Police finally busted David Roy Shepard on September 26, 1996, they arrested him in posses-sion of eleven pounds of DMT, eight pounds of MDMA, eleven pounds of MDA, five-and-a-half pounds of ergotamine tartrate, and about one-and-a-half ounces of LSD. It took authorities three months to unravel his true identity.

V.

"THERE WERE SIX," SAID LEONARD Pickard.

The half-dozen chemists to whom Leonard attached himself descended from a different tradition, parallel to that of Nick Sand and Tim Scully, Dr. Leary and the Bear, but with zero publicity. The Six learned from the mistakes of the Brotherhood of Eternal Love, though none among the Brothers ever knew the Six even existed. The Six survived through their silence.

"The Jungian analysts in Berlin were first, with their archetypes springing up from the unconscious," said Pickard. "They were among the progenitors, circulating LSD after Albert Hofmann's initial discovery. Dr. (Arthur) Stoll[1] was second. It went out from there like a Sea of Radiance, long before the CIA launched MKULTRA in 1951."

Pickard eventually wrote an entire book about the Six—652 pages without identifying a single chemist. *The Rose of Paracelsus*, written by hand from his prison cell and self-published in 2015, offers a fanciful travelogue with Leonard meeting face to face with five of the Six. His critics, including his avowed enemies within

---

1. Chief of the Sandoz labs where Hofmann discovered LSD; credited with developing migraine medicine from the same ergot alkaloids Hofmann used for Delysid.

the DEA, scoff at the existence of such a clandestine international cabal. Pickard just shrugs.

"Funny how people think *The Rose* is fiction, but perhaps that's best. A few people recently concluded that the Six are facets of One—one person who cannot otherwise speak."

The mantra of the Six, then and now according to Pickard, is as much omerta as it is mystic slogan: "Those who know don't tell and those who tell don't know."

Leonard purports to know, but tells as little as possible, as do the half-dozen psychonauts like himself scattered around the globe who have dedicated their lives to perfecting, extolling, and dispensing Dr. Hofmann's transcendent chemistry. He maintains that he stumbled into their midst while still in high school. The Six alone, he said, have the skill and purpose to synthesize pure LSD by the pound.

"The Six are of an entirely different order," said Pickard. "The system, if there is one, has no name. Their syntheses were the most advanced, and not published. The manufacturing, if there is any, clearly required advanced training of a special order. And the personal practices were such that great discipline prevented their detection for decades, and perhaps even now."

Leonard identifies these brothers (none are female) in arms only by color code, ascending the spectrum from Crimson to Indigo, Vermilion, Magenta, and Cobalt. Perhaps they exist only in his imagination, but then how does one explain the persistent availability of acid over decades despite the end of Delysid and all the failed efforts of the DEA thereafter to wipe LSD off the face of the earth?

Before Richard Nixon and Ronald Reagan declared War on Drugs, organic chemistry was a calling like any other. Youngsters were either suited to the craft or they were not; if they were not, they became firemen, preachers, songsmiths, janitors, doctors, or a host of other professions.

Wunderkinds like Leonard were born chemists—intent on unraveling the mysteries of the universe one catalytic reaction at a time. Even today, Pickard refers to the very best of this rarified fraternity as "the Westinghouse people": those forty high school students selected each year as the finest young scientists in America.

"The government liked to keep track of the Westinghouse people as some sort of wizard asset list," he said.

According to Pickard, he was not the only Westinghouse winner who went underground following the upheavals of the sixties. He implies that the Six may have sprung out of that chaos. The generational civil war that erupted during the Summer of Love ended chemistry's benign nature. By Watergate, when the political dust finally began to settle comfortably into the Me Decade, chemistry in general, and neurochemistry in particular, had evolved into a dangerous game.

"Interestingly, I was detained in 1976 for an MDA lab in Woodside," recalled Pickard.

Two days before Pickard's thirty-first birthday, San Mateo Sheriff's deputies stormed his wood-framed cottage near the Stanford University campus looking for drugs.

"Only traces were found," he said. "The precursor[2] for MDA—which is the same for MDMA—is also the precursor for the Parkinson's drug L-DOPA. My attorney in those years[3] petitioned the FDA for permission to work with it."

Because the DEA hadn't gotten around to forbidding MDMA, Leonard and his lawyer assumed correctly that he could experiment with the L-DOPA compound. The incident report the deputies submitted said they came looking for peyote but found none.

---

2. 3,4-methylenedioxybenzylmethylketone, a.k.a. piperonyl methyl ketone, a.k.a. 3,4-methylenedioxyphenyl-2-propanone. "All are synonyms for a substance that was legal through the seventies and eighties, but was scheduled in the nineties as MDMA prevalence grew."
3. "He is now a high federal official, and I would never compromise him."

Leonard was released without being charged, but he now knew that he was on law enforcement's radar. He assumed his cheerleading at the Sand and Scully trials probably put a target on his back.

The following year, Pickard moved south to Portola Valley and tried his hand at home chemistry again. This time, neighbors complained of rank odors rising through the floorboards—something akin to burning tires doused in Airedale urine. Deputies who were called to his apartment complex found Pickard's MDMA lab in the basement.

Pickard told them he picked up the lab equipment from a recycling center. It might once have belonged to a Brotherhood chemist, but Leonard, on the other hand, was just a Stanford undergrad tinkering with chemistry in his off hours. He knew nothing about any MDA, the so-called "love drug," which had been outlawed as a Schedule One substance at the same time as LSD. When that argument failed, he maintained he was producing the analogue MDMA which had a slightly different molecular structure than the illegal MDA.

"I had a delightful conversation with Leonard," said Alan Johnson, chief inspector for the Santa Cruz County DA.[4] "He struck me as a really bright kid. He was dressed in a little V-neck sweater. He was a little preppy. We're talking about a whole different culture back then.

"Today's cookers just get a recipe from some criminal. They mix a little of this and a little of that. They don't really know what they're doing. This fellow was trying to change the MDMA to make it legal. He was making the argument, and it was a new argument, that he's manufacturing an analogue."

The argument failed in court. Forensic analysis showed traces of MDA and he wound up with a three-year sentence in the county jail. He served half before agreeing to a *nolo contendre* plea.

---

4. Per Peter Wilkinson's July 5, 2001, *Rolling Stone* article, "The Acid King."

"The time served was the maximum under California state law, minus good time," he said.

Up to then, Pickard had lived a charmed existence out West. The only time he'd been arrested was in the spring of 1970 when police pulled over his '64 VW microbus[5] in the Southern California community of Norwalk. When they ran a routine check, the cops found he'd left Georgia without finishing his five years' probation for the 1965 auto theft.

"I do recall being picked up for violation, but released in a few days and probation being cancelled by a federal judge," he said. "It just went away, not even a court appearance."

On the strength of his trust fund, he'd been floating around the country when he wasn't working at his lab job at Berkeley or auditing one chemistry course or another. He passed through communes and college towns. Once, he ventured south of the border to check out the University of Guadalajara's medical school.

"I loved visiting with the students. They used to call and say, 'Come on down!'"

Another time, he crossed the same Canadian checkpoint where Nick Sand morphed into Ted Parody.

"I visited Victoria purely for affection and intrigue," he said. "I never saw Nick."

He once visited England, whetting his appetite for nineteenth century literature ("*Loved* the Age of Manners!").

By 1974, Pickard quit wandering and settled in the future Silicon Valley.

"Stanford was transforming," he said. "I found the density of talented people irresistible."

He regarded education as smorgasbord, enrolling in classes at Foothill Junior College, as well as San Jose State University, the University of California Santa Cruz, and, of course, Stanford.

---

5. "Only car I ever owned. Alas, it was no more by '84."

"Leonard was hanging out at Stanford with a lot of people who were in the know," recalled Talitha Stills. "He was beyond university before he ever got to university. He had a real interest in medicine and the chemistry and pharmacology underlying the drug movement."

With what was left of his dwindling trust fund, Pickard bounced between *bon vivant* and not knowing where his next meal was coming from. He became the eternal grad student. Calculus made him giddy; bio analytics, rhapsodic. In anatomy class, he empathized with the cadaver.

"Half her skull was sawn in a sagittal section, but her hair and eyelashes and one eye remained intact if you inverted the head," he recalled. "I could not approach her without a prayer or a blessing. I think the professor felt the same way."

He moved from class to class, choosing at whim which formula or technique he wanted to deconstruct. At some point, he decided to become a doctor. He collected pre-med credits the way Little Leaguers collect baseball cards.

"I had two hundred units from various places: about six years of undergrad science," he said. "I never took history or philosophy or English lit or politics."

On the social side, he needed no MDMA to fall in lust. A coed in halter top and short shorts did the trick, no chemicals required.

"Leonard had his little trust fund, so he could just dedicate himself to going out," recalled Talitha. "He was all over the place. It was almost impossible to keep tabs on him. He was a pretty serious ladies' man."

One compadre recalled Pickard hiring part of the Stanford marching band to serenade an ingenue. Pickard denies that extravagance, but does remember hiring an opera tenor once to sing a few arias. "At San Jose State, there was a girl in whose eyes I saw far fields of starry light," he waxed poetic. "We are still friends, and quite Platonic."

And yet, perhaps in deference to the Six, Pickard is defensively fuzzy about most relationships, male or female, through the 1970s and well into the eighties. He explains his reluctance as protective. He's wary about putting anyone else in the same jackpot where he wound up.

"In the years just after the sixties, we all shared and lived communally—though not in an actual commune per se," he recalled. "Those who had, gave. Those who had not, bartered or offered services. There was little money, but all was managed somehow.

"That said, in the circles I shared, there were several estates near Stanford. We lived in their cottages. My personal delight was a stone gatehouse in Portola Valley that led to some vast estate hidden in the hills that I never even saw. Turreted, spiral stairs, massive stone fireplace, stained-glass windows. Don't see those much in the States. Life was oddly cheap, with friends helping.

"Tai (Talitha Stills) found a huge place up on Mountain Home Road in Woodside. It had more horses than people. Places like that have now all been bought up by dot-com billionaires. Main house was gated; long oak-lined drive; several cottages, pool, meeting halls in upper floors. Owned by one of the last White Russian families that fled the Bolsheviks in the 1920s. Tai would host parties, driveway packed—the works.

"That said, I also once lived in chicken coop with only the clothes on my back, at the edge of a winery in Monterey country with an heiress. Just for a few weeks, but great fun. Earthy."

With Leary neutered, Owsley retired, Scully into biofeedback, and Nick Sand on the lam, underground sources for psychedelics appeared to dry up near the end of the Me Decade. Hippies became yuppies. Nihilism yielded to materialism. Pop historian Tom Wolfe wrote about EST, astronauts, and radical chic, but lost all interest in acid tests.

Even the CIA's enthusiasm waned. Called before Congress,

ranking officials of both Langley and the Pentagon reluctantly fessed up to two decades of MKULTRA. Yes, they had noodled with acid as a weapon and truth serum. Neither lawmakers nor the general public seemed especially surprised. The real lesson of Watergate and the sixties was that the government lies.

Washington's duplicity didn't lessen psychedelic condemnation. LSD had become inextricably meshed with Vietnam protest and dubious tales of people leaping from skyscrapers or staring at the sun until they went blind. Government propaganda that LSD could warp the DNA of the unborn was also proven to be patently false.

A general Baby Boom malaise settled over the submissive bent of the Silent Majority, but the latter still called the shots. With great fanfare and scant deliberation, the Congress that the Greatest Generation elected continued funding the War on Drugs.

While the government roundly condemned marijuana and LSD, far more addictive and deadly drugs like nicotine and alcohol enjoyed a commercial resurgence. Winstons tasted good like cigarettes should and leisure time was also Miller time.

Cocaine replaced LSD as the illegal drug of choice. A tsunami from Columbian cartels hit the US in the late seventies, swamping both law enforcement and hospital ERs. In the age of Disco, party-goers used coke to soar and MDMA to mellow out.

First synthesized in 1912 as a potential blood-clotting agent, MDMA, or "ecstasy," as it would come to be known, had to wait another sixty years before anyone paid much attention to its sublime side effects.

Dow Chemical pharmacologist Alexander Shulgin, subsequently nicknamed "Doctor Ecstasy," brewed his own version of MDMA in 1965, but didn't get around to trying it out himself until ten years later. When he did, he experienced "an easily controlled altered state of consciousness with emotional and sensual overtones." Shulgin likened MDMA to a low-calorie martini.

A shambling stork of a man, Sasha Shulgin resembled a mad

scientist straight out of Central Casting: Freudian chin bush, fluffy wayward brows over kind eyes, liver-colored lips curled into a perpetual grin. Leonard Pickard first began reading Shulgin's treatises in *Nature* and the *Journal of Organic Chemistry* fresh out of high school. Here was a role model well worth emulating.

As was routine among psychonauts, Shulgin was a scientific prodigy. He entered Harvard on scholarship at sixteen to study organic chemistry and took his PhD at Berkeley in 1954. He landed a plum position with Dow Chemical[6] as a research chemist in the late fifties, developing the biodegradable insecticide Zectran[7], which made him a corporate superstar.

At the same time, he experimented with mescaline and had a revelation.

"I understood that our entire universe is contained in the mind and the spirit," he later told *The New York Times*. "We may choose not to find access to it, we may even deny its existence, but it is indeed there inside us, and there are chemicals that can catalyze its availability."

Thence forward, Shulgin dedicated his life to discovering, analyzing, and ingesting psychoactive substances. He synthesized STP in 1963 and kept going, picking up the torch originally lit by Albert Hofmann. Eventually he created hundreds of such compounds—more psychedelics than anyone who'd come before or since.

He never dodged the irony that Dow made it all possible. Showing its gratitude for Zectran, the company that created Agent Orange and Napalm underwrote Shulgin's home laboratory as well

---

6. Known for a wide range of products from breast implants to Agent Orange, Dow seesawed with DuPont for a century as the nation's best-known chemical manufacturer until the two merged in 2017.

7. Shulgin got the credit but Dow got the cash. As with the method for making LSD perfected by William Garbrecht, his employer Eli Lilly and Co. paid $1 for the patent—the same price Dow paid Shulgin for Zectran.

as the first decade of his research. All they asked was that he leave Dow's name out of it.

Sasha first experimented with MDMA in the autumn of 1976. He was so thrilled with the results that he felt compelled to report his findings during a national conference the following December.

MDMA curbed inhibition and boosted empathy, he said. He told an audience of shrinks it spawned a brand-new breakthrough in psychotherapy. For angst-ridden patients unable or unwilling to put themselves into others' shoes, a dose of "Window," as Shulgin had dubbed his new wonder drug, would open their eyes.

And for a few years, Sasha's prediction seemed to come true. Among those with whom he shared his discovery, psychologist Leo Zeff grew so excited that he became the Al Hubbard of MDMA. The San Francisco psychotherapist spread the drug to over four thousand psychiatric counselors nationwide, developing a whole new protocol for putting patients under its spell. Like Sasha, he gave MDMA a pet name: "Adam," an anagram reference to the embryonic innocence of Eden.

But psychoactives seldom got a pass during the War on Drugs, and so it was with MDMA. By the end of the seventies, the DEA caught on to the analogue game. Every time a new drug surfaced, outlaw chemists came up with a variant. The moment that the government added another compound to Schedule One, a modified version hit the streets. Sasha Shulgin wasn't the only chef cooking up new recipes.

"We all were working in the same directions, but independently," said Pickard.

At the same time Shulgin and Zeff were trumpeting MDMA, an Indiana college chemistry instructor and a Nevada metallurgist were also synthesizing the drug. Purdue professor Dave Nichols and mining engineer Darrell LeMaire joined the growing ranks of psychedelic sorcerers replicating Shulgin's formulae, just the way that Pickard tried to do at his Woodside cottage and later on, in the basement of his Portola Valley apartment building.

"Serendipity?" asked Pickard.

Alas, MDMA's journey from promising panacea to banned party pill was roughly the same as lysergic acid's, only shorter. Whereas the FDA took twenty years to outlaw LSD, MDMA made the list in less than ten.

On March 30, 1979, Dr. Oscar Janiger gathered thirty of the earliest surviving psychonauts at a Beverly Hills house party to reminisce and assess the future of LSD. Captain Al Hubbard showed up in his khaki Boy Scout uniform, complete with an official-looking badge and revolver at his hip. Sans his long locks and signature flowing robes, a sobered Tim Leary came despite grumbles from peers that he'd done more damage than good by mouthing off to the Establishment and ratting out his friends.

The rest of Janiger's guest list read like a *Who's Who* of the surviving first generation of lysergic champions:

- Dr. Humphrey Osmond, the Canadian physician who first dosed Aldous Huxley, Alcoholics Anonymous founder Bill W. and other notables;
- Neurologist Nick Bercel, believed to be the first ever American to drop acid (1949);
- Dr. Sidney Cohen, who conducted UCLA's first clinical studies of LSD as therapy for alcohol abuse and end-of-life anxiety;
- Myron Stolaroff, founder of Menlo Park's International Foundation for Advanced Study, which soldiered on, experimenting with acid even after the ban;
- Dr. Murray Jarvik, inventor of the nicotine patch and early proponent of LSD as a tool for fighting tobacco addiction;

- Hollywood sci-fi producer Ivan Tors[8], who used acid to create *Flipper*, among other hallucinatory movie and TV animal characters;
- Willis Harman, co-founder of the human potential movement and founding president of Sausalito's Institute of Noetic Sciences,[9] an ongoing attempt to mesh science and religion, casting LSD as both sacrament and catalyst.

"We were there when the first pebble dropped and the ripple became a tidal wave," remembered "Dr. Oz" Janiger. "It was like living in Mesmer's time and seeing hypnosis develop."

The consensus was that LSD's story arc had been inevitable. Leary and Alpert should have been less confrontational. Enthusiasts like Owsley and Ken Kesey might have tamped down their hyperbole. Serious scientists like Cohen and Stolaroff might have done a better job extolling acid's positive potential.

But in the aftermath of the sixties, it was clear that all had played important roles in letting the genie out of the bottle.

"We *need* people like Tim and Al Hubbard," said Cohen. "They are necessary to get out, way out, too far out, in fact—in order to shift things around. We need people like Osmond to be reflective about it and study it. Then little by little, a slight movement is made in the total picture. So I can't think how things could have worked out other than how they did."

Despite the setbacks, all remained hopeful. At seventy-seven, Hubbard still hyped his favorite mind bender: "It seemed the only way that man could ever understand himself. You could take [LSD]

---

8. Tors introduced Dr. John C. Lilly to LSD. Lilly dosed dolphins, noting their subsequent affection for humans. His work inspired popular acid sci-fi films *Day of the Dolphin* (1973) and *Altered States* (1980).
9. Founded by NASA astronaut Edgar Mitchell, the sixth man to walk on the moon.

and you wouldn't understand me any better, but you would understand yourself."

But understanding was in short supply that season. The unacknowledged elephant in Dr. Oz's living room was the DEA. With each bust, sentences grew longer, penalties more severe.

The government had also made the LSD permission process so onerous that few even bothered to submit clinical proposals. Psychedelic study spelled career suicide. Only outliers like Sasha Shulgin dared dabble. Research wound down to nothing.

And yet, psychonauts remained optimistic. It was in their nature.

Nonetheless, those who persisted did so at their own risk and increasingly, outside of the law. Daredevils in lab coats. Fugitives at the fringe of academe. Chemists who vanished like thieves in the night.

Ghosts like Leonard Pickard.

VI.

On June 17, 1980, Dr. Lucille Georg Pickard collapsed at home. She was sixty-seven.

"Lucille died of a hemorrhage, quickly," said her stepson. "I returned for her funeral, but was unable to do so for my father's."

William Leonard Pickard Sr. died on Sept. 5, 1980, four months after his wife. He was fifty-nine, a suicide. When Lennie turned twenty-one, his father told him, "You're Leonard now, son," and never used his nickname again. He was not big on public displays of affection, but did leave Leonard somewhere in the neighborhood of $150,000.

"They had a pact that when one left, the other would follow," recalled Pickard. "Father put his affairs in order, made his will, gave away his dog, sold off the herd of Angus, phoned everyone he loved, and that was that. It was no surprise. I was told at fifteen that it would occur, and occasionally every few years thereafter. Such pacts were not uncommon in the Old South. A way of stating their love for each other."

His stepmother's funeral struck Leonard as something of a feminist celebration.

"During her memorial at the Unitarian Church, I was approached by Lucille's fellow CDC researchers, many of whom I had met as a youngster. I was amazed they remembered me. Crowds of young women post-docs and female students whispering, 'Dr. Georg, Dr. Georg. . . .'"

Her celebrity was rarified but significant. Over her lifetime, Lucille Pickard published more than ninety scientific papers. A bound compilation remains a permanent part of the CDC library. Several of her cites can still be found on the Internet.

Lucille Georg Pickard was a past president of the Mycological Society of the Americas. In 1982, the International Society of Human and Animal Mycology began presenting an annual lifetime achievement award in her honor. A microbe is named for her. "*A. georgiai* or some such," said Pickard. "One of the Actinomyces.

"She was the first to identify Valley Fever among migrant workers as being fungal in origin. This was a great unknown and effectively untreatable killer among Mexican field hands throughout the Southwest. It resulted in hundreds if not thousands of deaths annually. She called it 'coccidioidomycosis.'"

On a more nostalgic note, Leonard remembers two other women from that feminist funeral—each an anachronism straight out of *Gone with the Wind.*

"Our maid Gladys came dressed in her finest," he recalled. "She said of Lucille, 'She was a great lady.' I gave her an embrace, and thanked her for her many kindnesses to me as a boy.

"But it was Gala who I remember taking it hardest. She was easily the principal mourner."

Like Leonard, his older sister inherited Audrey Pickard's sturdy DNA, yet it was Lucille who shaped her destiny. Her stepmother taught Gala card games and chamber music; how to catch and cook crabs; the pleasures of beach combing and collecting shells. For her sixteenth birthday, Lucille hand painted a trousseau trunk loaded with silks and laces.

Under Lucille's guidance, Gala could have become either Blanche DuBois or a steel magnolia. She hadn't her kid brother's curiosity or genius, but all the pomp and gentility of an Atlanta debutante. She owed much of her identity to her stepmom, and wept hard.

"Gala was very distressed at her loss," said Pickard.

A moment passed before he added the afterthought: "That was the last time I ever saw my sister."

In an Aug. 31, 1980, story published in the *Austin American-Statesman* headlined "LSD Rears Its Acidic Heads for Dizzying Second Austin Engagement," staff writer Jim Shahin reported a local angle to what had become a national story:

> In New York and San Francisco, LSD—or "acid" as it is commonly known—has become fashionable again.
>
> No one is certain of the reasons for the LSD revival, but the theory most often advanced is that San Francisco manufacturers jailed in the early 1970s are being released.
>
> "It appears that the first part of last year several major manufacturers got out of jail and since then we've been seeing a lot of it," said Lt. Pete Taylor, head of the narcotics division of the Austin Police. "As far as we can tell, it's all coming from San Francisco."

"I did pass through Austin briefly, but it's a little foggy," said Pickard, his memory fuzzy on details.

Talitha Stills remembered clearly enough. Pickard landed in an Austin commune for quite a spell, probably in pursuit of a woman. It might have been during the summer of 1980, though no specific record linked Leonard to Austin's reinvigorated acid market.

One thing is certain: Leonard was preoccupied with mobile labs and legal matters. Perhaps that was why he couldn't get back home for his father's funeral.

Earlier in the year, months ahead of Lucille's passing, he'd been scouting Athens, home of the University of Georgia. It seemed a good place to land following his California jail time, but a change of address didn't keep trouble at bay. According to the police blotter in nearby Gainesville, he was arrested on Feb. 7 for meth possession.

"In Gainesville, I was detained for an unknown substance found during a routine traffic stop and search. Analysis indicated it was 3,4,5-trimethoxybenzaldehyde, an exotic and *legal* precursor for many *legal* compounds." As droll postscript, he added: "It's also a precursor for mescaline."

The police had to turn him loose, but Leonard remained indignant.

"I would never *dream* of making methamphetamine!" he said. "It's been a tragedy since its inception. I class it slightly under heroin and fentanyl in terms of the aggregate harm it's done to humanity." Mescaline, on the other hand. . . .

Four months later, and just days before his stepmother's death, Pickard was again arrested—this time in the Orlando suburb of Deland, Florida. The charge was MDA distribution, but again, police got the chemistry wrong. MDMA was not yet illegal. They had to let him go.

By year's end, it was clear that returning to his Southern roots had been a mistake. He'd skated past the courts and stayed out of jail, but his growing arrest record now resembled that of a bona fide scofflaw, not a misunderstood prodigy. He headed back to California and academic sanctuary.

"From remote places in the deserts and mountains, I tended to circle back to Stanford, auditing classes and other activities for many years."

From Leonard's perspective, the oak-studded campus with its Ivy League pretensions, world-class faculty, and nouveau riche roots was now his home.

"Gloryville!" he crowed. "The Quad. Afternoon coffee at Tressider Student Union. Hoover Tower. Memorial Chapel. The wonderful book store and the UGLY (undergrad library). Yes!"

For most of the remainder of the decade, Pickard hunkered down in Palo Alto and kept his nose clean. He traveled from time to time, but maintained a Stanford post office box. He learned to keep his hair neatly trimmed, dressed down, and drew no attention to himself.

In 1984, his faithful VW microbus finally gave up the ghost.

"She'd been through quite a few rebuilds," he said. "I loved the old thing. I had one of the first mobile phones in the early days when only pimps and physicians used them. A great black box the size of a briefcase on the floor, three channels for all of San Francisco, and a party line. Rotary dial."

Wheels or no wheels, he continued his travels. In September of 1986, he was stopped in Atlanta with a pair of brass knuckles in his luggage.

"The knuckles were a memento from my grandfather, who was among other capacities deputized in the county during the 1920s," Pickard explained. "I had no interest in them otherwise. Packed into my suitcase and forgotten until the X-ray exposed them at the Atlanta airport. Paid a $100 bond and it was dismissed."

Mark Dowie, a founding publisher of *Mother Jones* magazine, fell in with Pickard's crowd. Dowie befriended the introspective nerd with the Chris Hemsworth good looks. They were both runners and jogged together frequently, usually through the Point Reyes forest along Bear Creek trail near Dowie's beach front home. Dowie found Pickard disarmingly wry and wickedly wise, but outwardly as threatening as a dandy perpetually enroute to the faculty club. Pickard never discussed what he did for a living.

"He was, in a way, part of the love generation," said Dowie. "He really believed LSD and its derivatives could produce a better culture."

Pickard's long run of leniency at the hands of the law ended abruptly two years later, but not before his first close encounter with a chemical hero and his future role model.

"I was at Stanford in '86 doing coursework when I ran into a perplexing technical problem," recalled Pickard. "I wrote to Sasha and he invited me up to one of his lectures."

At the time, Alexander Shulgin taught social chemistry as part of the public health curriculum at the University of California, San Francisco. At the end of one class, as students shuffled out into the hall, a blonde, blue-eyed beanpole nearly as tall as the stoop-shouldered Shulgin ventured to the lectern. With scant small talk, he launched into a complex molecular monologue about Shulgin's recently outlawed compound, MDMA. Leonard Pickard was looking for a mentor.

In 1986, the War on Drugs had escalated once again. Congress passed the Anti-Drug Abuse Act, which pumped $1.7 billion into DEA enforcement. Nancy Reagan answered the international narco-politics of Pablo Escobar with "Just Say No" while her husband, the President, signed into law the Controlled Substance Analogue Enforcement Act, slowing underground chemists' perpetual game of staying one molecule ahead of Schedule One. MDMA was one of the bill's first casualties. Without flatly announcing his intent, Pickard sought Sasha's advice on how to keep cooking.

Shulgin bushed his brows. He grokked Leonard and suggested they continue their conversation in private, beyond eyes and ears that might eavesdrop inside the lecture hall.

An icon who lived every psychonaut's dream, Shulgin struck an early understanding with the DEA. He exchanged his chemical expertise for the freedom to pursue psychoactives without government interference. Bob Sager, chief of the DEA's West Coast laboratory, became so close to Sasha that he officiated at the Shulgins' 1981 marriage ceremony.

Through Sager, Sasha was granted a rare Schedule One license exempting him from the heavy penalties paid by the Brotherhood and other underground chemists. Shulgin reciprocated by sharing his knowledge with Congress and the courts.

He wrote a booklet on psychedelics that became a primer for every new DEA agent: *Controlled Substances: Chemical and Legal Guide to Federal Drug Laws* (Ronin Publishing, 1988).

"That was his Faustian bargain," said Rick Doblin, founder of the Multidisciplinary Association of Psychedelic Studies and a close Shulgin ally. "In order to do his work, he had to be useful to the DEA."

The Shulgins' hillside ranch in the East Bay community of Lafayette became a psychedelic oasis. Shulgin created a legal nether land where he openly tinkered with psychoactives in a brick shed he built fifty yards away from his kitchen door.

Leonard revered Sasha. To teach and tinker, free of fear was . . . ecstasy.

"Sasha and Ann invited me to the house on several occasions," he recalled. "He showed me his lab and the notebooks he'd kept for thirty years. I joined a class he taught at Berkeley. I was just so honored."

But Shulgin survived the War on Drugs through discretion. He understood and appreciated better than anyone his singular role. At any moment, some politician could yank his license, making him as vulnerable to draconian drug laws as Leonard or Nick or Owsley the Bear. Caution was paramount. He did not advertise nor flaunt his license and he selected his confidants with care.

Thus, he let Leonard into his life, but only time and trust would gain his young apprentice access to Sasha's inner circle.

Leonard regarded pure science a noble calling, but not a career. Men like Sasha Shulgin and Nobel laureate Paul Berg, who taught Pickard biochemistry at Stanford, were exceptional, but Leonard despaired of ever reaching their level. The deeper he dove into the fast-evolving science of neuropharmacology, the clearer it became that he would need a medical degree if he hoped to fulfill his psychedelic destiny.

Pickard began volunteering weekends in the ER at San Francisco General. There he witnessed a world far removed from textbooks and white privilege.

"I worked until four a.m. as a volunteer: blue coat, scrubs, latex gloves," he recalled. "Saw everything: ODs, mass casualties, cops, junkies, birthing mothers, strokes, PCP convulsions, baseball bat victims. Cooling down at some twenty-four-hour café, I'd watch the sunrise in my blood-speckled uniform. I have never felt so alive as on those nights."

Yet med school seemed out of reach. Dropping out of Princeton, then hopscotching from college to college did not look good on a résumé. He befriended a young resident who heard his frustrations.

"He suggested an offshore school like Guadalajara for breadth of experience," said Pickard. "That's where he'd gone and it hadn't hurt his career. He told me, 'I started at the bottom and now I'm at the top.' That cinched it. I fully applied. He even wrote me a letter of recommendation."

Despite his ER epiphany, misfortune continued to stalk Pickard. The dual life of grad student/volunteer and underground chemist caught up with him again. In October of 1987, he offered a passport to police when stopped and asked for ID. The passport turned out to be under an assumed name and earned him two days in the San Mateo County jail.

When US Customs was notified, officials took the incident far more seriously. He was charged with making a false statement on his passport application—a federal crime that got him a suspended sentence of six months plus five years' probation.

Even now, over thirty years later, Pickard has no ready explanation for his recklessness. He falls silent when reminded of the many times he got caught.

A fellow psychonaut who came to know him well in later years suggests Leonard had a fatal flaw. He refers back to the admitting shrink's notes[10] during his extended stay at Connecticut's Institute of Living in the mid-sixties:

"He was labeled a toxic narcissist with no core value. He therefore feels justified to psychopathic tendencies."

Indeed, Sasha warned him to be careful. Through his own back channels, the paterfamilias of West Coast psychonauts learned law enforcement was closing in.

Leonard knew better. He was careful. He was clever. He was untouchable.

Three days after Christmas in 1988, a neighbor smelled something funky seeping from inside a cinder block unit on the industrial outskirts of Mountain View in the beating heart of Silicon Valley. When police arrived, Leonard Pickard greeted them at the door carrying a box of blotter paper. He warned them not to enter.

"What's that in the warehouse?" asked one of the officers.

"An LSD lab," Leonard recalled answering. "But let me caution you. You must advise the forensic chemist and search team to wear full protective clothing, including gloves, moon suits, face plates, and respirators. Otherwise, you may experience unusual psychological changes."

Armed with a search warrant, they ignored Pickard. Inside, the cops found a small trailer similar to the sort often used at construction sites. Someone had gone to great lengths to mask the odors that gave the lab away.

Pickard's old nemeses, the San Mateo Sheriff's office, called in a contingent from the state Bureau of Narcotics Enforcement. They swarmed the bunker with black lights. Chemical dust glowed everywhere.

"It was a huge lab," said Ron Brooks, special agent in charge of

---

10. In a June 21, 2019, letter, Hartford Hospital wrote Pickard that no such records exist of his stay at the Institute of Living; all files are routinely destroyed after ten years.

the BNE's San Jose office. "He was making windowpane, microdot, and blotter."

Pickard also had apparently been experimenting with Shulgin analogues and synthesizing mescaline. When Brooks later told drug expert Darryl Inaba that he'd bagged a mescaline maker, Inaba scoffed: "No fucking way. That's just too hard to make. There are only a few people in the whole world. . . ."

Analysis showed that Leonard was one of those people. The white crystalline needles were indeed mescaline.

"Guys like him do that just as a challenge, just to prove they can do it," said Brooks. "It probably cost him way more to make than he could ever sell it for."

What boggled Brooks the most, however, was the scale of the operation: state-of-the-art lab equipment, including a roto-evaporator, heating mantles, and pill press.[11]

Boxes of blotter paper like the one Pickard was carrying when arrested were scattered around inside the trailer. Some bore designs of samurai shields, some of Grateful Dead album cover art. One box contained sheets of black-and-white kaleidoscopic faces like those featured in the M. C. Escher lithograph that Leonard gave Tim Scully a decade earlier.

In addition to the blotter acid, the haul included 89,802 acid tabs and another 123,278 of the larger acid pills. Estimated street value: $250,000.

"He was an excellent chemist," said Brooks. "Excellent and prolific, on par almost with Owsley himself in terms of output."

It turned out Pickard was correct about someone getting hurt. Even in full-body jumpsuit and respirator, BNE investigator Max Houser collapsed in convulsions inside the trailer. He'd nicked his

---

11. Along with analogues, precursors, and other chemicals, the DEA began monitoring sales of specialized lab equipment in the late seventies, making it increasingly difficult to experiment with anything remotely psychedelic.

neck shaving that morning and enough vapor filtered through a slit in his protective gear to send him reeling.

Upon his arrival at a nearby hospital, an earsplitting buzz drowned out the voices of the EMTs and nurses shouting at him. Houser had to read their lips through dilated pupils stung by the fluorescent lighting. Only after an IV of Valium brought him down was he able to identify the migraine noise as acid-amplified openings and closings of the ER's automatic doors.

Once released, Houser began convulsing again hours later while he was in the shower at home. For months thereafter, he suffered terrifying mood swings: anxiety to depression then back again. Interviewed twenty years later by journalist Lisa Winters, he maintained he still bore scars from the episode.

"I regret his difficult moments, although I suffered the same effects without the benefit of protective suits," Pickard told Brooks.

Had Houser been guided by an experienced psychonaut, suggested Pickard, there would have been no need for Valium.

"Anxiety can spin out of control when taken to the ER with a mind-set expecting psychosis and surrounded by people who are inexperienced," he said with clinical detachment. "Ideally, a talk-down should suffice. A meadow and friends would be a completely different experience than guns, radio, and fear, I am told."

In a suspect show of sympathy, Pickard coyly hinted at a worldwide web of acid acolytes who could help OD victims like Houser, were they not deterred by drug laws:

"Even now, it's almost impossible to study overdose phenomena like these," he said. "Sustained exposure to unknown but massive dosages of LSD, as experienced by the few unknown individuals worldwide who are responsible for its distribution, has no parallel in clinical settings. I understand various psychiatrists and pharmacologists would like to interview them, but they are, necessarily, unavailable."

Never admitting guilt or even acknowledging that the lab

belonged to him, Pickard spoke at length with BNE investigators. They remained baffled long after the session ended.

"I recall Mr. Pickard back in the interview room," said BNE agent Dave Tresmontan. "He played a lot of things close to the vest. I remember him sitting there with his legs crossed, very calm, very friendly, somewhat guarded. My thought was, 'Here's a very intelligent individual, maybe slightly eccentric.'"

During the subsequent investigation, one of the more curious allegations was that Pickard had a relationship with the DEA dating back to its inception. By one published account, he entered the brand-new San Francisco field office in the autumn of 1973 and offered to inform on the Brotherhood of Eternal Love. Agents declined his offer, but began building a dossier. Later, they took Pickard up on his offer. He was credited with helping shut down two meth labs and a rival LSD operation. The DEA officially closed out its relationship with him on May 2, 1988.

"Such allegations without reference to the case, name, location, and date are hearsay," said Pickard, who vehemently denied ever having worked with or for the DEA.

In a legal catch-22, the government is likewise forbidden to reveal whether Pickard ever cooperated with the DEA.

"DEA's absolute policy is never to reveal any information pertaining to confidential informants or SOIs (sources of information)," said Pickard. Hundreds if not thousands have tried to pry names out of the Department of Justice, including Pickard. None have succeeded.

The reason Pickard's alleged cooperation was leaked, he said, was retribution: no one likes a snitch. Pickard maintains that the DEA allegations—including the very specific date when his cooperation supposedly came to an end—are meant to do him harm.

"The problem is that just by airing the allegation widely, great personal problems can be created, and they would never go away," he said. "As they say: 'Easy to allege, hard to disprove.'"

According to Pickard, the facts ought to speak for themselves. Except for Scully and Sand, he's never even met any member of the Brotherhood of Eternal Love, let alone spied on them. He refused to cooperate with the prosecution of any of the drug cases brought against him, despite offers of leniency. He knew how to keep a confidence.

As he later attempted to explain in *The Rose of Paracelsus*, Leonard went full-throttle Ivy Mike:

"Actual informants send psychedelic people to prison, a matter of public record. Ivies by contrast claim complex relationships with DEA for their defense at hearings and trials, and DEA thereafter issues denials and confuses juries on the issue."

The Mountain View bust was Exhibit A. Leonard talked, but revealed nothing. He alone pled innocent to three counts of manufacturing LSD.

"How unusual then (or not), that the '88 seizure led nowhere," he said. "No houses, no apartments, no third parties, no additional warrants, no phones, no cars, no bank accounts, no lists of addresses or phone numbers or any threads whatsoever to exploit. Zero."

Ron Brooks and his entire BNE detail eventually had to admit defeat.

"We followed up leads in Daly City and in San Francisco, also out in the southern East Bay, but never had anything solid," he said. "He was very good about covering his tracks, and he and his circle of friends were all masters of using multiple identities and blind mail drops and phones forwarded to other phones."

Leonard reacted with a smirk.

"During a hearing in the '88 proceedings, the prosecutor brought forth a huge mass of interlocking rings of keys,[12]" he said. "They

---

12. Variously known as MIMA (mechanically interlocked molecular architectures) or olympiadane, the diagrams resemble interlocked Olympic rings (hence the name) and are chemical shorthand for complex compounds, equations, and/or reactions.

found hundreds of them in the trailer. He showed them to the judge and said: 'Judge, we don't know much about Mr. Pickard, but from what you can see, there must be something going on.'"

Indeed, the mystery deepened after investigators discovered a tantalizing memo tucked inside a brown vial that had also been found in the trailer laboratory:

> As I prepare my third kilogram of LSD, I think with amusement of our last conversation three weeks ago, when you called me a liar, and I had to walk you down the hall to get you the very first gram that was supposed to be offered to you preferentially. Since July of 1984, our friend has taken thirty grams in that year, thirty grams in the second year and seventy-five grams in the last six to eight weeks. The recent change indicates that someone close to you has accessed an existing system as well as its potential problems. I hope you can monitor these proceedings in some way, since you come from the finest psychedelic heritage, prior to being seduced by some sleazy cocaine and qualude [sic] nightmare.

Seemingly meant for a distributor or client, the note nagged at Brooks. Whether Pickard wrote it and for whom it was intended, never was determined. A lawyer's son, Leonard knew his rights, especially the one that guaranteed him silence in the face of questioning.

Following the code of Ivy Mike, he revealed nothing.

VII.

Shortly after the mountain view bust, Leonard overcame his sketchy academic record. Following twenty years of on-again, off-again classes, he finally made it into med school.

"I'd done all my required interviews with MDs in Los Angeles and was accepted at UAG in Guadalajara a few days after my '88 detention," he said.

Alas, there would be no enrollment. Under the recently forti-fied War on Drugs, his state offense escalated to a federal viola-tion. Within days of his arrest, he found himself facing a federal judge. Even if he got lucky, Pickard was looking at years in prison. Medical school was over before it began.

At his sentencing, US District Court Judge Marilyn Hall Patel showed little sympathy. After reviewing his extensive arrest record, she admonished the forty-four-year-old convict: "I hope that the years in the federal penitentiary will be spent wisely. You don't have much time left to straighten out your life."

Pickard did nearly four years of an eight-year sentence at Terminal Island, a mid-level LA prison that overlooks San Pedro harbor. TI had run-down tennis courts and a Native American sweat lodge, but hardly qualified as a country club. Pickard tried meditating in the law library, but ultimately had to count on fellow psychonauts to keep him sane.

"Ann (Shulgin) wrote me often, and told me that she and Sasha were working on *PiHKAL*," he said. "That was exciting. I got one of the first copies."

Shorthand for "Phenethylamines I Have Known And Loved," *PiHKAL*[1] was the Shulgins' 978-page self-published hybrid: part autobiography, part cookbook. The first half recounted the love story of Sasha and Ann—where they grew up, how they met, and their many drug experiences before and after marriage.

The second part, titled "The Chemical Story," explained in detail how to synthesize 179 phenethylamines, an especially potent family of psychotropic drugs. Each recipe included recommended dosages, trance length, and what to expect along the way, to wit:

> There was a strange devil-angel pairing. As I was being told of the ecstatic white-light ascent of my partner into the God-space of an out-of-body experience, I was fighting my way out of a brown ooze. She saw the young Jesus at the bottom of a ladder drifting upwards step by step to some taking-off place, and I saw all the funny gargoyles around the base of the ladder surrounded by picnic bunting. For me it was the 4th of July rather than Easter![2]

PiHKAL and Ann's letters were as close as Leonard got to altered states during his stay at Terminal Island. If he sought out-of-body experiences, he had to settle for fasting, yoga, and holotropic breathing.[3]

He appeared to have taken Judge Patel seriously. Middle age

---

1. Published in 1991, the underground bestseller was followed in 1997 with its sequel, *TiHKAL* (Tryptamines I Have Known And Loved)
2. A trance induced with sixteen milligrams of 2,5-dimethoxy-4-ethylphenethylamine.
3. A form of hyperventilation developed by psychonaut pioneer Stanislav Grof to approximate LSD's surreal state of consciousness.

and multiple run-ins with the law seemed finally to have mellowed his inner rebel. While inside, Leonard turned vegetarian, shunned anything addictive including caffeine, and became a Buddhist disciple of Alan Watts.[4]

He picked his prison peers carefully. Among other nonviolent career criminals, he befriended an affable Afghan rug dealer named Mohammed Akbar Bey. Akbar, who was doing fourteen years for narcotics trafficking, regaled Pickard with stories about embedding Kabul heroin inside carpet fibers then weaving them into rugs suitable for export.

Pickard applauded the ingenuity, if not the drug.

"I agree with Wavy Gravy," he said. "There's blood on heroin and cocaine."

It galled him that the DEA lumped his crimes together with those of Middle Eastern opium dealers and the Medellín coke cartel. Schedule One did not differentiate between psychedelics and bona fide killers like heroin. Under federal guidelines, none were acceptable for medicinal use, yet all allegedly had high potential for abuse.

Ironically, the street drug *du jour* then sending hundreds to jail and thousands more to the ER was classified as Schedule Two. Crack cocaine had the same high abuse potential as Schedule One, but with medicinal saving grace, or so said the government. In Leonard's experience, both as a San Francisco General volunteer and based on prison-yard scuttlebutt, crack killed more in a week than LSD had in half a century.

Two years into his sentence, Pickard paused one afternoon as he

---

4. The British-born philosopher/theologian wrote more than twenty-five books on religion and popularized Zen among the Beats during the early sixties. A proponent of mescaline, Watt experimented with LSD as early as 1958, agreeing with Aldous Huxley about the drug's mind-expanding potential or *kenshō*. "Some people get there from psychedelics, some from meditation, some from study, some from lineage."

passed through the rec room. A chubby middle-aged talking head pontificated over the TV. With receding hairline and full Shulgin-style beard, the fellow might have been just another C-SPAN policy wonk, but there was urgency in his argument. He spoke more like psychonaut than bureaucrat. Leonard settled into a chair and listened to the entire interview.

Author Mark Kleiman was hyping a book about the failures of the War on Drugs. *Marijuana: Costs of Abuse, Costs of Control* slammed DEA enforcement, stiff sentencing guidelines, and Nancy Reagan's "Just Say No" campaign.

"We've spent a lot of resources and not got the problem under control," he said. The better policy, he argued, was "grudging toleration": slacking off "punishment bankruptcy" and substituting rehab, education, and decriminalization instead. Junkies were addicts, not criminals. Discourage their habit, but don't lock 'em up and toss away the key.

Pickard recognized a comrade-in-arms. Kleiman might resemble Sydney Greenstreet, but he spoke like the Harvard-educated progressive that he was. That night, Leonard wrote to Kleiman, requesting his curriculum vitae and published papers.

Kleiman wrote back, according to Pickard. In the years ahead, grudging toleration would be Leonard's anthem, and his new pen pal would become another mentor.

After Pickard walked out of prison in November of 1992, he caught a Greyhound to San Francisco.

"I arrived at the Zen Center directly on the day of release carrying only a cardboard box," he recalled.

Pickard joined the Hoshin-ji[5] Urban Temple on Page Street in the Lower Haight, where he paid $350 a month for one of the

---

5. Translates as "Beginner's Mind," also the title of Chapter Two in *The Rose of Paracelsus.*

forty small cubicles that apprentices rent when preparing for the priesthood. For the next two years, he was up at four daily, rang the temple bell at five a.m., meditated for an hour and a half, chanted, swept the sidewalk, then ate breakfast.

"Monastic practice involves twenty-four hours a day," said Blanche Hartmann, better known at the Zen Center as The Abbess. "The bulk of the day he did whatever he was doing, and I have no idea what it was. I never felt fully invited into his personal life. There was always an air of mystery about him."

When he wasn't at the Center, Pickard studied neurobiology at Berkeley. Dr. David Presti, an authority on addiction, steered him away from psychedelics and focused him more on general drug abuse prevention. Pickard claimed to have turned his life around. He credited Presti, Zen, and Hartmann with helping him do so.

"She took my hand when I left prison," he said. "I lived there for two years as a monk. I also trained at the Tassajara near Carmel."

The first Zen monastery established outside of Asia, Tassajara is 126 acres of remote coastal wilderness located two hours south of San Francisco. The only way in and out is a dirt road sixteen miles from the nearest pavement. The place had a clandestine aura that appealed to Leonard: a secret training ground for sacred spies. Since it opened in 1967, Tassajara had fostered hundreds of apprentices seeking solitude, ranging from songwriter Leonard Cohen to Apple's Steve Jobs, and an ex-con named William Leonard Pickard.

"I lost contact with a large early portion of my life after the prison years," he said.

His new role models were holy men, like Brother David.[6] "When the Vatican instructed him to inquire into Buddhism, he left his hermitage to learn our practice at Tassajara."

Pickard did appear to reinvent himself. To hear him tell it, he

---

6. A celebrated Benedictine monk credited with melding spirituality and science, Brother David Steindl-Rast devoted his life and career to interfaith dialogue on a global scale.

entered the monastery an unfocused felon but emerged a penitent advocate of clean living.

"He seemed set on his science and doing something with his life," recalled Mark Dowie, who reconnected with Leonard after prison.

Blanche Hartmann was less sanguine.

"I assumed he had some money left over from his earlier days dealing, but I have no idea," she said.

According to Pickard, his mother left him "quite a sum" upon her death in 1991. A retired legal secretary who finished where she started in Atlanta, Audrey Johnson Hammond was 71 and had survived all four of her husbands, but hadn't seen her only son since the sixties.

"He was trying to change," said Hartmann. "I don't know how he felt about his manufacturing LSD, whether he thought it was good or bad. I never asked him about it. My guess is, even though its illegal, he didn't think it was wrong to make LSD, because he thinks there's something beneficial about making it, or he wouldn't have done it."

Pickard did not completely turn his back on psychedelics. He resumed relations with the Shulgins, who invited him to participate in a weekly psychonaut tradition.

"After an Easter gathering on Mount Diablo, they invited me to my first Friday night dinner," he said. "It was a life-changing encounter socially, to be received honorably and knowingly into the larger academic community."

Each Friday for as far back as most could remember, the Shulgins staged an informal dinner party where Sasha held forth on his latest discoveries. Hosted by Ann and her daughter Wendy, the relaxed, invite-only suppers became famous among the psychonaut cognoscenti.

"Leonard always showed up in formal dinner dress," recalled one of the regulars. "Nobody else did. It was odd."

Sasha and Ann hosted even smaller klatches among their most trusted friends. It was with these half-dozen loyalists that Sasha tested his newest potions. After trying an analogue out on themselves, the Shulgins shared among their fellow guinea pigs while Sasha carefully noted the results. He and Ann included their findings in *PiHKAL* and its successor volume, *TiHKAL*.

But Pickard was not invited. Ann empathized with their new acolyte, but did not fully trust him. Talking drugs was one thing; taking them was another. The War on Drugs was now in full swing and the stakes too high to take chances.

Too much a wild card to secure invitation into the Shulgins' super-secret inner circle, Pickard did manage to get his name on John Weir Perry's potluck list. A Harvard-trained psychonaut who'd once studied with Carl Jung, Weir also staged potlucks at his Marin home. As Perry's ex-wife, Ann Shulgin vouched for Pickard. He became a regular.

As with the Shulgins' Friday night dinners, conversation at Perry's potlucks dwelt on the nature of consciousness, narco politics, and recent shifts in drug policy, though drug use itself was tacitly forbidden. Always the threat of DEA infiltration loomed. No one was keen on sacrificing personal freedom for principle. Even Sasha had lost some of his fearlessness.

His legendary DEA invincibility ended the year Pickard left Terminal Island. *PiHKAL* became an instant underground bestseller, but amateur psychonauts everywhere were now cooking up a storm.

"It is our opinion that those books are pretty much cookbooks on how to make illegal drugs," said DEA spokesman Richard Meyer. "Agents tell me that in clandestine labs that they have raided, they have found copies...."

In 1993, agents descended on Shulgin's farm, combed through the house and lab and carted off anything that looked suspicious. Sasha was fined $25,000 for violating the terms of his Schedule

One license and was asked to turn the license in. He reached a compromise, but it wouldn't last.

"Once and only once did the local Contra Costa County sheriff bust Sasha for growing peyote," said Pickard. "He and Ann had a bucolic setting, with quite a variety of *Lophophora williamsii*[7] and the license to possess it. But during the raid, the cops crushed the cacti beneath their heels. Even as they served the warrant, rather than seizing the plants as samples, they destroyed them. Sasha was heartbroken."

Both the sheriff and the DEA apologized, but thereafter, Shulgin posted a sign on the door of his lab:

> This is a research facility that is known to and authorized by the Contra Costa County Sheriff's Office, all San Francisco DEA Personnel, and the State and Federal EPA Authorities.

Underneath were contact numbers and names of representatives for each agency.

Leonard paid his first post-prison visit to Esalen Institute the same year the DEA trampled Sasha's cactus garden.

"It was a real convocation—luminaries flying in from all over," Pickard remembered. "As the only member of the group usually awake at four a.m., I was designated to drive down from Hoshin-ji to pick up a Harvard Medical School professor of neuroscience. He'd flown in on the redeye from Boston. Some years later, he became provost. We drove into Big Sur just as the sun was rising. Glorious!"

The brainchild of a pair of sixties college dropouts, Esalen Institute occupied fifty-three breathtaking acres on a terraced cliff overlooking the Pacific. Birthplace of California's human-potential

---

7. Mescaline cacti

movement, Esalen attracted psychonauts the way compost attracts earthworms. Before it inspired a multitude of New Age motivational road shows, Esalen famously equated self-actualization with sex, drugs, rock 'n' Rolfing. When East Coast media wanted to depict California at its looniest, they dispatched correspondents to soak in Esalen's hot springs for a week.

The very first Esalen catalogue offered an introductory course in "Drug-Induced Mysticism;" the inaugural seminar in 1962 was based on Huxley's "Human Potentiality" lecture. Even after acid was outlawed, the Institute's trappings remained indelibly psychedelic.

Pickard felt right at home.

Over the years, Esalen's founding dropouts Dick Price (Harvard, psychology) and Michael Murphy (Stanford, philosophy) invited every aging Aquarian luminary from Tim Leary to Allen Ginsberg to lecture nostalgic Boomers about holistic yoga, improved karma, psychoneuroimmunology, and a host of other enlightened topics. Joseph Campbell spoke there about *The Tibetan Book of the Dead.* Gestalt therapist Fritz Perls publicly spanked Natalie Wood during a role play. Altered states abounded.

At the end of each day, most everyone wound up in a hot tub clutching an apple-chard smoothie or a chardonnay. Quizzed about the rampant nudity among its patrons, Esalen CEO Sharon Thom rationalized, "Being naked is a leveler."

Leonard was all about leveling. He seized the opportunity to chauffeur a future provost as one way to put himself closer to medical school. It didn't work, but schmoozing a Harvard don did indirectly help pave his way back into the Ivy League. First lesson: drop the proper names.

"Sasha and Ann were central to our small gathering that weekend," he recalled. "Our group included Nobelist Tom Schelling,[8]

---

8.   UC Berkeley economist credited with inventing Game Theory.

Lew Seiden,[9] Stan Grof, Mark Kleiman and Rick Doblin, among others. Rick had just started MAPS.[10] Brother David may have come down from Carmel to open with a prayer."

A fan since Terminal Island, Pickard hadn't met Kleiman face to face until a San Francisco psychedelic conference in April of '93. After his prison pen pal had quizzed Pickard on his academic background, Kleiman suggested that Harvard's Kennedy School of Government might be a better fit than med school. The suggestion nettled, but also gave Leonard pause.

"Not my first choice," he said, "but I thought a few years in Cambridge would help with med school admissions."

He didn't sleep alone at Esalen that weekend. After years of free love and casual relationships, Pickard had finally met The One at a Shulgin Friday night dinner. It was October, and Halloween was in the air.

"She had a peaked cap, as a witch," he recalled. "I was in my monk's robe."

Deborah Harlow was a honey-haired vixen with sober predisposition. An MDMA fan, she gravitated early to the Shulgins, who approved of her all-consuming advocacy.

"Debbie really loved brilliant, eccentric men," said Dr. Rick Strassman, an Esalen attendee. "She was really drawn to them, and could really turn on the charm. If they needed narcissistic replenishment, she'd deliver."

Dave Nichols, Strassman's contemporary and a leading neuropharmacist in his own right, remembered Harlow and her peers lobbying for MDMA under the tongue-in-cheek banner, "Madams for Adam."[11]

---

9. University of Chicago neuropharmacologist and Ecstasy psychotherapy pioneer.

10. Multidisciplinary Association for Psychedelic Studies, the leading lobbyist for legalizing psychedelics, was founded in 1986.

11. Before "ecstasy" caught on, MDMA's street name was the anagram ADAM.

Though eight years Pickard's junior, Harlow was far more sophisticated. Before MDMA was outlawed, she had already administered the drug to more than two hundred patients, surveyed twenty psychoanalysts who used MDMA in therapy, and addressed Congress in an impassioned, if ultimately failed, effort to keep Ecstasy (a.k.a. XTC) off of Schedule One.

As leaders among the second-generation psychonauts, Harlow and her first husband Robert Forte vowed to bring psychedelics back into the mainstream. Her second husband carried the acid torch even further when she first met Leonard.

"By that time, Deb was in the middle of a difficult divorce from Jaron Lanier, the computer maven who coined the term 'virtual reality,'" he said.

Leonard convinced her that the third time would be the charm. Her intellect was icing on the cake. Enlightened and bright she might be (she had her MA; Leonard still had only his high school diploma), but quirk and winsome smile counted as highly as academic credentials. She cocked her head just like Veronica Lake. Leonard held the door for her just like Cary Grant.

They had chemistry.

Leonard sought references from the Shulgins, David Presti, and the Esalen psychonauts in his bid for med school, but Mark Kleiman talked him into drug diplomacy instead. As an associate professor at Harvard's Kennedy School of Government, Kleiman had an inside track with admissions. It helped Leonard's case that he had hooked up with Deborah Harlow.

"Mark Kleiman had a crush on Deb," said a friend of all three. "Leonard wanted into the Kennedy School; Kleiman had a lot of influence. By helping Leonard, Mark got closer to Debbie."

Before falling under Harlow's thrall, Kleiman earned his reputation the hard way, combining humble roots with academic excellence. A Jewish kid from Arizona, he'd paid his dues. After attending prestigious Haverford College, he systematically climbed the ladder to the top of government service. He took his Master's in public policy at the Kennedy School, then served as aide to Congressman Les Aspin and Polaroid founder Edwin Land before being tapped to head the Office of Policy and Management with the Criminal Division of the Justice Department. He carved out a specialty as a drug policy expert, earned his PhD in 1983, then began making noise nationally about Ronald Reagan's War on Drugs.

Kleiman saw Pickard as apprentice. With his support, Leonard bypassed the normal hurdles and entered the Kennedy School in September 1994, Deborah at his side.

One year shy of his fiftieth birthday, Pickard had finally returned to the Ivy League. Simultaneously, he won a neurobiology research fellowship in the addictions division of Harvard Medical School—one step closer to his ultimate dream of becoming a physician.

With Harlow as his partner, Pickard seemed finally to have found his groove. They set up housekeeping in Cambridge and co-authored a series of academic briefs about social drug use, including a finding that New Yorkers liked LSD at their raves while Californians seemed to prefer Ecstasy.

But Leonard made his mark with heroin, not psychedelics. For his second-year project, he focused on the former Soviet Union. Theorizing that a growing global black market in opioids could be traced to unemployed Russian chemists following the collapse of the Berlin Wall, he set out to see whether a free-market economy had had the unintended consequence of unleashing a new synthetic heroin in the West.

First synthesized in 1959 by Belgian chemist Paul Janssen, fentanyl was a hundred times stronger than morphine. A rarity in the US, the drug had pandemic potential should unscrupulous chemists produce it in bulk. As a reformed underground cooker himself, Leonard felt uniquely poised to predict and prevent fentanyl's spread.

Kleiman signed on as his faculty adviser. He encouraged Pickard to turn a routine grad school Policy Analysis Exercise into a full-blown fentanyl inquiry. Leonard tested the waters in an eight-student seminar and again during a presentation at the Faculty Club. Then he took his study a step further, seeking support from the CIA's Counter Narcotics Center and the State Department.

"Now, as it happens, the Assistant Secretary of State for International Narcotics and Law Enforcement Affairs came to speak to our seminar," said Pickard. "I pitched him as a sponsor. He knew my background, and accepted on the basis of fentanyl's appearance in Moscow."

Assistant Secretary of State for International Narcotics Matters Robert Gelbard had visited Russia often and saw first-hand what Pickard was suggesting. He became a fan. When Pickard submitted an expanded fifty-page proposal that asked, "What Can State (Department) Do About Drug Problems in Russia?" Gelbard answered with approval of his project. Leonard's "Design of a System for Monitoring Trafficking and Use" got the green light.

Using Gelbard's State Department connections, Pickard began hob-nobbing with ranking Russian drug officials, gaining insight into fentanyl's alarming growth.

"I took the risk, career-wise, for it seemed like science fiction at the time," he said. "I asserted it would become fact and exactly why."

"Leonard talked to Russians," reported one of his Harvard associates. "He was obviously very good at that. He contacted various law enforcement figures, including the FSB, which is the successor to the KGB."

Despite his stand-out success, Leonard had his detractors who characterized him as a dilettante who talked a good game, but failed to carry through.

"He presented himself as a person who was well-connected and could see what was happening in the drug scene, but he was never able to make much out of that or demonstrate the truth of what he was observing," one of his professors later told *Rolling Stone.* "I ended up regarding him with a great deal of skepticism."

Indeed, Debbie Harlow's old friend and fellow MDMA advocate Rick Doblin[12] had a similar take. He visited the Pickards on occasion in their off-campus apartment, before and after Debbie became pregnant. She bore Leonard a daughter, whom the couple named Melissa.

"Melissa was born at Brigham and Women's,[13] and of course I was there," said Leonard. "Harvard paid for it, thankfully."

They appeared to be the quintessential Yuppie family, but Doblin had his doubts. A Kennedy School graduate himself, he watched Pickard operate more as skilled poseur than late-blooming academic:

"What can you say about somebody who always wears a suit and tie to meetings that are usually more relaxed? He wanted to pass in a lot of professional circles or responsible circles, even anti-drug-abuse circles. It felt like he was playing the role.

"He'd tell these shadowy stories that were somehow connected to Russians who had made out in privatization in perhaps less than completely ethical ways and who wanted to help out their country by studying drug abuse issues. I didn't know what to believe. I always felt there was more going on than he was saying. There were some major missing pieces in what he was sharing."

---

12. Harlow, psychologist Alise Agar, and Doblin formed the Earth Metabolic Society in the early eighties to solicit private funds for psychedelic research. EAS reorganized as MAPS after Harlow and Agar quit.

13. Adjacent to Harvard Medical School, "The Brigham" is one of the nation's oldest maternity hospitals.

PART TWO

If You Go Chasing Rabbits

VIII.

ONE MORNING IN THE SUMMER of 1995, Leonard Pickard showed up on Alfred Savinelli's doorstep. The owner of the Taos, New Mexico, aromatherapy emporium "Natural Scents" had been expecting Pickard. They'd met briefly some months earlier after Pickard made a heroic effort to search him out.

"All these years later, I still don't know how he got my name," said Savinelli. "The volunteer list was supposed to be confidential."

In the first FDA-authorized psychedelic study with human subjects since the seventies, Savinelli had been selected as one of five-dozen volunteers at the University of New Mexico medical school. Dr. Rick Strassman sparked new hope among psychonauts with his five-year pilot study. He'd begun testing in 1990, looking for a connection between DMT and the pineal body,[1] located at the very top of the spinal column. Somehow, Pickard learned Savinelli was subject number forty-seven among Strassman's first guinea pigs.

---

1. Dead center in the human brain, the pea-sized gland produces sleep-inducing melatonin, but also has an ancient reputation as a mysterious "third eye," connecting the individual to the cosmos. Strassman set out to see whether DMT triggers spirituality and whether the pineal gland plays a physiological role in the human quest for heavenly connection. Both pro and anti-abortion activists have challenged his contention that DMT release from the pineal gland forty-nine days after conception marks the entrance of the spirit into the fetus.

A rising psychonaut star, Strassman bucked the freeze against psychedelic research that started with Schedule One in 1970. From Esalen to Cambridge, scientists hamstrung for more than twenty years by the War on Drugs followed Strassman's progress closely. The young researcher chose DMT because it provoked hallucination and instant disorientation, but unlike LSD, the trips lasted only thirty minutes.

"DMT is ubiquitous in nature, if one knows where to look," said Leonard. "Common grasses, even the acacia tree. Heated in a tea with Syrian Rue from any health food store, you have a between-your-eyes psychedelic."

Strassman dubbed DMT "the Spirit Molecule." A veteran connoisseur of altered states, Savinelli knew the drug well.

"It's found in everything," he said. "Plants, animals. Human beings manufacture it in the lungs. It's everywhere. It just has to be activated."

A professional chemist himself, Savinelli had been in and out of trances often, just never before under such close medical scrutiny.

Among other things, Strassman hoped to fix a safe dosage level. He developed a sliding measure for severity and type of delusion—a gauge he called the Hallucinogen Rating Scale. He used Magnetic Resonance Imaging before and after to see how DMT affected his subjects' brains. Strassman made the entire process sound eminently clinical. Savinelli had a different take.

"He turned me into his Frankenstein," he said. "He wanted to see how much it took to get you to do the funky chicken."

In subsequent findings published in the *Journal of General Psychiatry*, Strassman stressed the serious nature of his study.

"I think hallucinogenic drugs are potentially quite dangerous and should remain tightly restricted," he said. His work, Strassman argued, might "lead to possibly developing drugs that could treat bad trips in emergency rooms."

That did not happen. As it turned out, however, the study did lead

Leonard Pickard to Alfred Savinelli, a.k.a. "DMT 47." Leonard was not just another psychonaut looking to get high; he was a Harvard grad student studying the effects of social drugs on international relations, or so he told Alfred. That was why they needed to talk.

Pickard repeatedly rang Savinelli's bell that morning. He nearly gave up before Savinelli finally answered his door. Ashen, bug-eyed and breathless, Alfred looked like he hadn't slept. In fact, he had not. A short, sinewy man with shoulder-length hair and faint mustache, Savinelli resembled a hungover Jesus.

He stammered that Pickard wasn't his only guest visiting from Harvard that weekend. He let the door swing wide and Pickard saw a man balled up in a corner of the living room.

John Halpern was a young Harvard psych resident Pickard had met briefly three months earlier in Cambridge. He'd shown up the previous evening, said Savinelli. Son of a prominent New York psychiatrist and—like Savinelli—a Strassman volunteer, Halpern was observing the DMT experiment, but was not above tripping himself. When Savinelli told him about ayahuasca, a potent new source of Spirit molecule he'd just imported from South America, Halpern had to try it out.

Halpern was twenty years younger than Pickard, but already making a name for himself. He'd recently published an essay titled "The illicit use of hallucinogenic drugs is a re-emerging public health problem, especially among well-educated adults and teenagers." At the moment, Halpern qualified as a living example of just such an adult. Covering his face with his hands, he howled through his finger mask. He struck Pickard as less a shrink than an ER walk-in.

John Halpern had a fascination with psychedelics that dated back to high school. He'd dropped acid, smoked hash, and eaten peyote with Navajo tribesmen, never with ill effect. Ayahuasca was different.

A hallucinogenic tea made from Brazilian rain forest plants, ayahuasca was the latest psychonaut rage during the mid-nineties. The foul brew was supposed to induce nausea followed by intense otherworldly spirituality, but all it did for Halpern was conjure demons and make him puke.

Pickard found Halpern keening like a tormented rag doll. His balding head was beet red; his horn rims magnified his horrified pupils to exclamation points. While he whimpered, Pickard administered psychic first aid. He'd taken "more LSD than anyone on the planet," he told Halpern. Not to worry: ayahuasca was aspirin compared to acid.

"Leonard starts massaging my feet, telling me everything is fine," said Halpern. "He was treating me in a way like a baby. If I burped, he would go, 'Mmm, yeah. Oh yeah.' Just to try to make it humorous."

From that moment forward, Pickard became "a brother from another planet," said Halpern. Leonard soothed him back to reality. They bonded in the days that followed, and Halpern confided the dilemma that prompted his ayahuasca nightmare. A Harvard-trained psych resident he might be, but the real world now intruded and Halpern doubted his own grit.

He was going to have to quit the psychedelic tourism he'd enjoyed since finishing med school. No more peyote by moonlight with Navajo elders. No more DMT pit stops inside the subconscious. He had to earn a living, pay off student loans and secure tenure. No more tripping. He would have to see patients, conduct rounds, and collect a salary like any other shrink.

Funny thing, said Pickard. He'd recently inherited a million bucks. He had even more cash squirreled away from "the old days"—a reference Halpern reckoned later to be code for untaxed profits Pickard earned before his 1988 acid bust.

"I've never met anybody in my life who would have hundreds of thousands of dollars just laying about," said Halpern. "Never in a safe; just—it's in a shoebox, you know?"

It did not occur to Halpern that Pickard might still be manufacturing the stuff. No way a Harvard Kennedy School grad student needed to break the law. Regardless, Pickard's offer of a loan sounded good to Halpern.

Years would pass before his ayahuasca terror resurfaced as Kafkaesque nightmare.

Leonard began spending more and more time in New Mexico, but kept up his ongoing research into Russian heroin. He split his schedule between Taos and Cambridge with a pit stop now and again in Eastern Europe. As his newest confidant, Halpern gained insight into the latest scoop on designer drugs. Drugs like fentanyl.

It was fentanyl, in fact, that led Pickard to the strange case of George Eric Marquardt—a cautionary tale he shared during one of his New Mexico sojourns with both Halpern and Alfred Savinelli.

A brilliant self-taught chemist, George Marquardt was arrested in 1993 as he was moving his lab from Boston to Wichita. During his subsequent trial, prosecutors connected Marquardt's synthetic heroin to some 250 deaths up and down the Eastern Seaboard.

In pleading guilty, Marquardt described his occupation as "drug manufacturing."

"Of what kind?" asked US District Judge Patrick Kelly.

"Clandestine," answered the forty-seven-year-old shambling lump who stood before the bench.

"Sir?"

"Clandestine," repeated Marquardt. He stroked his ZZ Top chin whiskers, shifted weight from one scuffed work boot to the other, and continued: "I don't know that I've had an occupation outside of being a career drug manufacturer."

Pickard was familiar with his legend. A Washington state narcotics agent once declared, "this guy can make dope out of the dirt in your pockets." Even while doing one-to-ten in an Indiana reformatory for car theft back in the seventies, Marquardt brewed up enough speed and hallucinogens to keep his cell block buzzed through much of his sentence. He never got caught cooking.

Like Owsley and Scully and Leonard himself, Marquardt began as prodigy. His initial brushes with the law were ironic, even quaint. In 1966, Marquardt passed himself off as a youthful exec with the Atomic Energy Commission. He was lecturing comely young physics students at an all-girl Catholic college in Milwaukee when the FBI arrested him. In reality, he was a twenty-year-old Waukesha High School dropout then on probation for stealing an oscilloscope from the University of Wisconsin.

"Things in his lectures did not ring true," said Sister Emelius, chair of the Alverno College chemistry department.

Pickard found empathetic points of recognition all over Marquardt's record. Marquardt never fit in at school, not because he was inept or lazy, but because he was obsessed with chemistry. Waukesha High expelled him a month ahead of graduation. He refused to study English or history. Even math made him cringe.

Like Pickard, Marquardt aced statewide and even national science competitions. At six, he was dismantling and rebuilding TV sets. When other kids played Little League, Marquardt was developing his own method for dating fossils with carbon-14. He was not so nerdy that he was immune to puberty. A high-tech surveillance system inside the girls' locker room turned out to be a Marquardt project. He had an early, prurient interest in the connection between sex and psychedelics.

His romance with LSD began at age twelve after he watched a junior high public health film. Dosed with acid, a mouse began chasing a cat through the movie. Marquardt was mesmerized. He cooked his first batch before his fourteenth birthday.

Classmate Clifford Goerke remembered a strange, angry kid who bucked authority and threw tantrums at the slightest provocation. Marquardt distanced himself from his God-fearing parents, retreating to his basement laboratory. When his father grumbled about all the electricity he was using, Marquardt rigged a cable to a nearby transmission line, bypassing meters.

He regarded his teachers as imbeciles. In a final effort to broaden his education, his high school counselor let him take college-level chemistry at nearby Carroll University. He found the professor as useless as his high school instructors and dropped out anyway.

Over the next couple of years, Marquardt lied his way into research positions at Marquette and Northwestern universities, as well as the Argonne Research Laboratory in Chicago, where Leonard had once interned.

While posing as a biochemist at the University of Wisconsin, Marquardt made off with $2,476 in lab equipment, including a radiology device he sold to a used labware broker in Chicago. The device wound up at the University of Illinois where a comparison of serial numbers led school officials back to Marquardt. He was arrested while honeymooning in Los Angeles and back in jail before his first child was born.

Pickard never copped to it, but the case history of George Marquardt hit very close to home. The biggest difference seemed to be that Marquardt got caught more often and paid a far heavier price. By the time Leonard took an interest, Marquardt had spent half his adult life behind bars.

There was one more significant distinction, according to Leonard. Before he ever set foot inside his first jail, George Marquardt showed the makings of a budding Nazi.

"I could never have anything to do with any of that, and here's one reason why," said Pickard. "I grew up with stories from my uncle who was a soldier near the end of the war and among the first to enter the death camps. Fourteen-year-old girls he saw there on meat hooks. Even in his old age, this fine old warrior and huntsman would cry at the memories."

Marquardt apparently grew up free of holocaust horror stories. He admired Adolph Hitler's "ruthlessness of purpose," and said as much to his parents and teachers. The end always justified the means. His adolescent heroes were a pair of nineteenth century Prussian chemists[2] who put science ahead of sentiment.

"They weren't about being good human beings or bad human beings," he said. "They were about being good chemists."

Like Leonard, Marquardt was a wanderer. He took to roaming between prison stretches, landing in college towns much the way Pickard did. He snuck into labs at the universities of Oregon and Wisconsin to brew his newest mindbenders. Along the way, he lost his own taste for drugs. His contempt spiked for those who did indulge. He had zero pity for addicts and saw nothing wrong with feeding their habits.

"He got off on the power trip of being able to make drugs and what people would do to get them," said his ex-wife, Peggy Dulaney. "Girls—well howdy, they'd do anything."

The oddball Peg Dulaney married and nicknamed "Squeak" reeked of chemicals. He dressed in faded overalls and tripped over his own feet, but she found him endearing. They remained together fourteen years.

"He could be an arrogant son of a bitch with other people, and he always kept a .45 stuck in his britches, but with me he was real sweet," she recalled. "He was real good to my daughter, paid for all her schooling. He loves animals. We had seventeen dogs at one time, and a bunch of cats too."

During his longest stint outside of prison, he befriended his pursuers. Much like the mighty mouse who chased the cat in that long-forgotten sixties LSD film, Marquardt toyed with and talked to narcs more often than his fellow felons.

"He says that he solves chemical problems by envisioning himself as a nucleus within an atom and picturing what reactions

---

2. Emil Fischer (1852–1919), 1902 winner of the Nobel Prize for chemistry and Justus Liebig (1803–1873), the father of modern organic chemistry.

might take place around him," said John Duncan of the Oklahoma Bureau of Narcotics. The Marquardt he came to know was a joker and rough-hewn mystic.

Marquardt saw himself as a pioneer hero lifted from legend. He described his life to the *Tulsa World* in 1978 as "the last American folk adventure: The light in the moon . . . narcotics agents chasing you all over the land. It's a fantasy made real."

The occasion of his newspaper interview, however, was his latest bust for cooking. This time, he'd set up a three-room lab in his Muskogee home to manufacture LSD, but with a twist.

"It was going to be the hallucinogen of the future," he said. "It combined the best features of amphetamines, but acted more like LSD. The results were spectacular, beyond the realm of anything I ever experienced on LSD."[3]

Once more, Marquardt did his time then vowed to go straight. He walked out of prison a changed man. He set up a used lab equipment warehouse outside of Wichita he called Prairielabs. It attracted scant attention until a traveling salesman called 911 in August of 1992, gasping for breath.

Joseph Martier[4] stumped the ER physicians. The forty-two-year-old Pittsburgh solar heating salesman who called the EMTs to Prairielabs nearly died from fentanyl poisoning, which made no sense because nobody outside anesthesiology even knew what fentanyl was. A hundred times stronger than heroin, a speck the size of a salt crystal could provoke instant respiratory arrest. The DEA came to know fentanyl as "serial killer of the drug world." Some

---

3. 2,4,5 trimethoxyamphetamine was synthesized just once on American soil, and never again.

4. A law school dropout, Martier teamed with a former Exxon chemist to corner the market on PCP in western Pennsylvania. Arrested along with members of the Pittsburgh biker gang that distributed their product, Martier and his codefendant were convicted in 1979 and sentenced to fifteen years each.

junkies died so quickly the hypodermics were still stuck in their veins.

"They died before they could get high," said a representative of the Philadelphia Health Department.

It took the DEA six months to link the dots which ran from Baltimore to Boston, Pittsburgh to Prairielabs. The final dot landed in George Marquardt's home laboratory. As Leonard did during his 1988 arrest, Marquardt stood by during the raid and offered fair warning to the task force that swept past him in HazMat suits. Breathe the fumes or touch the dust at your peril; this shit could body slam a whale.

Fentanyl was George Marquardt's Waterloo. While the Russian variety measured roughly eighty times stronger than China white, Marquardt's was closer to four hundred times as potent. The DEA priced a kilogram at between $240,000 and $640,000. By comparison, heroin went for $100,000 to $200,000 a kilogram and cocaine, a mere $20,000 to $25,000.

In court, he did not deny he made it, but took no responsibility for the dozens who OD'ed. They knew the risks every time they stuck a needle in their arms. Marquardt had no pity. He fascinated Leonard Pickard.

With Mark Kleiman's approval, and awareness of the Harvard Human Subjects Committee, Leonard located Marquardt in March of 1995. At fifty-one, he was beginning a thirty-year prison term in Oregon. Explaining in a letter that he wanted to more clearly understand fentanyl's effects, Pickard flattered Marquardt as the expert that he was. He enclosed a research questionnaire.

Was fentanyl pleasant? Would its use spread? Was Marquardt familiar with an ultrapotent form of the drug strong enough to flatten an elephant? What precursors did he use? How might the chemicals be monitored on a global scale?

After folding Marquardt's responses into his ongoing Russia project, and with Marquardt's permission, Pickard forwarded his findings to the UN Drug Control Program in Vienna.

"The gem of his reply," Pickard said later, was that the DEA hadn't confiscated his lab after he was arrested. It was still out there, somewhere in Kansas—a fact Pickard salted away for future reference.

IX.

DR. DAVE NICHOLS COUNTED AMONG the world's leading neuropharmacologists. In 1993, with seed money from Laurence S. Rockefeller, he cofounded the Alfred Heffter Research Institute—a Santa Fe nonprofit meant to fill the vacuum after government grants dried up for psychedelic study.

"I'd like to think it's the beginning of a renaissance," he proclaimed. "LSD and other hallucinogens are very important tools in helping us answer a very old and important question: what is man, why are we here, and who are we?"

Every academic psychonaut worth his or her salt sat on Heffter's board. Microsoft pioneer Bob Wallace[1] was an early benefactor and both Sasha Shulgin and John Halpern hired on as consultants. Named for the nineteenth century German biochemist who first extracted mescaline from peyote, the Heffter Institute funded clinical studies for federally-approved human experiments with psychedelics at the University of Arizona, Harvard, and universities in Switzerland and Russia.

---

1. Microsoft's ninth employee, Wallace coined the term "shareware." In 1996, Wallace and wife Megan Dana-Wallace opened Mind Books in Berkeley where Nick Sand re-emerged in his first public appearance following his years underground. Wallace died unexpectedly of pneumonia in 2002. He was fifty-three.

A jolly academic who devoted his career to resurrecting psyche-delic medicine, Nichols attracted grad students by the score to his medicinal chemistry classes at Purdue University—among them, Leonard Pickard.

During his first three months after settling in at the Kennedy School, Leonard gravitated to Purdue. At Shulgin's urging, Nichols spoke with him about his plan to spin his Kennedy School master's thesis into a serious, long-term study of the abuse of emerging drugs.

"He was *real* enthusiastic," said Nichols.

Pickard regaled both Nichols and his longtime lab assistant with his tales of visiting faraway places for his thesis. Pakistan. Russia. Amsterdam. He also hinted that the government—perhaps the CIA—might have a hidden hand in subsidizing Leonard's travels.

Unlike Nichols's other much younger grad students, Pickard was a contemporary. They were born a year apart. It didn't take much conversation for Nichols to recognize a fellow psychonaut. Thus, when Leonard proposed to visit his lab, Nichols was both flattered and in instant agreement.

"My assistant, Stewart, made the LSD we used for our rats," said Nichols, "so I introduced them. Leonard got to know Stewart pretty well."

Pickard's subject was among Dr. Dave's favorites: the alchemy of LSD. Like Sasha Shulgin and Rick Strassman, Nichols held one of the DEA's precious Schedule One licenses. Pickard planned to explore methods for detecting and controlling drug synthesis, he explained, and wanted to see first-hand how it was done in the lab.

"In the run-up to '96, I studied a wide range of substances in an effort to predict the next major drug of abuse," said Pickard. "To do so, I looked at things from different angles: the ease of synthesis, the availability of precursors, the number of synthetic approaches, the potencies, the 'pharmacokinetics' of each (how the body metab-olizes the material)."

Leonard arrived in Indiana the following July with exciting news. He'd been writing to a Norwegian chemist who, quite by accident, came up with a whole new method of improving lysergic analogues, as well as fentanyls, but with potentially dire results.

"I did correspond with (Dr. Paul) Froyen on some esoteric aspect of chemistry, then unrelated to LSD," he recalled years later. "Very interesting mechanism. Subtle, effectively unknown."[2]

Pickard reasoned that the more known about LSD architecture and fentanyl, the better. He later denied he was merely swapping recipes with Froyen.

Since moving to Harvard, Pickard had been building his library and expanding his database. His focus might be drug abuse prevention, but curbing Russian fentanyl was just the tip of his ambitions. He also focused on future designer drugs—addictive mind benders as yet unimagined.

In addition to his research fellowship and frequent travel, he busied himself deciphering foreign treatises on addictive and psychoactive drugs. Before summer session began at Purdue, he'd translated Czech, German, and Hungarian lysergic patents into English. He tracked down precursor chemical suppliers in a half-dozen European nations. He showed all the poise and dexterity of Victor Frankenstein stocking his basement laboratory.

Despite this feverish activity, some of his Harvard professors remained unimpressed. One said Pickard was more talk than action. Another grew wary of his Russian connections.

"I didn't know their reputations," said Mark Moore, Guggenheim Professor of Criminal Justice Policy and Management. "They were unfamiliar to me then and have remained unfamiliar with me now."

---

2. "Paul came into play because I read his brief paper on a synthetic mechanism that possibly could result in improvements in the routes to certain controlled and deleterious psychoactives, but also including LSD. This was the topic of a paper I wrote which relied upon synthetic difficulty or ease as major factors in future abuse scenarios."

Dave Nichols disagreed. Seldom had he met a more dedicated student. Under his longtime assistant's supervision, he gave Pickard full run of his laboratory. Clearly here was a biochemist destined to leave his mark on the science of psychedelics—perhaps a future fellow of the Heffter Institute.

After finishing his work at Purdue, Pickard went on vacation.

"I came up from Delhi to Kathmandu in the summer of '95, between semesters at the Kennedy school," he recalled. "My itinerary that summer was Boston to London to Delhi to Kathmandu, then Delhi to Tashkent/Mazar to Moscow to Washington, DC, and then back to Boston."

It was a working vacation that he lavishly described two decades later in *The Rose of Paracelsus*. Replete with mysticism and out-of-body experience, Pickard spun an encyclopedic yarn of chance encounters with a handful of outlaw chemists who—like himself—led multiple lives in service to the sacred, secret production of LSD. In the logic of *The Rose*, it made perfect sense that he might run into one of them during a morning ramble through the Himalayas.

Pickard maintained that he never knew when he might happen upon one of the Six, each designated by a color straight out of a box of Crayolas: Crimson, Vermillion, Indigo, Magenta, and Cobalt. *The Rose* never names the sixth chemist nor does he ever meet Pickard, leaving readers to surmise that Pickard himself might be the missing crayon.

With each encounter, his colorful cabal delivers a new instruction or "mythopoeic" insight from yet another exotic locale. They are identified only as "nameless numbered files lost in the massive databases of the UN Precursor Control Program."

In *The Rose*, Pickard questions each of the Six in much the same way David Carradine questioned Master Po in the seventies TV series *Kung Fu*:

Pickard: He mentioned experiencing the breadth of the human condition?

Magenta: So that he remains humble and focused, even with his consorts, and not distracted by the trappings of global mobility, the odd castle bedroom, and unabated sexuality. . . .

Pickard: And Indigo? We met in Salzburg and Vienna.

Magenta: Indigo considers ritual preparation of sacraments, the spiritual practices necessary to function while exposed to millions of doses.

The Rose opens in 1994 when Leonard, the forty-nine-year-old Buddhist trainee, trips through San Francisco at daybreak accompanied by the wise and enigmatic Crimson, just before Pickard is about to depart for his new life at Harvard's Kennedy School. According to *The Rose*, by the time Pickard arrived in Kathmandu a year later, he had already chanced upon Indigo (during a break in a UN Drug Control conference in Vienna) and Vermillion (during a stopover in Berlin). His assignations among the Six usually happened abroad because none dared cook LSD in the US.

One close associate from that time said that Leonard later claimed a Nepalese drug lord threatened to hold him captive as his personal biochemist. Not so, countered Pickard.

"No problems in Nepal whatsoever," he said. "I very much enjoyed Kathmandu and parts north. Many memories, some of which I described in *The Rose*."

He did run into a British expatriate on that trip known only as Magenta. As with each of the other Six, Magenta whipped Pickard into an allusive froth that left many if not most *Rose* readers scratching their skulls and asking, "Huh?"

The inevitable contact high from one of the Six seemed amplified by the devotional resonance of Bodhinath. Magenta's walking stick tapped unceasingly like some secret code. We circled the mesmerizing ancient clockwork, telegraphing peace throughout the ten directions and untold realms. We became trekkers on the sacred mountain Meru with its rubies and amethysts and harlots and sanctified streams holding up the skies. The spinning became a spiral of reveries until we soon nodded at the wailing wall of Jerusalem, prostrated ourselves before the golden crucifixes of Florence, and ceaselessly recited a thousand sutras in Dharamsala. We whirled with our arms out and faces upwards like dervishes, and cycled among unknown lovers in the holy orgies of the Epidaurians.

Pickard's peculiar memoir drowns the reader in florid prose while making no reference to Deborah Harlow, their daughter Melissa[3], or the daily routine of domestic existence in Cambridge. Neither does *The Rose* acknowledge his fast-evolving camaraderie with John Halpern and Alfred Savinelli.

Instead, the overstuffed *roman a clef* features four far younger Kennedy School companions—two women, two men—who idolize Leonard as "Captain Pickard," their older, wiser classmate. He nicknames them Surf, Hagendas, Hulk, and Hammer, and spies on their respective sex lives, vamping like a coy 'tween diarist who constantly fears that his elders are eavesdropping. All four students are as real as the Six chemists, Pickard maintained, but remain anonymous to spare them the stigma of having befriended a felon.

Naysayers may scoff, but *The Rose of Paracelsus* is absolutely true, according to Pickard. Like Leonard himself, his memoir tiptoes through minefields of fact and fantasy, trusting that some misstep won't trigger ruin.

---

3. Pickard maintained that he does recount vignettes involving loved ones, but cloaked them in anonymity to spare them the mockery of knowing a felon.

The question of money arose during the summer of '95 and persisted over the remainder of the decade. Pickard's adjusted gross income that year was less than $8,000. He didn't bother to file a tax return. Nonetheless, he was able to trot the globe on a whim. He possessed a couple of Visa cards, managing minimum payments that totaled $1,042 by year's end.

That he seemed to fly off regularly to Indiana, New Mexico, Moscow, or Kathmandu raised no eyebrows at the time because he was a student, after all, and travel was part of the curriculum. How he got around wasn't important. How he could afford grand gestures of generosity was more problematic, though not so much to his recipients.

"Leonard was terrible managing money," said Alfred Savinelli. "Just terrible."

A California transplant first lured to Taos by the high desert romance of *Easy Rider*, Savinelli was a latter-day hippie in desperate need of cash himself when Pickard first showed up on his doorstep.

Savinelli opened Native Scents in October of 1989. He advertised himself as a "wildcrafter" who extracted "oils, essence, homeopathic and ceremonial plant products" that Native Scents marketed in twenty-three countries around the world. Savinelli maintained a lab on the premises to mine his oils and essences from local flora and fauna. He regularly ordered test tubes and flasks, compounds and catalysts to facilitate the extraction process.

By 1995, the business was floundering and Savinelli's two original business partners balked. A bank loan to buy them out was unfeasible: no financial institution saw the upside of essential oils and scented candles.

No problem, said Pickard. When John Halpern needed cash, Pickard promised a cigar box containing $100,000. He could work similar magic for Savinelli.

It never occurred to either Halpern or Savinelli to question the

source of the money. Pickard was older, wiser, and besides, he confided to Halpern that he lived a secondary secret life as a CIA oper-
ative. Halpern believed him. How else to explain his "sometimes
bizarre and secretive behavior?"

With the wolf at his door, Savinelli ignored his instincts. Pickard
ponied up an interest-free $300,000 loan. All Leonard asked in
exchange was a few supplies now and again ordered through chemical and labware distribution houses with which Native Scents regularly did business. A rotary evaporator here; a three-liter receiving
flask there. Nothing that would arouse suspicion.

"I should have known better," said Savinelli.

At the time, Pickard was renting a house on the outskirts of
Aspen—a Colorado resort town with high tolerance for recreational pharmaceuticals.[4] He told Savinelli he was experimenting
there with mescaline synthesis—nothing illegal, though an over-
ly-curious narc might not see it that way.

Like Savinelli, Leonard had taken a shine to northern New
Mexico, with its Rocky Mountain highs, artsy ambiance, and New
Age tolerance. Pickard thought he might move his operation from
Colorado and become Savinelli's neighbor. As 1995 wound to a
close, Savinelli and Halpern had become two of Leonard's clos-
est compadres, though neither get a single mention in *The Rose of
Paracelsus*.

When Pickard travelled to Amsterdam on Nov. 26, 1995, Halpern
and Savinelli tagged along. They were there for the annual Cannabis
Cup, where more than 100 growers competed among 1,500 connoisseurs, who fly in from all over the world to toke the finest weed
in Europe.

"You pay $100 and are given several different types of marijuana,"

---

4. Drug obsessed celebrities like Hunter S. Thompson and Jack Nicholson
    called Aspen home.

explained John Wilson, a stoner from Waco, Texas. "You smoke it and rate it on taste, smoothness, quality, potency. These guys have spent years crossbreeding into hybrids."

Although technically illegal, marijuana and hashish flourished in the Netherlands during the 1990s. Some 2,000 cafés openly sold baggies and bongs as frequently as they did lattés or beer. Amsterdam was an excellent venue for mingling with fellow psychonauts. That was why the three amigos were there.

"After that trip, I started to feel like Pinocchio coming back from the island of the bad boys," said Savinelli. "I was in way over my head and realized I had to re-evaluate the clique I'd fallen into."

Following John Halpern's disastrous ayahuasca episode in Savinelli's living room, the trio had bonded over Pickard's quest to uncover new and legal psychedelics. In much the same vein as Sasha and Ann Shulgin, Leonard carefully skirted Schedule One prohibitions. He kept away from forbidden compounds. He'd learned his lesson and would not cross the line. He'd made many friends there, but had no wish to return to Terminal Island.

Savinelli was as open to mind expansion as Halpern or Pickard. In addition to participating in Rick Strassman's DMT trials, he'd gone so far as to visit northern Mexico in search of Sonoran toads that were rumored to secrete a hallucinogenic enzyme. Largely through Savinelli's efforts, a whole new branch of psychedelic tourism eventually brought dozens of toad milkers to Sinaloan pueblos in search of amphibian discharge.

His attraction to Amsterdam, however, was the same as Pickard's: locating like-minded psychonauts.

"Leonard was cultivating contacts in the Netherlands," said Savinelli. "He met with a number of professors, some German, some Middle Easterners. I remember we ate sushi one night. These unsavory types show up. Leonard knew them. They take one look at me and ask, 'Who's this Jesus Christ looking guy?' I ignored 'em, but Halpern's gotta show that he's a free-thinking American. He sparks up a doobie. Those guys were *not* amused."

Savinelli didn't mind a spliff now and again, but not on so public a display and not among thugs. Pickard didn't indulge in cannabis at all.

"While I have visited many coffee shops in Amsterdam, I have never smoked in them," he said. "In some settings of drug users, I have feigned use to be accepted (but) I have never had a positive drug test, in prison or elsewhere."

If Leonard had any addictions, they were of a different order.

"My lab assistant Stewart went to Amsterdam with him once," recalled Dave Nichols. "Leonard took him to the red-light district. Stewart thought it was just part of the sightseeing, but the prostitutes knew Pickard by name. They trailed him down the street yelling: 'Leonard! Leonard!'"

Three months after their Amsterdam visit, Pickard invited his two traveling companions on another European jaunt, this time for a February weekend in Heidelberg. The Second International Conference of the European College for the Study of Consciousness attracted an even stranger crowd than Amsterdam. Psychonauts galore. Distinguished academics mixed with goths sporting green Mohawks. Grunge rock and voodoo blues supplied the soundtrack. The occasion was the launch of the so-called Heidelberg Declaration:

NO JAIL FOR DRUGS
We condemn . . .

the often brutal methods of criminalizing, detaining and even sentencing people to death for the use and trade of drugs in Malaysia, Saudi Arabia, the US and other countries. These are irrational acts of social control without general preventive effect that violate human rights. Drug problems cannot be solved criminally, but only preventively therapeutically. So it's an overall social task. The same applies to the use of addictive and toxic drugs such as heroin, cocaine, amphetamines, etc. . . .

The guest of honor at the conference was Dr. Albert Hofmann. Acid's inventor was among the first to sign the declaration. Halpern snapped Pickard's selfie with the original psychonaut—a treasure Leonard had framed when he got back to Cambridge, where he seemed to be spending less and less time.

Pickard turned the rest of 1996 into an unofficial sabbatical, beginning with a spring ceremony in New Mexico where he officially graduated from Zen novice to Buddhist priest.

"I was visiting with Kōbun and his family at a little retreat in Taos where he practiced formal Japanese archery and skied Taos Mountain," Pickard recalled. "Kōbun was quite the man."

Kōbun Chino Otogawa was a legendary *roshi* (master) who'd instructed Steve Jobs[5], among others. On April 8, 1996, Kōbun ordained Leonard Pickard in a ritual staged at the Arroyo Seco zendo on the outskirts of Taos.

"Leonard asked me to be his sponsor," said Savinelli. "I stood at his right side while he took the vows."

"Kōbun and I were both robed," Pickard recalled, "surrounded by Zen students and visitors in an austerely elegant Japanese ceremony."

Dispatched in the early sixties by his own Japanese Zen masters, Kōbun immigrated to California and originated the Zen practices at Tassajara and San Francisco's Zen Center. Kōbun was as strict as he was wry. More than once he'd corrected Leonard's *zazen* posture with a long wooden awakening stick (*kyosaku*). Pickard

---

5. At a 1991 ceremony in Yosemite's Ahwahnee Hotel, Kōbun married the Apple Computer founder to Laurene Powell.

spoke reverently of a moment when the legendary *roshi* aimed at an archery target, missed, and watched the arrow plunge into the Pacific. "Bull's eye," said Kōbun.

"Zennies love that story," chuckled Pickard. "It speaks of remembering the right target: the ocean of mind."

For Pickard's ordination, *roshi* Kōbun had crafted a special gift.

"Kōbun spent days writing a lineage chart in Kanji, four inches by seventy-two inches, with my name at the end, above which was his name, above which were a series of teachers dating back through 1200 AD, and into the distant past to 2500 BC," said Pickard. "He gave me the dharma name of Eihei Shunko, meaning 'Eternal Dharma, Bright Spring (or Spring Light).' In monastic settings, I may use Shunko as my name."

Having witnessed his non-monastic behavior in Amsterdam and Berlin, Savinelli remained unconvinced.

"Some Buddhist," he said. "I don't know how you go from taking vows to budding sex fiend."

Nonetheless, Shunko Pickard sat *zazen* that day without Kōbun chastising his wandering eye or the drifting thoughts that Zennies term "monkey mind." Leonard Pickard had many a worry tangling his brain. One of them involved Afghan heroin, international prisoner exchange, and Stinger missiles.

In an effort to put his Kennedy School connections to practical use, Pickard recalled Terminal Island conversations he'd once had with Afghan drug dealer Mohammed Akbar Bai.

"We sat together on a prayer rug in prison, sipping sweet black tea from crudely fired handmade cups beneath the only tree—a wretched little birch with few leaves for shade," Pickard recalled in *The Rose*. "We watched as disoriented inner-city crack addicts stumbled in circles nearby."

A fine fellow with two wives and ten children, Akbar had taken the fall for an opium wholesaler back home in Kabul—a powerful warlord named Abdul Rashid Dostum whom Leonard described as "diminutive and comfortably plump." While Akbar cooled his heels in US prisons during the eighties and nineties, Dostum rose to the rank of General in the Afghan Army. In one of his many overseas junkets, Pickard made a point of meeting Dostum on his own turf. Together, they planned ways that they might repatriate Akbar.

"I began connecting Akbar Bai weekly through Cambridge to Dostum on his satellite phone in the far deserts or in his compounds in Tashkent, Uzbekistan, and Mazar-i-Sharif, occasionally greeting Dostum and listening in on their long conversations in Dari," recalled Pickard. "Their hypnotic exchanges recalled the old burnished faces of Central Asia, the crushing poverty and beauty of the royal city of Mazar, and Kabul itself—an *anus mundi* whose outskirts were littered with the whitening bones of its exiles."

In his exalted new role, General Dostum[6] controlled much of the arsenal left behind during the CIA's secret war against Russian invaders in the eighties. His munitions included thirty shoulder-fired, heat-seeking Stingers worth $400,000 each. Pickard understood the General would be willing to return four of them to the US in exchange for Akbar's freedom.

Operation Infrared commenced.

In the first real world test of the diplomatic skills he'd acquired at Harvard, Pickard brokered a Washington, DC, meeting with US Customs officials. He arranged for the Carnegie Endowment for International Peace to act as intermediary. Aside from seeking Akbar's freedom, the General was equally intent on warning the US against the rise of the Taliban, but his entreaties fell on deaf ears.

---

6. After his election to the Afghan Presidency in 2001, Hamid Karzai promoted Dostum to Deputy Defense Minister. He became Vice-President in 2014.

"Dostum asked for US consular presence in Mazar-i-Sharif, but was refused," said Pickard. "In retrospect, he turned out to be right."

Pickard angled for a more modest and pragmatic deal: removing deadly Stingers from the volatile Afghan civil war. With serial numbers that Dostum provided, he was able to verify the missiles' existence.

"The CIA liaison confirmed the authenticity of three of them, saying the fourth had already been returned," said Pickard. "At the time, CIA had $60 million for the return of thousands of missiles, but didn't want to get involved."

In the lead up to their meeting, US Customs still doubted Dostum.[7]

---

7. As recounted in *House of Trump, House of Putin: The Untold Story of Donald Trump and the Russian Mafia* by Craig Unger (Dutton, 2018), President Trump's longtime associate Felix Sater also swapped Stingers:

His most notable early operation took place in 1998, when he went on the hunt for Singer antiaircraft missiles that the CIA had originally given to the mujahideen for use against the Soviets during their occupation of Afghanistan, but which were at risk of falling into the hands of radical jihadists.

Felix went to work. His attorney Robert Wolf called David Kendall, then President Bill Clinton's lawyer, and told him that Sater had serial numbers for the Stinger missiles the Clinton Administration had sought. After President Clinton was informed, Wolf then spoke to CIA general counsel Robert S. McNamara Jr. and read out the serial numbers of the Stingers.

But the CIA was still skeptical. Next, Felix provided photographs of the missiles with their serial numbers and a copy of a daily newspaper to show the photo was contemporaneous. Meanwhile, Wolf began extended talks with two men in the CIA's clandestine division about al-Qaeda, Osama bin Laden, and the Stinger missiles.

When President Clinton authorized the August 1998 bombing strike against al-Qaeda in retaliation for the terrorist bombings of the US Embassies in Kenya and Tanzania, *BuzzFeed* reported, no fewer than ten current and former intelligence and law enforcement officials said Sater "supplemented US Intelligence by providing location coordinates for al-Qaeda camps that the US military ultimately bombed in Khost, Afghanistan."

"Well, Felix got play for those Stingers," said Pickard. "Sadly, Akbar did not."

"I replayed this information to Ambassador Gelbard, who said the Customs response was nonsense; that arrangements could indeed be made for the return," said Pickard. "I volunteered to escort the Stingers across the Uzbek border into the American consulate. Just as Gelbard was about to act on the Stingers, he was appointed envoy to Bosnia for the Dayton Accords, and that was that."

Leonard's first crack at diplomacy fizzled.

"I thought about running over to Bosnia and asking Gelbard for a job at State," he said. "At the time, he likely would have hired me."

When the Stinger deal failed, Pickard and Dostum tried a different tack for springing Akbar.

According to courtroom testimony delivered years later, Dostum and Pickard planned to swap Akbar for an Afghan peasant whom they intended to set up with eight hundred kilograms (1,760 pounds) of contraband heroin before he entered the US:

"This guy was going to go to jail," testified the prosecution's star witness. "Initially, Leonard told me that the man's family was being paid off and it was $1 million US dollars, and that he would . . . the man would voluntarily do this."

The witness said that Pickard wavered on the details of his story over time, but not the central idea. Dostum would "give" the US an Afghan peasant plus the heroin he muled out of the Middle East in exchange for Akbar's freedom.

"And I said, 'Leonard, do you realize this man has no concept of what it is to do life in prison in the United States?' He said, 'It doesn't make any difference because it's better than what life (he has) currently,'" testified the witness.[8]

His name was Gordon Todd Skinner.

---

8. In his defense, Leonard testified the heroin shipment was designed to track how Afghan traffickers got the payload past US Customs, not as a basis for prisoner exchange.

X.

"SKINNER LOVED TO BE THE candy man," recalled Alfred Savinelli. "He was a second-generation drug-pushing pedophile. He had nine lives and had already burned through seven of them by the time Leonard met him."

Gordon Todd Skinner went by "Todd," much the same way that Pickard used his middle name among family and friends. Todd and Leonard. Leonard and Todd.

When he introduced them, Savinelli had no inkling they would become the oddest of odd couples or that he—Savinelli—would be the unwitting matchmaker.

Leonard flunked out of Princeton the same year that Todd was born. Despite the twenty-year age difference, there were similarities. Both came from privilege, clashed early and often with the law, and were exceptionally tall. Todd stood six foot five and weighed in at 238 pounds. Leonard was three inches shorter and fifty pounds lighter.

Todd looked the part of a mad monk, tonsured and hunched as if newly released from the belfry at Notre Dame. He was prematurely bald and bearded whereas Leonard was clean-shaven and had a full head of long flowing silver. Todd was lethargic; Leonard, a marathon runner—the tortoise and the hare.

When first they met, Pickard sensed an ally in Skinner. He

might be young, but seemed as dedicated a psychonaut as Sasha or Dave Nichols, or perhaps even Albert Hofmann himself. Skinner wanted to turn on the whole world. The two men registered instant simpatico in the sense that each intuited opportunity in the other. It took a year or two, but when Leonard's opinion finally did begin to shift, it dropped slowly beneath contempt and kept descending all the way to hell.

"He's a kind of preserved infant, but gargantuan, his face empty as a zero," said Leonard with undisguised sarcasm. "We refer to him as 'Bozo.'"

Skinner cared spit-little about the opinions of others. As with virtually everything about their relationship except their shared passion for psychedelics, Skinner and Pickard differed on the facts, including the date and circumstances of their fateful first encounter.

Skinner maintained under oath that he made Pickard's acquaintance at a San Francisco shamanic botany conference in late October of 1996. He distinctly recalled Leonard wheeling a suitcase containing $700,000 in cash through a hotel lobby. When Leonard haltingly asked Todd to help him with his, uhm, "laundry," Skinner heard the mumbling solicitation of a stuttering giraffe.

"You can't ever tell what's going on with his strategies," said Skinner. "He's usually double dealing on both sides."

Pickard takes a moment to catch his breath. Double-dealing? And from the lips of the greatest double dealer since Benedict met Arnold? Leonard insists he didn't actually meet Todd until February of 1998, during a session of the American Academy of Forensic Scientists . . . and the stuttering giraffe, by the way, was Skinner, not Pickard.

"He only appeared during that last year, really," insisted Pickard. "He lurked at a few earlier conferences, but he had *nothing* to do with big LSD, even though forever after he claimed otherwise."

Todd—not Leonard—was the aggressor, said Pickard. Right off

the bat, Skinner sucked up with promises of drugs and money. He hooked Leonard with the Big Lie.

"Basically I just made up quite a story and told him that we could possibly get some money from (billionaire Warren) Buffett," Skinner revealed later on the witness stand. "And I had quite a bit of fun with that one, but it really, in the end, upset him quite a bit."

His curiosity piqued, Pickard gave Skinner his full attention, but maintained his interest was purely academic.

"I found him a subject of interest for my research in novel drugs of abuse (e.g., Marquardt)," he said. "He was very familiar with variations of ayahuasca. Skinner attached himself with numerous members of the (psychonaut) community, and promoted himself as an heir with an interest in research."

Alfred Savinelli remembers the Skinner/Pickard link in less dramatic terms. As the person most responsible for putting them together, he remains almost apologetic. John Halpern once praised Skinner as "the world's greatest liar." Savinelli agrees, but would hardly characterize that title as praise.

"The very worst kind of human being," he said.

As with Halpern and Pickard, it was Rick Strassman's DMT study that first brought Skinner knocking at Savinelli's door. Skinner wanted some of that Spirit Molecule. He simply *had* to meet Strassman.

Alfred made the introduction. Strassman has never thanked him.

"Skinner showed up at my office at the University of New Mexico in '92 or '93," said Strassman. "He talked about all the drugs he had made and all the drugs he had taken. It was not a conversation but more like me listening to a guy possessed. I didn't get a good feeling. It was one of the few times my instincts were right."

Gordon Todd Skinner was born to the manor, Oklahoma-style. He and his family moved to Tulsa in 1967, when he was three. His father, also named Gordon, operated a chiropractic clinic. His mother, Katherine, ran a successful industrial spring manufacturing firm.

An imperious woman with a head for business, Katherine divorced and remarried thrice before her son entered high school.[1] In between weddings, she raised Todd. He came to understand that the father figures in his life were expendable.

Skinner attended private Cascia Hall Catholic Preparatory. He was eccentric, even as a freshman. He wore blazers and ties, fur coats, and switched over to full tux on free dress days. His second stepfather, Gary Magrini, chauffeured him to campus in a 1957 Bentley.

Skinner spent off hours at the Peace of Mind bookstore, the closest thing Tulsa had to the Brotherhood of Eternal Love's Mystic Arts World. He haunted the shelves devoted to sorcery.

At Cascia Hall, Todd excelled at all the traditional geek pursuits: chess, martial arts, mathematics. One classmate remembers Belushi behavior in the cafeteria. He'd capsize lunch trays, then run off giggling.

He gravitated early to altered states. While peers made papier-mâché volcanoes, Skinner extracted tryptamines from tumbleweeds. One friend's father, a NASA engineer who helped design the space shuttle, found Todd and his son synthesizing DMT in the basement. He warned the boys against messing in Pandora's box. Todd ended that friendship.

Skinner saw himself as Promethean—stealing fire from the gods and dispensing it in the form of mind-blowing sacraments to convert the Great Unwashed, starting with his school chums.

"All of my high school friends just lined up to take anything that I had," he recalled. "I was just a scientist saying, 'Try this out.'

---

1. Married and divorced twice from Skinner's chiropractor father Gordon Henry Skinner, the second time after she caught him molesting a child. She then married William Imholf for eighteen months, and finally IRS agent Gary Magrini.

And unfortunately, they were all just guinea pigs in line. Some of them thought it was great, and some of them don't talk to me to this day. . . ."

His Cascia Hall yearbook featured Todd in all-white karate jumpsuit. The caption read, "REMEMBER: His penmanship, the wing-tip collar, 'How's the Universe?' and N2O (nitrous oxide)." Classmates recall Todd lugging tanks of laughing gas to school and offering free huffs in the boys' room.

After graduation in 1982, Skinner's parents sent him to Heidelberg for an expensive international education,[2] but like Pickard, he flunked out first semester. He returned home angry, ashamed, but unapologetic. He worked half-heartedly but only occasionally at his mother's Gardner Springs Company. He had zero interest in mechanics. He preferred staying up on the latest New Age chemistry through a loose knit "neuro-network" of like-minded psychonauts.

Like Leonard, Todd eschewed narcotics. Street drugs were for losers, though he didn't mind selling them. Skinner was a capitalist, after all, and what the people demanded, he gladly supplied.

For himself, however, Skinner maintained higher standards. During one of several Mexican marijuana treks through Laredo, Texas, he'd also loaded 10,000 peyote buttons in gunnysacks and hid them in the trunk of his car. He told himself he was on a mission for the Native American Church, though none of its 250,000 members were aware of his magnanimity. He planned to extract the mescaline, which he regarded as a sacrament, then sell it to the Navajo, but felt dutybound to sample it first. The Doors of Perception opened.

"I was in a room that was small and all of a sudden it was like a

---

2. Skinner attended Schiller International University. He majored in finance and supplemented his income by exchanging currency at prevailing rates and charging a service fee. He dealt drugs, but rarely went to class.

set on the Ponderosa!" he recalled, his awe as fresh as a nosegay of Morning Glories.

As a newly-enlightened psychonaut, Skinner began attending any and all psychedelic conferences. Though Savinelli insisted he doesn't remember, Skinner maintained they first met at the annual Telluride Mushroom Festival in 1984, when Todd was only nineteen.

The following year, Skinner attended Mycophile IV, another 'shroom celebration staged in the San Juan Islands off the coast of Seattle. Mycophile drew many a heavy hitter from the hallucinogenic fringe: holistic health guru Dr. Andrew Weil, fungi expert and future TED talker Paul Stamets, PhD, and Albert Hofmann protégé Jonathan Ott,[3] English translator of Hofmann's German memoir, *LSD, My Problem Child*. Skinner felt right at home.

His stepfather's profession commanded much of young Todd's non-psychedelic attention. Gary Magrini was a career IRS agent recently assigned to the DEA—a glamour job in Skinner's eyes. Magrini worked at the periphery of tracking cartels, contributing to national intelligence and conning con men. He also spent a lot of time keeping his stepson out of trouble.

When Las Vegas police arrested Skinner the summer after high school for trying to pass bad checks, Magrini sprung him and got the charges expunged. He also forgave the lad for making off with Magrini's government-issue sidearm.

But he could not check his stepson's appetite for drug trafficking or spinning truth into fiction.

One day in the spring of 1984, Skinner called the Tulsa FBI office with an offer to bring down an international money laundering

---

3. Credited with coining the term "entheogen" as a psychedelic synonym, Ott moved to Mexico where he established a medicinal herb business akin to Savinelli's Native Scents. He once boasted his LSD was superior to Pickard's. In 2010, an arsonist burned his business, including rare volumes willed to him by Albert Hofmann.

operation. He told the agent who answered that he'd recently struck a deal with a Texas con artist named Sam Merit. Posing as heir to his mother's Gardner Springs Company, Skinner offered to loan Merit $300,000 to purchase an interest in a Caribbean charter airline and to develop a bogus Arizona gold mine.

Skinner offered the FBI few details as to how a nineteen-year-old college dropout got involved in so far-fetched a scheme, but his story did check out. The case would take years to successfully prosecute, but Merit eventually fled to South Africa after he and five of his cronies were indicted in an elaborate penny stock fraud.

Meanwhile, Skinner enmeshed himself in a fraud of his own. Claiming once again that he was heir to his mother's fortune, he opened an account with a Philadelphia brokerage house that specialized in foreign currency options. Skinner boasted to the *Tulsa World* that he sat on the Philadelphia Stock Exchange and operated a currency trading company called FINIX, but when his margins were called six months later, it turned out Skinner owed over $1.5 million.[4]

And he did all of this before celebrating his twenty-first birthday.

But Todd Skinner was just getting started. He moved easily between highbrow and lowlife. During the mid-eighties, he bounced between Tucson and Little Rock and Hot Springs, Arkansas, attending psychonaut conventions and hatching get rich quick schemes. In between, he snitched for the Department of Justice.

Todd befriended Boris Olarte, a Colombian cocaine dealer who'd bought a business from his mother.[5] Olarte was subsequently

---

4. In 1992, a jury found him and his mother guilty of bankruptcy fraud, awarding defendants $1,150,950.50. Skinner's mother paid $100,000. Skinner filed for bankruptcy.

5. In the mid-1980s, Katherine Magrini sold custom chocolates under the brand name "Okie Power." After Boris Olarte bought the business, was arrested, and made his deal with the government, his wife flew to Aruba with FBI agents to set up Olarte's supplier.

busted, then consigned to the Tulsa County jail. Using his step-father's connections, Skinner persuaded the DEA to put Olarte into the Federal Witness Protection Program as a first step toward turning him against the Medellín drug cartel.

His role in helping bring down the Colombians could not have happened at a better time for Skinner, who was simultaneously smuggling drugs himself. He got caught, first crossing the Mexican border with marijuana at Sells, Arizona, in November 1986, then peddling grass in Boston with a high school chum.

His drug dealing climaxed Jan. 26, 1989, with his arrest in the lobby of a Hyatt Hotel in Camden, New Jersey. Bail was set at $1 million. Charged with being a cannabis kingpin, Skinner was sentenced to three years' probation. Jersey authorities were less forgiving than Tulsa police or the feds. Skinner spent his twenty-fifth birthday in jail before he reached out once again to his stepfather. Gary Magrini advised his boy to make a deal.

Skinner turned snitch and gave up his customers. While the New Jersey Narcotics Strike Force eavesdropped, he wore a wire during the sale of thirty pounds of weed to a trio of hapless Jersey pot dealers. Skinner would later testify against John Worthy, his wife Willie Mae, and sidekick Lamont Briscoe. The case ultimately turned out to be tainted[6] for the government, but Skinner walked free, right into another sting.

He cooperated next with the government on a Jamaican drug case against the Morgan brothers of Montego Bay. Dennis, John, and Horace Morgan controlled a string of gas stations as well as a hotel, a car rental, and the Fairfield Plantation resort on the north-west coast of Jamaica. Though Fairfield could accommodate up to sixty tourists at a time, the Morgans limited occupancy to tamp down risks to their far more lucrative side business. According to the DEA, they had a lock on the hash, grass, and cocaine market.

---

6. In 1995, the New Jersey Supreme Court threw out the wiretaps and testimony: "The credibility and character of Skinner was . . . questionable."

Skinner's assignment was to persuade John Morgan to meet him in the nearby Cayman Islands on the pretense that Todd had a boat to sell: a vessel suitable for smuggling bales of grass. In the Cayman capital of Georgetown, Skinner was told, local police could arrest Morgan, then send him to the US to face charges.

On Dec. 7, 1989, Todd flew to Grand Cayman accompanied by two Gloucester County detectives and a DEA representative from the Miami office. They set up the sting.

On Feb. 20, 1990, Skinner flew to Jamaica to woo Morgan. Using a string of aliases,[7] he chartered a seventy-eight-foot oil tanker. All looked perfect until a hurricane intervened, wrecked the tanker, and ruined the ganja shipment.

But Skinner wasn't done stinging in the Caribbean. He met a South Dakota Bible banger during one of his Jamaican visits. A former minister of the Des Moines-based Open Bible Standard Church, Everette LaVay McKinley set up the World Fidelity Bank on the island of Grenada, promising a 48 percent return on investment. Two hundred twelve church members gave the Reverend a total of $5.5 million to invest. They never saw it again.

Skinner testified about McKinley's attempt to involve him in his scheme, and the court gave McKinley twenty-seven years.[8] At his sentencing, McKinley invoked Proverbs 29:27, which warns against partnering with a thief:

The fear of man bringeth a snare,
but whoso putteth his trust in the LORD is safe.

---

7. James Young, Charles Fletcher, Gerard Terrance Finnegan, P.C. Carroll, and William Good, among others.

8. McKinley pled down to four months in prison and had to pay $4.89 million in restitution. He ran unsuccessfully for the South Dakota House of Representatives as an Independent in 2016 and died two years later on April 20, 2018. He was sixty-four and still a member in good standing of the Open Bible Church.

"Scripturally, I was wrong," muttered McKinley, "but I won't make that mistake again."

In 1992, Todd said that he ruptured a disc in his back. He went on prescription pain meds: Soma, Carcipital, Percocet, Demerol, Flexeril, Parnate . . . and became addicted. He came to loathe opioids. By November of that year, he maintained that he'd kicked his habit, but a habit he vowed never to kick was psychedelics. He did not smoke or drink or snort speed or opiates, but never, *ever* did he turn down an opportunity to trip.

In answer to a prosecutor's question about his recreational drug use, Todd carefully parsed his courtroom response, as if God were listening in: "I seem to have an idiosyncratic response to entheogens. That they are—have—(maybe that's arrogant, so I've got to be careful) . . . they are very spiritual and sacramental things. I do not use these—I think you put it, 'recreationally.' And I take offense to that, unfortunately, because I do not take these things recreationally. These are sacraments to me."

From PCP-A receptors to 5-fluoro-alpha-methyltryptamine, *amanita muscaria* to *psilocybe cubensis*, Todd had tried every sacrament he could lay fingers on—163 different compounds, once he sat down and counted them all. He meshed the best into a potion he called the Eucharist, which he served up in communion wafers to disciples at his very own Masses, recommending an ergot wine chaser in a golden chalice just the way Skinner fancied it must have been done 2,000 years ago.

One disciple later described the experience as sitting in a circle on the floor for about an hour while Skinner played ocean sounds and rainstorm LPs. He'd set up his altar and invite each communicant to step forward and get a hypodermic of his latest mystery serum.

"After the shot," said the disciple, "everyone was really drugged and would just lay around. Afterward, everyone said they had had very vivid dreams."

It was in this spirit that Skinner reconnected with Savinelli. DMT had always been on his menu, but his growing neuro-network emboldened his inner entrepreneur. In partnering with Savinelli, he came up with a scheme for synthesizing desert grasses into a domestic ayahuasca. Skinner figured he could sell the noxious brew to members of Santa Fe's fledgling União do Vegetal Church.

Portuguese for "Union of the Plants," the UDV Church had been founded in Brazil in 1961 with ayahuasca as its cornerstone. By the late eighties, when the New Age religion had spread to the US, ayahuasca's two essential ingredients,[9] which grew only in the Amazon rain forest, had been banned by the FDA. A twenty-year battle in the courts ensued, ultimately ending the import taboo,[10] but during the interim, Skinner tried repeatedly, if unsuccessfully, to fill the demand with his homegrown version.

Since his high school days, Skinner had maintained a lab at Gardner Springs where he tinkered with psychedelics. He searched for years for a synthetic sacrament. With role models like Sasha Shulgin and Owsley Stanley, Skinner concentrated on the chemistry of DMT, which occurred naturally in most plants.

Savinelli pursued a similar alchemy. A self-described "bad" (i.e. mischievous) shaman, Savinelli stalked mind-altering molecules in all living things. Alfred ate ants, milked toads[11] and smoked hemp, all in the service of connecting with his higher self.

"DMT is mother's milk," he was fond of saying. Like Todd,

---

9. The ayahuasca vine (Banisteriopsis caapi) and a shrub called chacruna (Psychotria viridis).

10. On February 21, 2006, the US Supreme Court ruled unanimously in favor of the UDV, allowing ayahuasca to be used as a sacrament by members of the church.

11. Skinner later refuted "the common story of people licking the toad, which is not what you do, that is dangerous, causes foaming of the mouth. But the Sonoran Desert Toad has this excretion that if you excrete it onto a glass slide, you can scrape off this material and you'll get the main constituent being 5-methoxy and dimethyltryptamine."

he'd consume almost anything to become one with the universe. He experimented with ketamine and Hawaiian baby woodrose seeds, which contain d-lysergic acid amide, approximating an LSD experience.

But the mother lode remained pure Delysid-grade acid. From Sandoz to Eli Lilly, from the Bernards to the Bear, the modern-day alchemist's holy grail was perfect triple-set[12] LSD-25. Many tried to make it. Few succeeded.

"There are less than ten chemists who manufacture LSD, and they all know each other," said Skinner.

And the best known, Todd came to understand after years of sniffing around, was an ex-con named William Leonard Pickard. Like Owsley, he'd done his time and appeared to have retired, but Todd believed otherwise.

His instincts weren't wrong. However well-meaning he'd been in heeding Judge Patel's advice, Leonard found psychedelics as irresistible as did Skinner or Savinelli. After following Sasha Shulgin's career and studying Dave Nichols's lysergic formulae up close and in the lab, Pickard had to dabble.

By the time he met Todd Skinner, he'd fallen into a Jekyll and Hyde routine: Harvard Fellow by day, alchemist whenever he could get away. Following Nick Sand's example, Dr. Jekyll maintained the appearance of a happily married Boston policy wonk, while Mr. Hyde perpetually kept on the move.

---

12. Reworked three times to increase purity.

XI.

TIM LEARY SUCCUMBED TO PROSTATE cancer on May 31, 1996. He was seventy-five.

Acid's original Messiah had abandoned the Witness Protection Program twenty years earlier for a D-list Hollywood existence. *Hustler* publisher Larry Flynt and his rival Hugh Hefner befriended him. Winona Ryder was his goddaughter. Leary wrote books, made talk show appearances, pontificated, and partied on demand. When he wasn't schmoozing at the Playboy Mansion, Leary and his old Millbrook nemesis G. Gordon Liddy hit the campus debate circuit, turning their respective roles in the War on Drugs into carnival sideshow.

Schedule One, preached Leary, ushered in "an inquisition, a moral crusade against individual freedom and choice." While failing to acknowledge his own significant role in dropping a two-decade shroud over psychedelic study, Leary cried in the wilderness for the rest of his life.

"LSD is obviously a very important tool in understanding the brain and human consciousness," he said. "The suppression of that search by the government is a political scandal."

But America was too busy embracing disco in the seventies and neoconservatism in the eighties to hear what he had to say. Psychedelics were passé. Near the end of his life, Leary announced that genetics and space migration would be the next big things. The Internet and virtual reality fascinated him. He called the personal computer "the LSD of the 1990s." His followers needed to "turn on, boot up, and jack in."

"Instead of 'justice,' he used to say 'just us,'" recalled his disciple Leonard Pickard.

Dr. Tim never reclaimed the bully pulpit he had during the sixties. "Question authority" was replaced by "Greed is good," and Drop City became a ghost town. Leary's personal life suffered as much or more than his public persona.

In 1990, daughter Susan committed suicide, as had the first of his five wives. The last divorced him in 1992. He and son Jack were estranged.

And yet Leary remained the eternal optimist. His final words were "Why not? Why not? Why not?" His ashes were shot beyond the ionosphere, along with those of *Star Trek* creator Gene Rodenberry.

It was the human brain, not space travel, that would be "the number one challenge of the twenty-first century," Leary insisted. "We're the licensed owners and operators of it, and we should learn how to use it. Psychedelic drugs are the tool to do that."

For those few still willing to listen, one of his final admonitions contained more than a hint of "tune in, turn on" defiance:

"Scientific study of drugs that expand consciousness and accelerate mental activity is a threat to any authoritarian state because it encourages innovative and creative thinking."

Leonard heard his swansong, and he agreed.

On September 26, 1996, Tim Leary's favorite chemist surfaced in a warehouse laboratory in the Vancouver suburb of Port Coquitlam. The Royal Canadian Mounted Police arrested David Roy Shepherd and five others with five kilograms of DMT, three kilograms of MDMA, five kilograms of MDA, forty-three grams of LSD, and fifteen kilograms of ergotamine tartrate. Mounties also confiscated a small arsenal, $500,000 in cash, and a pile of gold and silver bullion. It was the largest, most sophisticated psychonaut hub ever busted in the Western hemisphere. Overall value: more than $60 million.

It took authorities two more months to figure out that David Shepherd had been on the lam for nearly twenty years and that his real name was Nicholas Sand. His lab was deemed so extensive and hi-tech that Canadian drug busters turned the crime-scene video into a training film.

As for Sand, he was tried, convicted, and began serving his Canadian sentence before the US extradited him to San Francisco to face bail-jumping charges. Nick's old nemesis, Judge Samuel Conti, came out of retirement just to nail him, only to find that the extradition terms limited the size and weight of the book he could throw at Sand. The maximum was a disappointing five years to run concurrently with the Canadian sentence. In total, Sand did three and a half years before parole.

Leonard followed press reports about Sand's legal woes closely, but dared not reach out to his original role model. At the same time that Columbian cocaine was fading from the headlines, the DEA had inexplicably turned up the heat on LSD.

Another case Leonard quietly tracked at the time involved a forty-year-old Oregon entrepreneur with a reckless bent whom Pickard regarded as an existential threat to the whole acid underground.

Following a two-year investigation, DEA and local authorities combined forces to bust Bruce Michael Young on April 15, 1997, in the rural coastal community of Kerby, Oregon. Young and partner Bruce W. Kasten had gotten careless. They stiffed their landlord, who found several footlockers that his tenants left behind, loaded with labware. He also discovered barrels of ethanol, which he subsequently learned from the DEA is a bonding agent used to fix LSD to blotter paper.

"The bottom line is that this is a well-organized group that has produced millions and millions of hits of LSD," said Dan Durbin, spokesman for a joint DEA/Kerby task force. "This is not some fly-by-night afterthought."

The wayward son of a retired Missouri police chief, Bruce Young had been a self-styled chemist since his pot-smoking youth in the suburbs of St. Louis. Convicted twice on marijuana possession, he moved west in 1984. Giving his occupation as "Product R&D," he thrived beneath law enforcement's radar until 1995, when he bought an RV for $35,000 cash, moved to Kerby, and registered his mobile lab to a nearby residence, also purchased for cash: $165,000.

As the saga unraveled, details emerged linking Young[1] to Central American money laundering.[2] More names surfaced and the investigation grew.

After the bust, Leonard's interest spiked. He followed Young's case more closely, taking note of Young's associates. On the back of a Super 8 motel receipt dated Aug. 15, 1997, he scribbled some of the names: Robert Riep, Ernst Tüting, Ostermann Chemical Company.

Quizzed years later about their connection to Bruce Michael Young, Pickard remained mum. Those who know don't tell and those who tell don't know.

Pickard paid over $15,000 to American Express, Citibank, and MBNA in 1996, but sent nothing to the IRS. He filed no Form 1040 that year or the next, nor for the remainder of the decade. He

---

1. Young bonded out, jumped bail, and was arrested two years later in the Northern California town of Rohnert Park. When cops responded to a domestic disturbance call, they found Young and girlfriend Traci Michele "Butterfly" O'Rear in their motel room with two pounds of marijuana and $563,812 in cash. The couple later married while Young was in jail. He maintained that he'd found Jesus and gave up on LSD.
2. Skinner said he'd once seen Pickard mail packages of $10,000 to $30,000 to the Harris Corporation in Central America.

later explained that he either tapped into the tax-free trust left him by his parents or earned below the annual $10,000 filing minimum. He was a poverty case far too busy trotting the globe, making new friends, and warning the world about fentanyl to concern himself with money matters.

A huge benefit of studying at the Harvard Kennedy School was his exposure to second-, third-, and fourth-tier government officials: career apparatchiks characterized as essential members of the Deep State, but rarely recognized beyond Washington, DC.

CIA operations officer John Kenneth Knaus was just the sort of superspy Leonard would never have met outside Harvard. Best remembered as the agent who helped extract the Dalai Lama from Tibet in 1959, Knaus was a research associate at Harvard's Fairbank Center for Chinese Studies when Leonard approached following one of Knaus's lectures. Breaking the ice, Leonard mentioned that he'd once met the CIA's Robert Rewald[3] in Terminal Island.

"Oh, you mean that thing in Hawaii?" Knaus had asked.

"Yes, that thing in Hawaii."

Pickard quickly explained how he made Rewald's acquaintance while in prison. Leonard told Knaus that a government misunderstanding over "errant lab equipment" landed him briefly behind bars. He'd been mistakenly found guilty of drug manufacture and did a little federal time. He met several remarkable characters while inside including Akbar Bai and Rewald, but once Leonard walked free, he'd flipped over a new leaf. Voila! He was now a Harvard fellow.

"Knaus nodded somberly," recalled Pickard, "but with a detectable

---

3. An ex-pro football player who operated an elaborate Ponzi scheme in Honolulu during the 1980s, Ronald Ray Rewald maintained that his firm was a CIA front. Until it was unmasked as a fraud during a lengthy trial, Rewald's company—Bishop, Baldwin, Rewald, Dillingham, and Wong—was believed to have bilked investors of millions on behalf of the Agency. Rewald became a talent agent after leaving prison in 1995. He died in Hollywood in 2018.

air of guardedness, for this CIA operations officer had forgotten more secrets than most remember."

Pickard could tell by the hesitancy in Knaus's voice and the subtle shift of eyeballs behind his bifocals that he'd switched from chatty to cautious.

"He concluded that his new visitor, presumed at first to be an innocent HKS matriculant, had perhaps a roguish background that, as in Heisenberg's uncertainty principle, might shift perspective the closer it was observed. . . ."

Knaus twitched his mustache. "I'll check with Langley," he told Leonard.

Knaus wasn't the first, nor would he be the last, Kennedy School adjunct to hold Leonard at arm's length. If he'd checked with Langley as he said, Leonard heard nothing further about it. He and Knaus never spoke again. From thence forward, Leonard convinced himself to be more circumspect. He might be under government surveillance.

Nonetheless, Leonard used his other newly-developed CIA and State Department contacts to gain further foreign introductions. The Russian head of the MVD[4] (Ministry of Internal Affairs) was the first to grant him an audience in Moscow.

"An inroad," he said. "I kept recordings of those interviews."

The MVD contact led to others: Major General Alexander Sergeev, chief of MVD's drug division; Minister of Drugs Eduard Babayan; Vladimir Sorokin, chief chemist for the Russian National Forensics Laboratory. . . .

Pickard became a regular Russophile. The rise of fentanyl was now a cornerstone of his Kennedy School studies. In addition to profiling George Marquardt and surveying hundreds of Boston

---

4. Much like the American FBI, MVD was responsible for investigating and apprehending criminals and maintaining public order, but was also mandated to stop public intoxication, supervise parolees, and manage prisons and psychiatric hospitals, among other state functions.

addicts about their opioid habits, he began conducting similar analyses of strung-out Muscovites.

According to Skinner, he also took an active interest in studying Russian women. He may even have fathered a child with a Russian expat.[5] But at the same time Jekyll explored Moscow, Hyde was allegedly cooking acid in the Rockies.

When Skinner testified that he first heard about Pickard's moveable lab, it was still located in dilapidated quarters on the outskirts of Aspen. Leonard supposedly paid $15,000 a month rent.[6] The story Pickard told him was that he originally bought his lab equipment with winnings from a high-stakes poker game. Through his neuro-network, Skinner heard otherwise.

"Leonard somehow got into [Dave Nichols's] lab through saying he was going to do research work and he synthesized approximately sixty-six grams of LSD," he said. The street value, according to Skinner: $200,000.

Leonard could clearly afford the astronomical Aspen rent, but one icy winter in the Rockies was quite enough. He also had a standing rule: he moved his lab every other year no matter what. He wasn't going to wind up another Bruce Michael Young. From the Bernards through Scully and Sand, the biggest danger of getting caught came from remaining in one place too long.

In the fall of 1996, according to Skinner, Pickard began scouting the mountains of northern New Mexico for new digs.

With an introduction from Savinelli, Leonard came across David Haley, a Taos contractor/carpenter.[7] The sometime artist was

---

5. A Skinner fabrication, according to Pickard: "I had no children by an unknown party."

6. Another Skinner lie: "Aspen was beyond my means," said Pickard. "Generally, the Gordon Todd Skinner ravings ... are a panicky school of red herrings, created while he was being interrogated."

7. Savinelli maintained that Haley and Pickard met during an ayahuasca session at the New Buffalo bed and breakfast in Taos.

working on a landscape oil when Leonard stopped to admire. He struck up a conversation.

"He indicated he had a degree from Harvard and did work in the field of pharmacology," Haley recalled from the witness stand.

Pickard identified himself as John Connor[8] and his female companion as Edwina Chang.

"I found Edwina to be a very beautiful person and Mr. Connor very knowledgeable and well-traveled," said Haley.

The conversation turned to Mr. Connor's need for a writer's retreat. He didn't know the territory, but it was apparent that Haley did. Would he be interested in helping lease a quiet out-of-the-way place where Connor could craft his memoirs?

With that, Pickard produced $1,100 in cash—quite enough to convince Haley he was serious, but not so much that it might arouse suspicion. They shook hands, exchanged contact information, and Haley left with purpose and a pocket full of currency.

He also accepted that Mr. Connor could only be reached locally through Box 289 at the Taos Mail Boxes Etc. Connor was new in town, after all, there were no cell phones in those days, and Massachusetts was 2,000 miles away. It turned out later that a John Connor had, indeed, rented that mailbox, using a Visa card and a Georgia driver's license, but the photo on the license was that of one William Leonard Pickard.

Beginning with Haley and the house in Santa Fe, Pickard's dual existence began slowly to unravel.

"I visited several times when staying over," he later admitted. "There were couches and a stereo, nothing else. No LSD. But it makes a good story for the Drug Enforcement Administration, which had no explanation at trial why no evidence of a lab was ever found."

Innocent or no, Leonard's cloak-and-dagger lifestyle afforded

---

8.   Pickard also used the alias James Clark Maxwell.

Skinner ample opportunity to spin the saga of the Acid King, and he took full advantage.

"Skinner wanted to host ayahuasca sessions like Alfred's, and asked me to rent the Santa Fe house," Leonard explained. "I did so, with his money. . . ."

In Pickard's telling, simple, rational, and blameless explanations exist for every misstep, but Skinner got to the government first; his version prevailed.

Leonard was not a complete stranger to New Mexico. Back in Boston, he'd cemented his friendship with Dr. John Halpern, another frequent New Mexico visitor. Since their first nauseous meeting in Alfred Savinelli's living room, Halpern and Pickard conferred often on psychedelic evangelism. While it wasn't entirely clear to Halpern how a Harvard grad student could afford to bounce between Cambridge and Moscow and Santa Fe almost on a whim, all of Pickard's many and varied associates had come to accept that Pickard had money—especially Halpern. Pickard's $100,000 loans had become an annual routine. The source, maintained Leonard, was Todd Skinner.

David Haley became aware of just how much money Mr. Connor had when a FedEx box landed on his front porch several months after their first exchange. In furtherance of his agreement with Mr. Connor, Haley testified that he'd dutifully scoured the multiple listings for a likely writer's hideaway, but the $20,000 inside the FedEx box accelerated the process.

"This money is for the work we'll do together," read the simple note that Haley found inside along with the cash.

Pickard wasn't the only psychonaut who swore that he'd turned over a new leaf in the nineties. Todd Skinner filed for Chapter 7 bankruptcy to wipe clean the debts he'd racked up over the previous ten years. His drug-running past behind him, he married a twenty-six-year-old Oklahoma State medical student on July 18, 1992, and vowed to settle down.

Skinner swept Kelly Sue Rothe off her feet, wooing her with wine, jewelry, and fibs. They honeymooned for four months along California's Mendocino coastline before returning to Tulsa where Kelly settled in as a researcher at Lifton Laboratories while she finished her doctorate in osteopathy.

Her husband was absent much of the time, allegedly testifying in court cases and traveling on behalf of his mother's business. Kelly bore him two children—a daughter quickly followed by a son.[9] The new Mrs. Skinner was tolerant of his absence, if vaguely suspicious. Todd had been a philanderer before their wedding and she kept coming across signs that he might not have given up his dalliances.

"He wasn't the money magnet he was proclaiming to be," recalled Alfred Savinelli. "He had an old beat-up van and lived in an old single-family home, but Kelly made him look normal: two kids and wife. He ingratiated himself in ways that were interesting though, and got people to commit."

In July of 1996, Todd Skinner bought a decommissioned USAF Atlas E missile silo at 16795 Say Road on the outskirts of Wamego, Kansas. Anachronisms of the Cold War, such missile silos still ring Topeka. Once SALT treaties and new technology made them obsolete, the Defense Department sold the silos to the highest bidders.

Skinner came up with $40,000 to put down on approximately twenty-eight acres. He created the Wamego Land Trust to act as owner of record and installed his junior high school science tutor, Graham Kendall, as trustee. On its face, the purchase looked legitimate. Representing his mother's company, Skinner maintained that he planned to outfit the silo with the latest in Japanese robotics. With assembly-line efficiency and minimal labor costs, the new subterranean machine works would crank out industrial coils and other Gardner Springs gadgets.

---

9. Katherine Elizabeth Rothe-Skinner and Morgan Rothe-Skinner. Kelly accused Todd of doping both children on long trips rather than having to put up with their whining.

But 115 feet beneath the bleak surface of the Kansas flatlands, Skinner also created lavish living quarters for himself and his closest *campañeros*: a surreal cavern featuring colorful Mexican artwork, a twelve-line phone system, a king-sized bed mounted on an oak pedestal with mirrored ceiling, humongous Italian marble hot tub, and a $100,000 sound system. He put in a mezzanine where he could survey his realm like the great and wonderful Oz. He also converted the fenced-in acreage above into a petting zoo: four llamas, a pair of Clydesdales, three miniature horses, and a tiny donkey. In all, Skinner's remodeling and menagerie cost over $300,000.

Todd told Kelly the silo was for business and the menagerie was for their children, but Kelly kept hearing that Skinner's underground Disney World was as much for head-tripping orgies as it was manufacturing custom springs. After months of his pathological excuses, she finally had had enough.

Kelly quit the marriage and spent the rest of the nineties fighting for custody.

Years later, after she'd remarried, become a doctor, and moved her family practice to upstate New York, Kelly heard from Leonard about Skinner's duplicity. She was sympathetic, if cynical.

"Don't worry," she told him, "he's done it to many people before you."

About the same time that Pickard graduated from the Kennedy School, Mark Kleiman quit Harvard and moved west. In the summer of '97, Kleiman invited Pickard to join him at UCLA's Drug Policy Analysis Program as Kleiman's deputy. He suggested Pickard might want to expand upon his theories about the growing opioid threat in Eastern Europe.

Kleiman had initial reservations about his star pupil. He found a disturbing reprimand in Pickard's academic file. Leonard had once submitted a research paper written by another student—one step short of plagiarism, but still a violation of the academic honor code.

Pickard sheepishly confessed his shortcut. He'd been extremely busy, you see, and, well . . .

Despite the black mark, Kleiman saw no further evidence of dishonesty. He hired him as his assistant.

Pickard didn't exactly start out with a bang. He rarely kept office hours, travelled frequently,[10] and finished little of the research assigned him—the same transgressions that got him into trouble at Harvard.

"That was making me nervous," recalled Kleiman.

But Pickard's knowledge of biochemistry was extensive and his Rolodex, formidable. His research veered toward synthetics, which Kleiman agreed were probably the next big threat. Pickard called his project the Future and Emerging Drugs Study . . . or FEDS.

FEDS delivered almost immediately. Pickard dug deep into Russian plans to step up fentanyl manufacture. Kleiman advised him to alert former DEA chief Robert Bonner,[11] whom Kleiman knew from his own DOJ stint. As a courtesy to Kleiman, Bonner referred Pickard to a current DEA official, who never got back to him.

Still, Pickard seemed eager and his FEDS work promised to be groundbreaking. How to fund his project remained a problem. The university had no budget.

"Then I got a letter one day from some guys I didn't know," recalled Kleiman.

The letter bore a Russian postmark. Two benefactors named Igor Beskrovny and Rachid Usupov sent Kleiman two checks totaling $140,000. UCLA kept 10 percent as an administrative fee, but

---

10. Leonard flew to Amsterdam March 10, 1997, and stayed for two weeks. According to the DEA, he carried an attaché case with a false bottom. His Amex and MBNA payments for 1997 totaled $19,637.61. Again, he filed no Form 1040.

11. A DOJ prosecutor and former Federal judge, Bonner ran the DEA from 1990–93.

Kleiman earmarked the remainder for FEDS, including Pickard's $30,000 salary, which Leonard summarily signed over to Deborah Harlow.

But as the weeks passed, Leonard fell into a pattern that had grown all too familiar. He missed required deadlines. He was always out of his office and often out of town. Kleiman began using the $140,000 he received from the Russians to pay the other associates on his staff instead of Leonard.

Acting as John Connor's leasing agent, David Haley located the perfect hideaway. The adobe bungalow at 110 Vuelta Herradura was conveniently close to Santa Fe, but far enough removed that nosy neighbors wouldn't be a problem.

Mr. Connor was exultant. Referring to his writer's retreat as "the swimming pool project," he moved in on Sept. 29, 1997, the same month that Leonard Pickard moved into his new offices at UCLA.

The yearlong lease called for rent of $2,500 a month, but almost immediately, Mr. Connor upped the ante. While David Haley did not object to Mr. Connor's generosity, he did wonder about a gradual escalation in the lease payments. The first payment was the agreed upon $2,500, but Connor followed it in October with $3,000.

By March of the following year, the payments had doubled. Haley noted the discrepancy, but the money kept on coming. In July of 1998, Mr. Connor gave Haley $7,000; in August, $12,000. Haley later told authorities that it never occurred to him to question why he was receiving so much additional cash. A bonus, perhaps?

Alfred Savinelli, on the other hand, brimmed with questions. He'd been able to repay only $25,000 of the $300,000 that Pickard loaned him to save Native Scents. Not to worry, Pickard told him. There was no rush on satisfying the full debt. Just keep letting him order chemicals on Savinelli's supplier accounts and everything would be fine.

Savinelli didn't even know about the Mr. Connor alias until he ran into David Haley one day at a Taos cafe. Haley told him the whole strange saga of the swimming pool project.[12] Mr. Connor told Haley his hobby was chemistry and that he was developing a Viagra knockoff in his new lab. Top secret. Hush hush.

Savinelli knew instantly that Connor and Pickard were one and the same. He told Haley as much. Since his Buddhist ordination the previous year, Pickard hadn't been around much . . . or so Savinelli believed. He regularly ordered chemicals through Native Scents, though.

It was true that Pickard was rarely in town, but when he was, he cooked, according to Savinelli. He'd set aside two weeks, keep the shades drawn and stock up on enough emergency Valium to drop a racehorse. Confronted by Savinelli, he admitted that he aimed for a minimum yield of six hundred grams.

Of Viagra?

Already deep in his debt, Savinelli was reluctant to question Pickard further. Over time, Savinelli came to realize that the project had nothing to do with swimming pools or erectile dysfunction. Pickard, Halpern, and Todd Skinner—the trio Savinelli unwittingly brought together—were producing up to a kilo every five weeks.

---

12. Over time, euphemism became code. "Alice," "garage," and "car" meant laboratory; "white light" meant DMT; "possessions" meant lab gear. Leonard's favorite password was "LOVE" and he used PGP (pretty good privacy) encryption on his computer.

XII.

On Oct. 21, 1997, the Oklahoma Highway Patrol caught Todd Skinner weaving through traffic. He was cited for driving under the influence, but Skinner was not so intoxicated that he could not pass himself off to the arresting officer as Gerard Terrence Finnegan. He had a driver's license that said so.[1]

The ruse worked. Nobody checked. Finnegan/Skinner appeared on Dec. 22, paid fines with $1,140 in cash, and no further questions were asked.

The Oklahoma justice system could be faulted for so grievous an oversight, but seldom did it have to contend with so clever a miscreant. For a very long time, Todd Skinner seemed to lead a charmed existence. With his stepfather's help, he continuously skated past the law. He never appeared to want for cash. His marriage might be on the rocks, but Todd looked as if he took even that calamity in stride.

He always found ways to keep an overactive libido satisfied.

---

1. From the witness stand six years later, Skinner described the equipment he and high school chum William Wynn used to create phony ID: "A Genesis MP multiple processor computer made by Daystar for parallel processing. A Newgen disublimation printer, a Ryna type L scanner, high res and simple equipment for cutting and trimming and physically cutting things down. And a heat lamination device to laminate over the graphics work."

Beneath his pretense beat a BDSM heart. He dosed his children's babysitter with blotter acid that summer. When she alerted the Pottawatomie Sheriff, her testimony got the same attention as Gerard Finnegan's DUI. "Not credible," said police.

During the first year that he split with Kelly, Skinner took up with seventeen-year-old Emily Ragan, a hyper-bright STEM student who lived in nearby Manhattan with her parents, both professors at Kansas State University. Diminutive, dark-haired, and sweet-natured, she was disturbingly comparable to Kelly. Skinner preferred suggestable dewy-eyed coeds, but was not averse to pricey hookers. In *The Rose*, Leonard wrote that he fantasized about being "smothered in girls."

Todd liked playing roulette with a lady on his arm. He frequented Topeka's topless Cabaret Club fishing for the latter, but gambled at Harrah's Prairie Band Casino on the nearby Pottawatomie Indian Reservation. He visited Vegas often.

And despite his soon-to-be ex-wife's sour indignation over his missile silo, the Skinner boondoggle turned out to be a bona fide hit. The Wamego outpost of Gardner Springs Inc. had been fully accepted by the locals. Several went on the payroll. Skinner hired off-duty cops for security. There were rumors at the Friendly Cooker café of meth labs and odd Satanic rituals down deep in the earth, but rarely any disturbances topside. Prairie stoicism prevailed. No harm, no foul.[2]

But 1998 would differ dramatically from 1997.

As the new year began, Katherine Magrini had a falling out with her son.

"One day he tells me to move out, at enormous cost," she said.

She did not advertise her reasons, but Mrs. Magrini angrily ordered all Gardner Springs machinery, materiel, and employees

---

2. Pickard later established that the Kansas Attorney General subpoenaed Skinner's phone records in July of 1997, suspecting narcotics activity at the silo. Nothing came of it.

pulled back to Tulsa. A business that once pulled in $2 million a year was losing ground in Wamego. The good times slowly ground to a halt.

Todd kept a game face. Both of his Porsches remained parked out front, conspicuous displays of his declining wealth. He planted a state-of-the-art windmill in the vegetable garden that he'd ordered as accompaniment to his missile base menagerie. He partied hard, especially on weekends, when all sorts of middle-aged flower children assembled in Wamego before descending into his subterranean sin den.

But the hard truth remained: Todd was nearly broke, and growing desperate.

Leonard wasn't.

Ever the Samaritan, Pickard insisted on keeping the cost of a single 100 microgram hit down to a very affordable 29.7 cents—or so said Skinner. The economics of scale still made even a modest markup a gold mine. Profit margin per batch could approach $3 million.

The challenge was, and always had been, distribution. Unloading Santa Fe "Viagra" to paying customers could get dicey. Amsterdam contacts handled the European market well enough, but domestic sales were a whole different matter. Reliable traffickers were hard to find. If any shred of the Brotherhood of Eternal Love remained, neither Pickard nor Skinner knew where it was. Those few Brothers Leonard located through his Kennedy School research were either retired or buried so deep underground that they almost never surfaced.

Paranoia struck deep in the mid-1990s. No one was safe, not even Sasha Shulgin, who'd been operating in plain sight and without a license since 1993. Witness the cautionary tale of Bruce Michael Young. With a dramatic rise in income, dealers all too often succumbed to profligacy.

Ultimately, Pickard turned to an ex-Marine who'd been

transforming acid into cash along the California coast for the better part of a decade. A jolly, unassuming retiree, Alec "Petaluma Al" Reid was a sometime art dealer with seven kids. He laughed from the belly, puttered like a grandpa, and philosophized with flair, combining the best parts of Wilford Brimley and Wavy Gravy. Everyone knew when Al came to town. He drove a big red Cadillac convertible with a hidden compartment suitable for a single kilogram of LSD.

Through a tried-and-true network of Grateful Dead loyalists, Reid had been spreading lysergic cheer for years in a region known to the DEA as the Acid Triangle. With a straight line from Monterey to Castro Valley forming its hypotenuse, the triangle came to a point at Bolinas Bay. It was within these boundaries that Reid peddled his elixir. In brown vials labeled "Wild Oats Vitamin C—100 grams," a dose could be purchased through mail order or from salesmen strategically stationed outside rock concerts. He also shipped frequently to Amsterdam.

Following established protocols, Pickard periodically met Reid at the Buckeye Roadhouse in Sausalito or Lyons Restaurant in Petaluma. There, Skinner testified, he exchanged acid for cash. Al spurned small bills. Too bulky. He liked to print tiny hearts on $100s so he could track where the money went.

Once in early '97, the Secret Service paid Reid a visit. Did Al know he'd been spending bad bills? Not many, but enough that the Treasury Department wanted to know where they came from. The agents gave him a crash course in what to look for and told Reid to stay vigilant.

Al wasn't sure who was passing him phony money, but from that day forward, he had his kids weed out counterfeits with ultraviolet light. Rejects went in a bad money trunk that the children were forbidden to loot.

Acid might be a family affair, but Reid was no Fagin. He established trust funds for his heirs. He invested in gem mining. He was a capitalist, after all, and made personal responsibility a cornerstone of his home teaching, with a curriculum heavy on math. Until he sprang for a counting machine, Reid trusted his youngsters to tabulate the take. They banded stacks with strips decorated in crayon. Hearts. Flowers. Stars.

It was only after Al caught his seventeen-year-old son skimming that he bought the automated counter. Even then, the sheer volume could be taxing. The larger and better product that Leonard produced, the harder it was to discreetly sell all of it, and the more currency there was to be laundered.

Leonard didn't know how Al managed to raise a family and run a million-dollar business, but he remained a big admirer. He, too, understood the demands of multitasking. He also appreciated that the time had come to give Petaluma Al a hand.

Todd Skinner was more than happy to oblige.

The swimming pool project presented dire risks beyond distribution and dirty money. Working closely with lysergics could prompt a condition Tim Scully once referred to as "Acid Makers' Queasy": a loopy lack of logic that kept chemists perpetually loaded and provoked careless accidents.

In August of 1998, Pickard suffered a serious chemical spill that nearly killed him, according to his partners. Reminiscent of the convulsions endured by Bureau of Narcotics Enforcement investigator Max Houser during the 1988 Mountain View bust, Leonard lay twitching alone on the floor of the Vuelta Herradura bungalow for two days, hallucinating nearer to the afterlife than he'd bargained for.

After a similar mishap with a broken flask once in Aspen, Pickard allegedly dodged injury by leaping into a hot tub. That time, he'd hired illegal immigrants to clean up. Lingering fumes in that lab house hastened his move to New Mexico.

Following the Santa Fe spill, Pickard was not so fortunate. He was laid up for days, his hands quaked, and his behavior changed.

"He became more reckless, if that was possible," recalled John Halpern. "The secret agent thing got way out of hand. Grandiose one minute; paranoid the next."

Savinelli noticed too. Pickard saw DEA everywhere. He hid video cameras in a potted plant and a wall hanging at the lab house. Stereo speakers secretly recorded conversations. His memory lapsed. Alfred came home from Native Scents once to find that Leonard had been there and left the gas on his kitchen stove. The house reeked. Had Savinelli lit a match, he would have been toast.

"Exposure to hundreds of doses has got to have an effect," he said. "He was just not right. I would compare it to electroconvulsive therapy. It's such a reset that part of his self or ego has dissolved to the point where he had to reconstitute himself."

Skinner, too, recalled his accidents and their aftermath in trial testimony.

Pickard called their memories "myth" and defied them all, as well as the DEA, to prove he'd ever overdosed. "No corroboration of any lab was ever found, not a billionth of a gram," he declared.[3]

Queasy or sober, Pickard did get production down pat, according to his partners. Despite his denials, all three maintained that Leonard cranked out quality crystals with regularity.

Still, business hit a wall in Santa Fe. There could be no expansion based solely on Petaluma Al's distribution. Pickard looked to

---

3. In *The Rose of Paracelsus*, he quoted the chemist Indigo's similar experience with acid overdose: "I saw the constant creation of the most perfect world imaginable by the mind of God, the luminous air of delicious gases like the perfumes of lovers and goddesses, the rich earths made of gems, the fecund ground of being. I saw the union of all dualities, the crystallized souls of heaven, the galaxies of consciousness, and all life as mythic and sublime."

While Halpern, Savinelli and Skinner were stoned on "pharmahuasca," Leonard told them the Indigo story. He concluded that was how all three assumed he overdosed, and not the unidentified underground chemist he would one day conjure in the romance of *The Rose*.

Halpern for help. For 10 percent of the profits, Halpern persuaded a childhood friend to join their enterprise.

Heir to a New York fashion design fortune,[4] Stefan Wathne agreed to spread Leonard's faux "Viagra" to London, Paris, Moscow, and beyond. He'd then arrange to send untaxed profits back to the US.

At first, Halpern told Wathne that Pickard inherited the capital to produce his Viagra knockoff. Later, he confessed the truth when he was certain Wathne "could tolerate accepting money from ill-gotten gains; that this would be illegal money."

Wathne got into the game. Leonard nicknamed him "Ice" for his native Iceland. The Harvard-educated *bon vivant* developed a method for converting drug profits into Russian bonds then sending them back to the states. The mystery contribution of $140,000 to Mark Kleiman's Drug Policy Analysis Program appeared to be a successful early example of Wathne's laundering skills.

But it wasn't long before "Ice" echoed Al Reid's complaint about small bills. Wathne wasn't about to mule a buttload of $20s through customs. His minimum transaction was $1 million. A month before Leonard's acid spill, he met Wathne in New York with $750,000. Wathne grudgingly accepted the money but warned him that $1 million meant $1 million. Whenever Leonard tried fudging, Halpern let him know that "Ice" was pissed.

During one inelegant exchange, Leonard flew to LA, booked into the Beverly Hills Hotel, and delivered two grocery sacks of cash to Wathne's boutique on Rodeo Drive. A puzzled female employee accepted the money on Wathne's behalf. Leonard flew back to San

---

4. The thirty-one-year-old jetsetter's mother and two aunts (known as the Triplets for their consistently matching outfits) operated high-end boutiques in Beverly Hills and Manhattan and sold their designer goods through Ralph Lauren, I Magnin, and Bergdorf Goodman, among other luxury retailers. Wathne was also a trustee of the American Ballet Theater, the American Russian Youth Orchestra, and founder of the Moscow Institute for Social and Political Studies.

Francisco nine days later after running up a $16,253.66 hotel bill, oblivious to his own profligacy or Wathne's fury.

Skinner was the perfect buffer. Combining years of fraud with friendly decadence, he successfully bridged the gap between mad scientist and dilettante. After he'd agreed to add Skinner to his growing enterprise, Pickard's extravagance worsened. Everyone flew first class and stayed at the finest hotels. During one acid exchange, Pickard roomed at San Francisco's Pan Pacific, Skinner stayed at the nearby Hyatt, while Wathne checked in across the street at the high-end Campton Place ("Best rack of veal in the City!").

The following day, Skinner rose early and cheerfully chauffeured Pickard to a storage locker north of the Golden Gate. There, he said, Pickard extracted $400,000. On their way back, Skinner deftly lifted $70,000 when Leonard wasn't looking.

Back in the hotel, Pickard counted the cash before turning it over to Wathne. He frowned, then confronted Skinner: $50,000 was missing. Skinner threw up his hands. Besides flatly denying that he'd taken the money, Skinner also took note of Pickard's lousy math. He wanted to tell him $70,000 was missing, not $50,000, but bit his tongue.

Leonard was so loopy he didn't even know how badly he'd been robbed.

"The women, the money, the recklessness. . . . All of that spun out of control after Pickard's exposure to the chemical spill in Santa Fe," recalled Halpern. "He changed. He started believing every bullshit lie Skinner told him."

Skinner was as spontaneous as he was pathological. He could spin fabulous hooey into high-stakes ambrosia. At a point when government and academic funding for psychedelic experimentation hit an all-time low, Todd let it be known at psychonaut conferences, mushroom festivals, and other gatherings of the hallucinatory cognoscenti that *he* could secure grants for projects like Rick Strassman's DMT study.

"Dave Nichols was out of money," testified Skinner. "Everyone was out of money as far as that group was concerned. They needed money. Savinelli didn't have enough and Strassman couldn't get more. Money was scarce."

Scarce for everyone except Leonard Pickard. Separating him from his cash became Skinner's singular focus.

Somehow during the early days of their collaboration, Todd convinced Pickard that he was Warren Buffett's sub rosa bagman and that he could persuade the billionaire to help Leonard stage an international drug trafficking conference at Harvard.

Nonsense, said Pickard. Warren Buffett indeed. What kind of fool did Skinner take him for? And yet, Leonard remained intrigued.

Over many months, Skinner embroidered his story with back-channel baloney: he was able to move Buffett's money around *because* he seemed so unlikely! Dontcha see? A hulking doofus with a head for numbers and a buccaneer's gift for crossing state lines. Who better to carry Warren's water?

Pickard listened dubiously to Skinner boast about transferring $1 billion from Buffett's Swiss accounts to a Caribbean bank in exchange for a $5 million commission. Skinner and Buffett were tight. Warren kept Todd on a $225,000 quarterly retainer. Todd had Mrs. Buffett's private number on speed dial. He hitched rides on the Berkshire Hathaway jet whenever he liked.

When asked later how he could possibly have believed that a Neanderthal like Skinner hung out with a Fortune 500 billionaire, Pickard said, "I was hanging on because I really wanted to do this project."

Slowly, Leonard came around to the prospect of a Buffett-backed drug summit. Skinner sweetened his hopes with the promise of persuading his good friends Sting and Paul Simon to furnish the soundtrack. Gathering together the *crème de la crème* of medicine, academia, and government in one place … it was all just too delicious.

And Leonard would get the credit!

He needed $440,000 to underwrite his unprecedented dream gathering of psychonauts, cops, neurobiologists, spies, and diplomats. It might be titled "The Cortical Revolution: upcoming epidemics from erotogenics, memory drugs, and addictive designer compounds." He could almost taste the canapes and Chardonnay. Among the keynote speakers: Vladimir Putin and US Drug Czar Barry McCaffery.

Pickard put in $100,000 seed money from the swimming pool project, then hit a wall. No contributions. Scant interest. Nobody shared his vision.

Buffett sounded more and more like a godsend.

As 1998 commenced, Leonard's academic career was at a standstill. Despite its early promise, FEDS had gone nowhere. Nonetheless, when he wasn't cooking in Santa Fe, Pickard soldiered on. From Amsterdam to Acapulco, he attended conferences, patiently posting his banner for, "The Future Drug Study—Drug Design and Policy Implications."

"Several researchers from Harvard's McLean Hospital and Hopkins were reading it," recalled Pickard. "Pinned to the cork board were cards from universities and industry, and one from the Chief Pharmacologist at DEA."

He dreamed of legitimacy. Proud of his new role as Mark Kleiman's deputy, he continued to bask in the Harvard mystique. His dodgy past behind him and his Kennedy School degree on the wall, he'd finally mastered the duality of Jekyll and Hyde. Were it not for the grandiose tangle Skinner wove for him, Pickard might have slid right into the twenty-first century as the wise, witty prognosticator that he so longed to be.

"If they had left me alone, I would have been a neurologist long ago," he sighed.

Skinner had big ideas. As he later described his role from the witness stand, Todd skyrocketed overnight from Pickard's junior executive to Chief Operating Officer:

> I was involved in money laundering, I was involved in trying to locate places that the labs would be at. I was involved in making decisions of where money was to go for what we called "charitable operations." I was also involved with communications decisions. I was involved with making decisions of security issues. Pickard referred to me as (the man in charge of) "worldwide security for the Brotherhood of Eternal Love." I was the document keeper, to the best of my knowledge. I looked and would make decisions that had to do with—Was this a good decision? Was this going to cause a problem? Constantly sifting through errors of seizure. . . .

Among Skinner's first orders of business was lassoing Ivo Kaanen, an old Heidelberg college chum, into Pickard's organization. Kaanen was to set up a lab on the Dutch-German border, where Leonard would furnish him with the Viagra recipe. The aim: quadruple European output. Wathne was tapped to handle the international sales increase.

Skinner testified that he organized domestic finances through an elaborate Vegas-style laundering system. Leonard loaded cash in storage lockers until Skinner could get to it. The easiest method was to hand wash Petaluma Al's $100s through casinos, using smurfs: friends, relatives, or Gardner Springs employees who would "gamble" just beneath the $10,000 federal reporting threshold. They'd cash in their chips and—voila!—clean cash.

The problem was the sheer amount. Leonard had storage lockers all over the country. Turning untaxed cash into clean roulette winnings worked well enough if done in the thousands, he said, but not millions of dollars.

As the alleged brains of the outfit, Pickard left the dirty laundry to Skinner, with whom he developed a love-hate relationship. Looking down his patrician nose, Leonard sneeringly referred to Todd as Paul Bunyan, Bozo, or Jelly Bean.[5] Nonetheless, he grew dependent upon Skinner's money juggling, even while criticizing his conspicuous consumption.

Older, wiser, and convinced that he was far more cautious, Pickard liked to believe that he stayed beneath the radar. No bling. No flashy clothes. No big bank deposits or fast cars or sudden and inexplicable displays of wealth. Crediting Skinner's generosity, he lived well and traveled extensively, but always in the service of higher academic purpose.

As is often the case with guilt-plagued captains of industry, Pickard wanted to give back. His master plan called for renewed respectability for and eventual legalization of psychedelics. It didn't occur to him that philanthropy might be as obvious a road map to unlaundered cash as smurfing.

When John Halpern, Sasha Shulgin, and others needed their studies funded, Pickard FedExed an anonymous gift of $97,700 in stock certificates[6] to Heffter Institute board member George Greer with instructions on how to disburse the money.

Heffter turned Shulgin down. He was "too hot," said Greer. The Institute delivered similar bad news to UC San Francisco research

---

5.   Skinner also used aliases to identify associates:
     Alfred Savinelli—Pseudo Indian.
     Ganga White—The Pretzel.
     Deborah Harlow—The Cobra.
     Sasha Shulgin—The Elder.
     Dennis McKenna—The Scientist.
     Jeffrey Bronfman—Poor Fuck.

6.   Greer returned the AT&T, Southern Bell, and Lucent Technologies shares. Heffter attorney Jerry Patchen later denied receiving the money, maintaining that the Institute carefully complied with all federal laws and had no connection to Pickard. Skinner ordered the shares sold in February 1999.

chemist Peyton Jacob and a Russian research team developing designer drugs in St. Petersburg. Only Halpern got his funding.

Pickard had better luck without the Institute acting as middle man. He gave $30,000 in cash to Bob Jesse,[7] a San Francisco software pioneer who'd quit the vice-presidency of Oracle in order to become a full-time psychonaut. Like Microsoft's Bob Wallace, Jesse willingly sacrificed entrée into the Steve Jobs/Bill Gates/Paul Allen pantheon[8] of Silicon Valley billionaires in order to concentrate on the connection between God and chemicals.

"None of these people were in it for the money except for Skinner," recalled Halpern. "I guess that should have been the big tip off."

Skinner was unapologetic about profiting from acid. He always came away from each transaction a little richer. He was equally derisive of Pickard, whom he privately regarded as a fiscal imbecile and an arrogant fop. Todd saw himself forever bailing Leonard's sorry ass out of one catastrophe after another. Pickard saw it the other way around. Theirs was a rocky symbiosis.

---

7. Around the same time, Jesse launched his own nonprofit Council on Spiritual Practices.

8. Among many other Silicon Valley pioneers, Gates, Jobs, and Allen admitted tripping on acid before sparking the PC revolution.

XIII.

Leonard's brain trust—Halpern, Savinelli, and Skinner—met infrequently, but when they did, the huddle resembled a coven of hippie Sopranos.

Over breakfast one morning in Taos, Leonard began by demanding that Halpern get the Social Security numbers of his oddball friends for future use in smurfing and/or phony passport production. Then he started in on the guy who got busted in Oregon.

Skinner handed Pickard a newspaper story about Bruce Michael Young's arrest. Young needed a muzzle, he remembered Pickard telling him at the time. The fear was that he'd blow the deep cover of a longtime and absolutely essential cog in Leonard's acid enterprise. While Bruce Young had made most of his money through cannabis, he used much of that capital to buy acid precursors from the same underground wholesaler who supplied Leonard. Scuttlebutt had it that Young or one of his partners might even be talking to an Oregon grand jury about the so-called ET (ergotamine tartrate[1]) Man.

So deep was the ET Man's cover that he'd allegedly had plastic surgery done in Canada to disguise his true identity. He'd been

---

1. In addition to LSD, the chemical is also the basic ingredient for several migraine headache medications.

operating beneath the radar for over twenty years. When he wasn't in Oregon, the mysterious ET Man lived in Italy.

DEA files indicated that a James Edward Miller (a.k.a. Klaus Kurt Mueller) held Irish, British, and Macao passports, yet hated to fly. He also had several drivers' licenses, but never ventured out on the road when visiting the US. Allegedly a fifty-ish Mafioso, he was graying at the temples and married a Eugene schoolteacher who—like Bruce Michael Young—had been called before an Oregon grand jury.

Leonard leaned in, lowering his voice. The schoolteacher and Young in front of the same grand jury? *Way* too close for comfort!

Skinner said that Leonard explained his relationship with the ET Man this way: he would pay him $100,000 in Dutch Guilders per kilogram of ergotamine tartrate; Miller would then smuggle the powder out of Czechoslovakia hidden inside machine tool crates; the shipments crossed the Atlantic and next went to a middleman in Chicago, after which the final leg of the journey was made by truck to Santa Fe. There, Leonard transubstantiated the magic powder into lysergic gold.

Leonard maintained that he scrutinized every detail along the journey. He even had an inside man with US Customs.

According to Skinner, Pickard then pushed $300,000 across the table at him and told him to eliminate the threat of Young's testimony. Skinner balked. He half-heartedly suggested a woman named Jessica Guinn. Perhaps she might be a potential assassin?

After cooling a bit, Leonard switched the conversation to kidnapping. Might Young be exiled to Central America?

Savinelli chimed in that he knew a dealer who could bring Rohypnol over the border. Hugo De La Llave[2] made the Mexico run regularly. Dose Young with a handful of roofies and he'd still be asleep when they dumped him somewhere south of Yucatan.

---

2. Llave got caught at the border Feb. 22, 1997, with thirteen tablets and was fined $500.

Leonard didn't dismiss the idea, but kept options open. Perhaps threatening Young's parents would keep him quiet. If Leonard ingratiated himself to Mr. and Mrs. Young, he could snap a selfie with them. Then he could mail it off to Bruce, who'd get the message: we know where your family lives!

"Oh, for crying out loud," said an exasperated Pickard years later, long after Skinner had sworn in open court that all his recollections were true.

They were true—sort of. According to the other two "conspirators" who were present that morning, keeping Young mum had indeed been discussed. But *eliminating* him? Come on. Both Savinelli and Halpern recalled a version quite different from Skinner's.

The actual conversation was spurious if not flat-out tongue in cheek, they both agreed. For all his Queasy-inspired lunacy, Leonard was still capable of sarcasm, even irony. What went on over breakfast that morning was adolescent role-playing, not murder most foul. Such hokum, like most of the other outlandish elements in the mythos of the Acid King, sprang directly from the fertile imagination of Gordon Todd Skinner.

For the better part of the next two years, Skinner kept alive the illusion of his personal wealth. Through the magic of credit cards, he'd graciously pick up Pickard's hotel and travel bills, only to recoup the money later, almost always with a hefty surcharge. Meanwhile, he one-upped the boss. When Leonard stayed in a luxury suite, Todd roomed in the penthouse. When Leonard rented a sedan, Todd got a sports car. When Leonard traveled business class, Todd chartered a private jet.

Todd boasted that he entertained shamelessly on Leonard's dime. In April of 1998, a former Brotherhood member and his mate came down from Bolinas to visit Todd and his teen fiancé Emily Ragan while they luxuriated at San Francisco's five-star Mandarin Hotel. Then a freshman at UC Berkeley, Ragan put

Dr. Albert Hofmann synthesized LSD and, later, psilocybin in his Swiss laboratory, launching the psychedelic age at the end of World War II.

Author Aldous Huxley became acid's first well-known advocate.

During the 1950s, con man Al Hubbard, a.k.a. "Captain Trips," carried his briefcase pharmacy all over the world, turning on celebrities and civilians alike everywhere he traveled.

Growing up in Georgia, William Leonard Pickard learned about psychedelics through pop culture and scientific study, in which he excelled.

Headed for success, he was selected "most intellectual" by his peers at Daniel O'Keefe High and played varsity basketball.

Winner of the prestigious
Westinghouse Science award as
a senior, he went to Princeton
on scholarship in 1963, but
flunked out the first semester after
stealing a car and winding up in a
Connecticut psychiatric hospital.

Around the same time, Dr. Timothy Leary
launched his acid revolution, urging America's
best and brightest to "tune in, turn on, and drop
out."

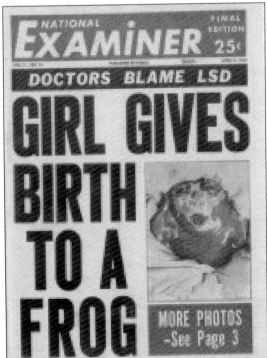

For the remainder of the 1960s, scare headlines and draconian legislation outlawed LSD and drove psychedelics underground.

(PLEASE TYPE OR PRINT)

DEPARTMENT OF STATE

PASSPORT APPLICATION

(Before Completing this Application, Read Information for Passport Applicants on Page 4)

PART I - TO BE COMPLETED BY ALL APPLICANTS

I, AUGUSTUS OWSLEY STANLEY 3RD, a citizen of the United States, do hereby apply to the Department of State for a passport.

STREET: P O BOX 29029

CITY: LOS ANGELES 29 STATE: CALIF

DATE OF BIRTH (Month, day, year): JAN. 19 1935   PLACE OF BIRTH: WASHINGTON, D.C.

HEIGHT: 5 FT. 7 IN.   HAIR: BROWN   EYES: HAZEL   APPROXIMATE DATE OF DEPARTURE: FEB 1963

OCCUPATION: STUDENT

MY PERMANENT RESIDENCE: SAME   COUNTY OF RESIDENCE: LOS ANGELES

(Passport Office Use Only)

D 1 3 5 2 5 5

PASSPORT

JAN 2 '63

B

PERSONS TO BE INCLUDED IN PASSPORT

No 4 2442

C

STAPLE ONE PHOTO BELOW
DO NOT MAR FACE

HAVE YOU PREVIOUSLY APPLIED FOR A U.S. PASSPORT: YES

LOCATION OF ISSUING OFFICE: WASHINGTON D C   DATE OF ISSUANCE: APR 17 1958

NUMBER: 964242

1-2-63
1-2-63

(Passport Office Use Only)

FORM DSP-11

(OVER - YOU MUST COMPLETE PAGE 2)

Chemist entrepreneurs like August Owsley Stanley III became outlaws, manufacturing psychedelics in back rooms and basements.

CALIFORNIA DEPARTMENT OF JUSTICE
BUREAU OF NARCOTIC ENFORCEMENT

WANTED

The Brotherhood of Eternal Love became the first and best-known distribution network for LSD, psilocybin, and other psychedelics, along with hashish and marijuana.

After he went to jail, Owsley's two chief assistants, Nick Sand and Tim Scully, carried on without him, creating Orange Sunshine, the best-known and purest version of LSD ever to hit the acid underground.

Pickard entered the acid underground during the trials of Scully and Sand in the early 1970s, carrying on their legacy after they were convicted for manufacturing psychedelics.

Alexander "Sasha" Shulgin, at right, was the premiere psychedelic chemist of the last half of the 20th Century. Pickard tried stepping into his shoes, but with catastrophic results.

MAPS (Multidisciplinary Association for Psychedelic Studies) founder Rick Doblin and Deborah Harlow, the first Mrs. Leonard Pickard, during a psychedelic conference in the early 1990s.

Dr. John Halpern, Pickard's junior partner from Harvard in the psychedelic manufacturing venture.

Alfred Savinelli, Gordon Todd Skinner and Skinner's second wife, Kelly Roth, during the days leading up to the Wamego LSD bust.

Trais Kliphius, New Mexican artist/ environmentalist who bore Pickard's son Duncan weeks before the Wamego LSD bust.

Krystle Cole, Skinner's girlfriend and third wife.

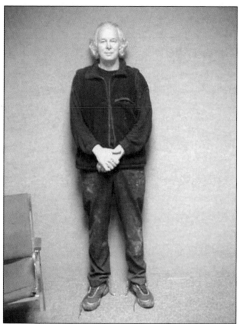

Pickard during the late 1990s, after his
graduation from Harvard's Kennedy School
but prior to the Wamego LSD bust.

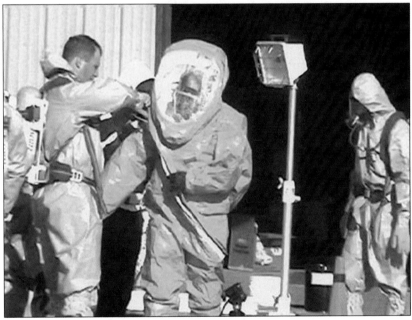

DEA agents in HazMat suits raid the Atlas Missile silo outside Wamego, Kansas, on Election Day, 2000, in what was incorrectly called the biggest LSD haul in history.

Federal Judge Richard Rogers who sentenced Pickard to two life sentences for manufacturing LSD.

"Petaluma" Al Reid, alleged distributor of the Skinner/Pickard LSD.

Clyde Apperson, Pickard's codefendant.

Gordon Todd Skinner in Oklahoma state
prison after his conviction for the kidnapping,
drugging, and maiming of his wife's boyfriend.

Leonard Pickard and author Dennis McDougal at Tucson Federal Prison.

her trust in Todd. He'd taken her down the Wamego rabbit hole regularly, dosing her and her friends on Eucharist, consummating their passion on the old oaken altar that Skinner called his bed. One besotted lass declared that Skinner "made the rain fall."

Money was no object. Life was a nonstop thrill ride. When he suggested he and Emily join the Bolinas couple on a little acid trip, she agreed.

In his quasi-defense, Skinner later maintained that he believed the little brown vial the ex-Brotherhood member pulled from his pocket was LSD. Actually, it contained a white powder called 2-CB, first synthesized by Sasha Shulgin in 1974 and known by the street name "Nexus." Dissolved in alcohol, Nexus approximated MDMA in its initial rush, though larger doses could bring on cartoonish hallucinations, weird voices, and a neon afterglow. The Dutch called the tablets Erox and sold them as an aphrodisiac stamped with little hearts.

But there was no ecstasy that April evening. By the time the symptoms of overdose developed, Emily lay stupefied on the bed, naked from the waist down. Skinner masturbated in another room, while the Bolinas couple blanked out in another bedroom.

Neighboring guests on the thirty-eighth floor began complaining downstairs to hotel management just before eight p.m. The front desk discreetly notified San Francisco Police.

When officers arrived, the suite door was open. Skinner was lying on the floor naked, hollering, "Somebody give me a blowjob! I wanna be fucked!" All four keening guests were handcuffed to gurneys and hauled off to the ER.

Police turned the entire incident over to Alameda County narcotics for follow up.

Had he been present, Pickard might have effected a different outcome. His ER training at San Francisco General could have deterred cop involvement. A veteran of many an OD, Leonard might have recognized the contents of the little brown vial as non-lysergic and its antidote easily administered. Valium cured all ills.

As it turned out, Pickard was indirectly involved in the Mandarin Hotel incident, just not in any obvious way. Skinner, Emily, and the Bolinas couple slid past police, but not their hotel bill. Todd said he asked Leonard for a little help and he sent $5,000 in cash. Tulsa police intercepted the FedEx package as suspected drug money, so Todd went back to the well. Leonard fronted him an additional $70,000.

As it turned out, Tulsa police could prove no connection between the $5,000 and drug sales. They finally gave up and released the cash to Skinner. Banking on Dr. Jekyll's short-term memory, Skinner said nothing. He kept it all—both the $5,000 and the $70,000.

"Didn't happen," said Leonard. "I sent Skinner exactly zero. It would take a real rube to swallow that story."

Providing endless details in the spinning of his yarns, Skinner claimed that Pickard stayed busy traveling the remainder of that year. In June, he was in Denver for two days before renting a car then spending the next three weeks tooling through the Southwest: Albuquerque, Scottsdale, Tucson, Santa Fe. . . .

When coffers ran low, he always gravitated back to his writer's retreat on Vuelta Herradura, whipped up a little Viagra, then went off again . . . all according to Todd.

Leonard flew to Boston for a week in July, then back to Kansas City and a meeting with Skinner at the Manhattan (KS) Holiday Inn. All four brethren in the swimming pool project—Skinner, Pickard, Halpern and Savinelli—convened in Telluride the following month for the annual Mushroom Festival.

Had Leonard ever filed an income tax return (he never did),[3] the

---

3. Pickard put $33,915.09 on credit cards in 1998.

festival would have fallen under Schedule C as a business expense. Sponsored by the free-form Telluride Institute, the weekend event promised "all things mycological, from the newest advancements in mushroom science to our famous mushroom cookoff." Skinner and Savinelli had been attending the annual event since its inception in 1984. During the festival, psychonauts owned the city. Leonard felt right at home. By Skinner's reckoning, it was also a great place to swap *psilocybe cubensis* and pick up hippie chicks.

Psychonauts flooded the Netherlands that season as well. From Sept. 26 through Oct. 20, Pickard and Halpern flew to Amsterdam for an ethnobotany conference.

"They were spooks and academics at the same time, thinking they were smarter than everyone else," said Savinelli.

Another obvious business expense, the conference was the perfect venue for drumming up support for Leonard's Harvard drug policy dream. He and Halpern put up posters at the Amstel Hotel Maatschaapij, inviting inquiry and creating their own psychonaut database—a future resource for FEDS.

Still, interest was only lukewarm. On Oct. 16, Skinner wired them both enough money to get back home.

As Leonard's bursar-in-chief, Todd purported to know his every move. Before the year wound to a close, Leonard was back in Santa Fe with the swimming pool project. While dropping in and out of his writer's retreat, he'd let the place go. Even in the high desert where lush lawns and rose gardens simply didn't exist, the exterior of 110 Vuelta Herradura had become unsightly. Walkways were shabby; shuttered windows, forbidding. Indoors, the place reeked. Nonetheless, David Haley convinced its absentee landlords to accept a lease extension for another year.

As 1998 ended, Leonard was off again. This time, he flew from San Francisco to Frankfurt, allegedly with a false-bottom attaché case his only luggage. He returned to San Francisco twenty-four hours later and spent New Year's Eve at the Palace Hotel. When he checked out a week later, he settled his $10,640.09 bill with cash. Next stop: the Kansas City Ritz Carlton. He bivouacked with Skinner at his missile silo, then headed back to Santa Fe.

"Skinner played a dangerous game," said Savinelli. "He'd intentionally overdose people with opiates, then play the life-saving doctor by giving them Narcan."

On April 28, 1999, Todd was down in his silo, chatting up Leonard in a transcontinental phone call. From the corner of his eye, he noticed a forty-one-year-old computer engineer that he'd hired the day before. Paul Hulebak drove up from Tulsa for a couple days work on Skinner's IT system.

"Skinner was on the phone to me at the time describing his latest drug episode," recalled Pickard. "He stopped midsentence."

Skinner watched Hulebak wobble then slump over his keyboard. What came next, Leonard assumed to be typical Todd histrionics.

"I've got a problem," he told Pickard in a panicky voice. "Call you back."

But he never did. After he hung up, Todd was preoccupied. Hulebak had gamely taken a couple of the drugs Skinner offered earlier. Now he lay face up, glassy-eyed and unresponsive on the silo floor. He slapped his face, yelled at him to get up, and checked his pupils with a flashlight.

Skinner later told Pottawatomie County Sheriff's detectives that Hulebak seized from an overdose of self-administered methadone and hydromorphone. How he'd acquired the cocktail was anyone's guess. Todd said he immediately took Hulebak to the ER.

Todd did no such thing. He first tried shooting Hulebak up with Benadryl and his own homespun remedies he called "antigens." When the engineer seemed to be breathing better, Todd ordered three of his employees—Hobbs, Guinan, and Kendall Graham—to help haul Hulebak to a hospital thirty miles away. He reasoned that suspicion surrounding drug use at his missile silo wouldn't be a factor outside the city limits.

But Skinner changed his mind upon arrival. Hulebak was breathing so well, he did a U-turn and came back to Wamego. There, Skinner and his crew stood vigil, monitoring Hulebak's recovery.

Only when he stopped breathing, nearly eight hours after the initial seizure, did Todd haul Hulebak to Wamego Hospital, a five-minute drive from the silo.

He was DOA.

"Todd Skinner is evil," said Hulebak's sister Kirstin Reynolds. "He considers himself very smart, but I can tell you from speaking with him numerous times that he's used to dealing with stupid people."

The Pottawatomie County Sheriff's detectives weren't stupid, but they also knew they didn't have enough to charge Todd. They turned Hulebak's body over to the Shawnee County Coroner for autopsy.[4] Skinner drove back to his missile silo, which he'd instructed employees to sanitize: no needles, opiates, psychedelics, etc.

Hulebak was not Todd's first guinea pig. Over time, he became so sophisticated at estimating dosages, potency, and antidotes that he literally thought of himself as a physician bringing zombies back from the dead. His father practiced medicine after a fashion at his chiropractic clinic. Why shouldn't Skinner follow in his footsteps? He even set up IV stations down in the silo for weekend recreational use.

As with Hulebak, Skinner similarly shot up John Halpern's assistant. A young Boston College undergrad who'd apprenticed himself first to Halpern and then Pickard, Mike Bauer fell beneath the thrall of Leonard's lysergic romance and became a junior member of the swimming pool project.

---

4. Weeks before his death, Hulebak had been assisting the DEA in its investigation of a Tulsa pill-mill doctor.

"Mike was John Halpern's 'stack rat,'" said Savinelli. "Pickard hired him to research volatile governments like Afghanistan in reference to their drug trade."

Bauer inevitably met Skinner. Todd took a shine to the lad. He invited him to visit the silo. During his first trip to Wamego, Bauer let Skinner talk him into an IV drip.

"Skinner liked touting the psychedelic aspects of opiate use," said Halpern.

Only later did he learn he was being overdosed on fentanyl. When Bauer convulsed and began to fade, Skinner brought him back with Naloxone, the generic version of Narcan. Unlike Hulebak, Bauer revived.

"Mike learned his lesson, though," insisted Savinelli. "He never trusted the son of a bitch again."

Others were neither so lucky nor so chastened. Bauer's resuscitation only encouraged Skinner. Elmer Gantry paled beside him. In white lab coat with stethoscope looped round his neck, Skinner proudly put the "con" back into conversion. He presented himself as the psychotropic Kildare.

"More like Mengele," muttered Halpern.

Pickard liked the ladies as much as Skinner, though it might be argued that he was slightly more selective. Leonard counted among his scientific role models Kary Mullis and Richard Feynman—both shameless voyeurs when they weren't pursuing Nobel prizes.

"I loved his book, *Surely You're Joking, Mr. Feynman*,"[5] said Pickard.

In a chapter titled, "Topless Bars and Other Ways to Have Fun," the Nobel laureate recalled leering as a nearby couple's foot

---

5   "The title derived from the Dean's wife at afternoon tea among the mathematicians at the Graduate College at Princeton," said Pickard. "She asked him if he wanted cream or lemon and Feynman said, 'Both.'"

massage advanced toward casual sex one afternoon during the 1980s. Feynman lounged beside them in the spa at Esalen:

> He starts to rub her big toe. "I think I feel it," he says. "I feel a kind of dent—is that the pituitary?"
>
> I blurt out, "You're a helluva long way from the pituitary, man!"
>
> They looked at me, horrified . . . and said, "It's reflexology!"
>
> I quickly closed my eyes and appeared to be meditating.

Pickard smiled at the passage. Most men were dogs, truth be told. Feynman the physicist and Pickard the chemist needed pleasuring as much as the next guy. And from Leonard's point of view, there was no aphrodisiac quite so affecting as the illusion of sexual control.

Halpern recalled him once telling Harlow, "You know honey, we should hire surrogates around the world, and they can carry your egg and my sperm and we can have little Leonards and Debbies all over!"

Pickard allegedly told Skinner that he wanted to have many children by many different women.

One of his favored San Francisco haunts was the notorious Mitchell Brothers' O'Farrell Theatre,[6] where he met Martina Schenevar (stage name Selin), Deanna Luce (Marisa), Athena Raphael, and Sita Kaylin (Natasha). Their pet name for Leonard was "Fancy Pants." He wined and dined them during their off hours. Martina once accompanied him on an expedition to Bangkok.

According to Skinner, Pickard checked into the five-star Auberge

---

6. San Francisco porn pioneers, Jim and Artie Mitchell opened the O'Farrell in 1969, evolving from topless to bottomless to full frontal over the next twenty years. Leonard befriended several of the dancers, inviting one them along on a two-week "research" trip to Bangkok in February 1999.

du Soleil in Napa Valley one April weekend for a ménage with Luce and Schenavar. Skinner said the lovefest ended when hotel management had to kick all of them out.

"Skinner has a rich fantasy life, dwelling inside his own hallucinations," said Leonard.

Whenever he stayed in Santa Fe, Pickard unwound at gallery openings and at a favorite lounge in Albuquerque. He gravitated to one artist in particular.

An environmental trainee employed by the air quality department of the state of New Mexico, Trais Kliphuis (pronounced Trace Clip-house) had recently staged a one-woman show in Santa Fe she called "Flesh Off the Easel." Leonard had struck up conversations with unusual women before, but this one was different.

"I'm not a very literal person," she said. "I'm more interested in the sublime and the mysterious, and in seeing what comes through me rather than having a concept or an image."

Thirty-something, intriguingly multifaceted yet fiercely independent, Trais clearly was no bimbo. By the time he wooed Kliphuis, Leonard and Deb were already on the rocks. Motherhood suited her, but abandonment did not. They hadn't exactly split, but Leonard's lysergic wanderings had taken their toll.

"Deborah liked to snoop though my notes, clothes, car, everywhere, even while I bathed," complained Pickard.

Trais, on the other hand, had as free a spirit as Leonard's. During their on-again, off-again year together, Leonard proposed marriage more than once. Tapping into Skinner's wealth, he plied her with gifts and offered to retire the $135,000 mortgage on her new house in Santa Fe. They flew twice to Amsterdam and London on his dime, as well as the resort island of St. Maarten in the Dutch West Indies. Later, when she was asked to identify him from the witness stand, Trais pointed at Leonard and sighed, "He's that beautiful man over there."

Trais was no Blanche Dubois. She grew up on Long Island,

studied chemical engineering at Tufts, and worked variously as cancer researcher, physicist's assistant, and senior WIPP[7] technician, while frequently opting for art over science.

"I always enjoyed her stories of dropping thousands of feet below the surface of the New Mexico desert into the vast salt mine storage facility for nuclear waste from Los Alamos," said Pickard. "Railroad tracks like a honeycomb, geologic eons passing on the way down: ancient oceans from 250 million years ago."

Trais might support herself as a scientist, but she made her name as an artist.

"Paint inspires me," she told the *Santa Fe New Mexican*. "I just love playing with it and seeing what comes through that I've never done before...."

Her reluctance to answer Leonard's marriage proposals might be traced to similar pleas that she got from Todd Skinner, who promised diamonds, sapphires, and a visit to Bora Bora aboard his G5 jet. That he had no jet or any hope of showering her with gems eventually became apparent, but would not have persuaded her in any event. Trais was an artist first, paramour second.

Leonard didn't wait for her to change her mind. Call it mid-life crisis or momentary self-awareness, but at fifty-four, Pickard was suddenly in the market for a wife. He fell next for a Ukrainian pre-med student whom he'd first encountered in St. Petersburg.

Natasha Kruglova was six years younger than Trais and ten years younger than Deborah Harlow. As Leonard grew older, his taste in women clearly trended younger. He began dating an emigre literally half his age.

"Relative youth is not what I was seeking," he said.

Kruglova came to the US to study medicine, but couldn't afford university tuition. She started out working the front desk at San

---

7. Located twenty-six miles southeast of Carlsbad, the Waste Isolation Pilot Plant is the nation's only deep (2,150 feet underground in an ancient salt formation) geologic long-lived radioactive waste repository.

Francisco's Pan Pacific Hotel. She'd brought her father with her from Russia. They set up informal housekeeping in a one-bedroom rent-controlled apartment that fronted directly on California Street.

"Mattress on the floor, Korean grocery on one side and a coin laundromat on the other," said Pickard.

Soon, Leonard began staying over whenever he happened to be in San Francisco, which was often. Natalya[8] accepted Leonard's cloak and dagger ways as if they were second nature because they were. She'd grown up in the USSR in a family grounded in intrigue. A retired trauma surgeon from Odessa, her father, Grigory Vorobee, had been assigned to Cuba during the 1962 missile crisis. Skinner said that when Pickard introduced her at receptions or cocktail parties as Selene or Martina or Natasha Vorobee, she went right along with the pointless ruse.

"I introduced Natasha exactly as she was," he said. "People were fortunate, and delighted, to meet a woman of her quality and bright spirit."

Todd took notice, inventing the perception of the Vorobees as KGB. Following his pattern of lusting after all Pickard's women, Skinner schemed after Natalya just as he had Trais. He offered her jewels and jet rides. Like Trais, Natalya wouldn't give Skinner the time of day.

---

8.   Natasha and Natochka were nicknames.

XIV.

On May 21, 1999, US Customs traced thirty gallons of Brazilian ayahuasca tea to the Santa Fe home of Seagram's liquor heir Jeffrey Bronfman. No arrests were made, but the DEA seized the tea. In his role as president of the North American União do Vegetal Church, Bronfman demanded its return. He sued the Department of Justice, setting the stage for an eventual showdown before the US Supreme Court.

Though newspapers completely missed the raid, Pickard circuitously got wind.

Skinner told Pickard he'd recently given Santa Fe entrepreneur Andrew Ungerleider[1] three grams of swimming pool Viagra, but according to Todd, the most recent batch had major volatility problems. One vial actually exploded. They didn't need any more accidents.

Skinner said that when he showed up at Ungerleider's door to retrieve the Viagra, his wife Gay showed him in. She didn't have the Viagra, but she did have a delicious rumor. It seemed that her brother worked for the New Mexico Attorney General and the scuttlebutt was that the DEA had just raided Jeffrey Bronfman's place.

---

1. In addition to developing New Age glassworks as CEO of the Earthstone and Growstone corporations, Ungerleider also produced the documentary *Dying to Know: Timothy Leary and Ram Dass* (2014).

When Skinner relayed the rumor to Pickard, he imagined agents crawling all over Santa Fe. It didn't help that the lease on the Vuelta Herradura house was coming up for renewal. In anticipation, the landlords were already demanding a routine property inspection, David Haley told Pickard. His panic hiked another notch. He ordered Haley to keep inspectors out at all costs.

How? asked Haley. It was their property.

Pickard thought a minute. How about dressing in drag and passing himself off as John Connor's sick mother? Haley could cough and wheeze like Anthony Perkins in *Psycho*. Literally bar the door.

Skinner was more sanguine. Perhaps the Bronfman bust was just a sign that the time had come to move on. Had it not been for the Hulebak case, he would have suggested transporting the swimming pool project to his missile silo. Unfortunately, the Pottawatomie District Attorney had Skinner in his sites as a person of interest. It seemed only a matter of time before Todd graduated to full-fledged murder suspect. The Wamego silo had to remain squeaky clean. Relocating there was not an option.

But there was more than one silo in Kansas. In fact, Skinner acquired his from a Wichita broker who happened to own one.

Tim Schwartz and partner Ed Peden made a business of buying and selling decommissioned silos. They called them "20th Century Castles." Schwartz invested in a castle of his own near Wichita.

"It was an actual silo," said Pickard. "A vertical cylinder surrounded by military fencing with an eighty-foot disc that blew off when the missile launched."

An Atlas F missile silo sunk into the earth in 1960 at a cost of $3 million, the former Air Force installation consisted of 15,000 square feet buried beneath the prairie next to the tiny settlement of Carneiro, Kansas. The vertical launch tube was separated by tunnel from its control center—a perfect venue for the swimming pool project, far from the prying eyes, ears, and noses of the DEA.

Unlike Skinner's Wamego circus, the Carneiro site was a virtual morgue. It attracted zero attention from surrounding farmers.

During the summer of 1999, Skinner claimed that Pickard gave him $650,000 and told him to find another lab location, preferably in Santa Fe. Skinner pocketed the cash and began lobbying for Carneiro. While Skinner secretly negotiated with Schwartz, Pickard called on a trusty sidekick to begin breaking down the Santa Fe lab.

Clyde Apperson was a machinist from San Jose whom Leonard had known since the seventies. They'd worked together on the Mountain View warehouse lab where Leonard was busted in 1988. Sticking to his Ivy Mike oath, Leonard spilled nothing to investigators about his partner. When Linda Apperson read about Clyde's close call in the newspaper, she supposedly forbade him to ever speak with Leonard again.

Apperson promised he'd get a legit job. He worked for Apple for a time and eventually opened his own machine shop, but once a psychonaut, always a psychonaut. Clyde felt the same visceral challenge to master MDMA and mescaline in the lab as did Leonard. They remained in contact over the years.

With his typical overabundance of caution, Leonard referred to Apperson as "C". He called upon "C's" expertise only when he needed to move his lab. Skinner maintained that Clyde's typical fee was $100,000 for set-up and $50,000 to break one down. Leonard flew him in from San Francisco and Apperson had the swimming pool project ready for transport in two days.

Though Savinelli had been the resident overseer in New Mexico, Apperson was not able to count on his help. He and Pickard were on the outs. Once in his debt, Alfred was now Leonard's creditor. Native Scents had been picking up the ever-growing tab on Leonard's chemicals. Pickard had gotten to the point where he wouldn't even answer Alfred's emails. He currently owed Savinelli $10,000.

As Leonard's new bagman, Skinner arranged to pay Savinelli

with $10,000 worth of DMT. The drug was a dingy brown and of dubious quality.

Skinner processed it himself in a kitchen coffee grinder at the home of one of Pickard's strippers. He packed most of it in a brown bottle so that Alfred wouldn't notice and told her she could keep the rest.

But Savinelli did notice. He had absolutely no confidence in Skinner. When Alfred's son Robert developed a summertime crush on fellow high school senior Emily Ragan, Skinner made a show of swooping in and stealing the girl away. Never mind their twenty-year age difference. Skinner reveled in breaking Robert's heart. His piss-poor excuse for DMT was just the latest insult he added to Savinelli's injury.

Savinelli distanced himself from Skinner and the swimming pool project. Once he learned John Connor and Leonard Pickard were one and the same, more alarms went off. As Halpern's friend, he warned him that he was consorting with conmen and clowns. He described Skinner as "the devil incarnate."

He later groused, "John (Halpern) is a dupe and a fool, but he didn't cause this all to happen."

Alfred's personal paranoia surged during the summer of '99. He kept most of his psychedelics and cash hidden in a safe beneath the tile walkway to his garage, but he buried the hottest drugs out in the yard. His alpha ethyl tryptamine was tucked into a creek bank near his property line and a baggie of Czechoslovakian ET that he said Leonard had given him a year earlier was hidden in a culvert behind his house. After the Bronfman bust, he relocated a fifty-five-gallon drum of ayahuasca root that he'd kept in inventory at Native Scents.

He wanted nothing further to do with the swimming pool project.

Skinner said that he paid his very first visit to Leonard's lab after Apperson had broken down the equipment. While Pickard prepared to leave for Europe on another FEDS mission, Skinner rented a room at the Santa Fe Hilton. He commuted daily to 110 Vuelta Herradura. In Savinelli's absence, Skinner got the cleanup detail. Nausea, he said, greeted him at the front door.

David Haley warned that there'd been a lot of damage, but when Skinner did a walk-through, he felt like he was gagging his way through a war zone. Acid stains streaked the bathroom. He brought in one of his day laborers to scrub it clean.

Lupe Tenorio-Matias reported back that the tile was ruined. It would have to be replaced. Skinner gave him three Valium and promised $1,000 cash if he could fix the bathroom and bring the entire house back to some semblance of normal.

Skinner was working against the clock. Under the terms of Haley's lease, they had to return the house to its owners by Sept. 10. Skinner summoned Gardner Springs employee Mike Hobbs from Tulsa to lend a hand. To hear Skinner tell it, the two men had to don latex gloves, swallow a handful of Valium, and pant past the worst of the fumes. While Tenorio-Matias cleaned, they loaded an eight-by-four trailer with Apperson's boxed-up lab gear.

Before he left for London, Pickard made it clear that he was not convinced Kansas was the answer. According to Skinner, he preferred relocating to another residential neighborhood in Santa Fe, where the DEA was not likely to snoop. Skinner told him he'd found another home comparable to Vuelta Herradura nearby for $800. He did not say it was temporary.

Once Pickard was gone, Skinner and Hobbs moved the trailer again, this time to a Storage USA unit located in an industrial zone on the edge of town, not unlike the one in Mountain View where Leonard got busted in 1988.

There the equipment would remain for the next three months.

When Pickard returned from London on Oct. 21, Skinner was ebullient. With the Santa Fe emergency behind them, he planned a celebratory wing ding like no other.

He started by renting a secluded party house located on a ridge overlooking Bolinas Bay. The one-time hideaway of late Grateful Dead founder Jerry Garcia, San Souci offered spectacular views of the Pacific peeking through stands of redwood, cypress, and eucalyptus. In addition to black-bottom pool, sliding glass walls, and psychedelic lighting, the split level four-bedroom spread stood on an acre of sparsely populated Stinson Beach—the perfect venue for an army of psychonauts to trip the light fantastic long into the night.

Using Mike Hobbs as his alias, Skinner put down a deposit for a month's stay. He invited several dozen of his closest pals to a Nov. 9 bash honoring rock star Sting, who was then in the Bay Area on a concert tour.

Sting's debut inside Leonard's inner circle occurred a couple years earlier, when the British supernova landed in Southern California and purchased the Malibu beach house of "Dallas" TV star Larry Hagman. Sting adapted instantly to the New Age lifestyle, which included a growing fascination with psychonauts and such Esalen-approved disciplines as yoga.

He gravitated to Ganga White, widely regarded as *the* premier yoga master on the West Coast. White maintained his studio in the Santa Barbara foothills under the aegis of the White Lotus Foundation.[2] Sting became a regular and eventually, a member of its advisory board.

Leonard approved. "I always thought Ganga was a fine teacher," he said.

So did Skinner, who maintained that Ganga was a reliable

---

2. Founded in 1968, the California non-profit propagated Ganga's philosophy: "I got into yoga for spiritual, mystical reasons. I had no idea there was a physical practice. Some of my first teachers were hatha yogis. They told me if I wanted to see the world from a different point of view I should try standing on my head."

customer for controlled substances.[3] As a matter of fact, a grand jury scheduled White to spill what he knew on the subject the first week of January, and both Skinner and Pickard thought it might be a good idea to listen in. Like several other guests at the San Souci party, Ganga was unaware of the swimming pool project. They tried to wire him with a transmitter microphone disguised as a pen, but it was another James Bond scheme gone awry. They heard only garble.

Money, it seemed, had become the root of all evil. Before the party, Petaluma Al dropped by to see Pickard about bringing his account up to date. According to Skinner, Leonard separated Al's $750,000 delivery into stacks of $100s and hid them at San Souci—money earmarked for the ET that Pickard had ordered during his recent London trip. Unfortunately, Skinner found the cache first.

After months of coddling Pickard, Skinner said he was getting sick of his cloak-and-dagger nonsense. Around the time of the San Souci gathering, Skinner recalled picking up the phone and hearing Pickard on the other end disguising his voice: "This is Carlos. I need a precursor out of Aldrich. A couple of kilograms of it or more."

Translation: Leonard wanted Todd to order more supplies from Sigma-Aldrich Chemical Co. Why couldn't he just say that? Everything with Pickard smacked of second-rate James Bond, said Skinner.

"A convenient, unverifiable tale," countered Pickard. "Skinner could go on for hours like this, once he knew what you wanted to hear."

During Leonard's absence from San Souci, Skinner continued, he went on a scavenger hunt. He found a bunch of bills buried inside a tool box in the garage. They included Dutch Guilders and a pile of Canadian cash, as well as lots and lots of good old American

---

3 "I never purchased, nor was gifted, nor received any controlled substance in any way from Skinner," said White.

greenbacks. Substituting $20s for $100s, Skinner topped each bundle with a Benjamin. He guessed that Pickard would not bother to count it all. Later, Skinner estimated he made off with between $200,000 and $300,000. He justified the theft as half the rent on San Souci, plus ongoing reimbursement for Pickard's lavish travel expenses.

It was harder to justify renting a Porsche for $20,000. What of it? Skinner deserved a nice ride.

And Sting deserved the best sound system. To that end, Skinner hired the Sacramento audio engineer who installed his high-end stereo in the missile silo. Chris Malone was only too happy to oblige. Todd had recently ordered a pair of $80,000 speakers from him and usually paid in cash. San Souci was no exception.

"He carried around one of those silver bulletproof briefcases full of cash," recalled Malone. "When me and the guy I brought with me to put in the system finished, he tipped me $2,000 then turned to my helper and handed him $1,000."

Basking in Sting's reflected celebrity, Todd recalled Leonard behaving particularly squirrelly during the party. Superstars, particularly scientific luminaries, seemed to reduce Leonard to a groupie who already stood out from the crowd in his full-length black leather overcoat and cowboy boots.

Pickard steered the very comely Natasha Kruglova from klatch to klatch, introducing her as his latest protégé—a Russian doll with a medical mind. She was applying to Berkeley, and Leonard curried favor on her behalf among the assembled psychonaut royalty. He aimed to see her past all admission obstacles.

For her part, Natasha clung to him like Scarlett to Rhett. Meanwhile, Todd skulked nearby, young Emily Ragan hanging on his every word.

Beside Sting and his entourage, Skinner said that the guest list included Kary Mullis, who'd earned a Nobel since the days when he and Pickard had experimented with bathtub acid at Berkeley.

"Kary attributes his insight into PCR (Polymerase Chain Reaction) to his acid experiences," said Pickard. "The DNA image won him the 1993 Nobel Prize[4] in chemistry."

He added, however, that Mullis was not on the guest list. In fact, he did not attend the party at all except in Skinner's imagination.

In Todd's version, Pickard nudged Mullis and asked him if he recalled that first time they'd synthesized a gram together.

"And Kary split," muttered Skinner, "because Nobel laureates don't want that kind of baggage on them."

While the swimming pool brass partied in Bolinas, their minions were on the move in New Mexico.

Clyde Apperson flew in to Albuquerque on Nov. 5. Two days later, Mike Hobbs rented a truck in San Rafael under the name "Bill Martin." He then began the cross-country drive to rendezvous with Skinner and Apperson in Santa Fe, making a stopover to visit Ganga White in Santa Barbara on the way.

Skinner had secured Tim Schwartz's silo the way he sealed most deals: by supplying Schwartz with drugs and lying. He promised to remodel the former missile base and turn it into another Wamego fantasyland in exchange for free rent. Schwartz responded with a signed handwritten permission slip: "Todd Skinner has permission to do anything with my missile silo—he is the boss."

Pickard headed for Carneiro too, according to Skinner, but followed a different itinerary. A week after the party, he flew commercial to Colorado, where he boarded a charter to Santa Fe. There he

---

4. Fame did not dull his eccentricity. Moments before delivering his 1993 Nobel lecture, Mullis said he'd rather talk to the Swedes about AIDS than DNA. He refused to believe that HIV was the cause. In 1992, Mullis founded the Star Gene company to make and market jewelry that contained the amplified DNA of dead celebrities like Marilyn Monroe and Elvis Presley.

picked up Trais Kliphuis and flew on to Manhattan, where they spent the Thanksgiving weekend at a Fairfield Inn.

He also called Natasha twice on the sly, said Todd. Ignorant of his tryst with Trais, Natasha arranged to meet Leonard at Lake Tahoe from Dec. 28 through Jan. 2. They would follow their New Year's holiday at Hyatt Incline Village with two more days at the San Francisco Hilton, then another week and a half at the Las Campanas luxury resort outside of Santa Fe.

Leonard paid for it all under the name Todd Ragan. When he wasn't using cash, he routinely stuck Skinner with the bills. Even so, Pickard chalked up $41,602.96 on his personal credit card accounts during 1999. He spent an additional $20,119.34 on money orders for Clyde Apperson. And still, Leonard never paid income taxes.

In between women, he did manage briefly to get down to business during the first week of December. Apperson and Hobbs drove the lab equipment from Santa Fe to Kansas. According to Skinner, Pickard joined him at the Atlas F silo in Carneiro, new home of the swimming pool project.

While Pickard and Apperson set up inside the Control Center, Skinner kept watch over the south Kansas flatlands for any suspicious vehicles. He loved Leonard's magic, but lysergic chemistry was beyond his skill set, he said. Once he rekeyed the doors, his job was done.

Todd's specialty wasn't chemistry; it was disinfecting dollars. The compulsion he apparently shared with Leonard Pickard was multiple partners, if not indiscriminate sex.

Shortly before Christmas, Skinner met an eighteen-year-old pigtailed pole dancer from Burlington, Kansas (pop. 2,674). Krystle Cole performed nightly at the Club Orleans. Blonde, blue-eyed, tall (5'9"), thin (120 lbs.) with a butterfly tattooed on her left ankle,

Krystle had her act down pat: small-town gal with swivel hips and alfalfa in her teeth. Skinner was instantly smitten.

At first, Krystle regarded her nerdy new admirer as less than unlikely.

"Do Amish men really go to strip clubs?" she wanted to know.

Once under his spell, Krystle's homespun cynicism melted. Skinner later insisted that he wasn't slumming; he was an investment banker interviewing her to become Emily Ragan's assistant.

"Krystle was a great valet," he told journalist Michael Mason. "She was very well organized."

Skinner quickly proved to be Krystle's new candy man; she, his willing guinea pig. She swallowed, smoked, and injected anything he prescribed, including hallucinatory suppositories. Krystle loved getting high. She was Vanna White to his Satanic Sajak. During the psychedelic Masses that Skinner regularly celebrated at the silo, Krystle tended his altar. She became as devoted to Todd as Natasha was to Leonard.

As both the year and the century wound to a close, neither Skinner nor Pickard seemed to notice that their lives might be spinning out of control. Having one babe for public consumption and another on the side seemed as routine as laundering Benjamins by the butt load. Like the proverbial frog in the proverbial pan of slowly boiling water, each soldiered on. Y2K was bound to be the best year yet.

XV.

As the new century began, Skinner spent more and more time at Harrah's Prairie Band Casino on the nearby Pottawatomie Indian reservation. He advertised himself as a billionaire, arrived in his Porsche, and always seemed to win.

On Jan. 8, 2000, Todd turned in an unusually large pile of chips. Challenged by an impudent cashier, he identified himself as a Treasury Department official. He flashed an Interpol badge, collected his payout, then went about his business.

But suspicions had been aroused. The following day, Pottawatomie Sheriff's deputies showed up at his missile silo and arrested Skinner for impersonating a federal officer. They kept him at the Sheriff's office until a Secret Service agent drove in from Kansas City. The agent accused Skinner of trying to plant a bomb.

"Do you track the President?" he demanded. "Do you follow the President? Do you go to areas where the President goes to? Are you interested in killing the President?"

Skinner sweated out the ordeal until four a.m. Once again, he got lucky. Just before dawn, the agent gave up and went home. Skinner faced federal charges, but as with Paul Hulebak's death, he was released pending further investigation.

Todd decided that gambling in Kansas might be imprudent. In the first of many trips, he flew to Nevada on Feb. 25. Skinner returned again and again to the Strip over the next several months, extending his winning streak to the Paris, Mirage, Treasure Island, and Bellagio. Wherever he went, a Currency Transaction Report[1] (CTR) seemed to follow. All told, he estimated he took home $750,000 in winnings—roughly the same in Dutch Guilders that had been wired from the Netherlands.

Once, he tried to swap a 1,000 Guilder note at Kaw Valley Bank in Wamego for a quick infusion of greenbacks, but the teller said she couldn't exchange Dutch currency. The manager explained that the nearest bank authorized to do so was 100 miles away in Kansas City. Skinner sniffed at such rubes. He took his Guilders to Vegas.

While Skinner laundered, Leonard wandered.

To help his new partner make above-limit currency trades during his frequent travels, Skinner introduced Pickard to a boyhood chum. Bill Wynn had matured into a skilled provider of all sorts of identification. He even had his own equipment. For laughs, Wynn made Leonard a driver's license under the name of Oklahoma state representative Bruce Niemi. The real Niemi never knew that Pickard also carried a library card and ID from the Tulsa election board, all in Niemi's name.

But it was John Connor—not Niemi—who squired young Natalya Kruglova from Vegas to Frisco to Kansas and beyond during the winter of 2000. Following their extended New Year's holiday, Pickard returned to Carneiro in February. According to Skinner, Apperson was still there tinkering with the swimming pool project. Leonard leant a hand.

Using his alter ego, the silver-maned Connor and his mistress checked in at the nearby Salina Ramada Inn from Feb. 11 through 19. Over the next four months, the Connors returned periodically, according to Skinner. While in Kansas, Leonard and

---

1. The Bank Secrecy Act of 1970 requires financial institutions including casinos to report any transaction over $10,000 to the federal government.

Natalya scrupulously followed the first rule of Ivy Mike: draw no attention.

In Leonard's version, they drew no attention because they weren't there.

"Natalya was never at Carneiro," he said. "She was at university."

Pickard's one Kansas visit had been a mercy mission. At Skinner's insistence, he and Apperson traveled to Carneiro to retrieve Todd's Mexican tile man, who was trapped inside the silo.

"Skinner had locked him inside for weeks to work on the tile," insisted Leonard. "If we hadn't gone to get him out, Lupe might have starved."

While both Skinner's and Pickard's stories tried credulity, Leonard pointed out that nowhere did his or Apperson's fingerprints appear inside the Carneiro facility. By contrast, Skinner's and those of his employees were everywhere. In Pickard's version, he and Apperson were being set up.

"In retrospect, it's apparent to me that Skinner needed a witness to say he saw us there," said Pickard.

Similarly, Skinner made up a story about paying Natasha's college tuition with a $27,000 cashier's check from the Mirage Casino. Natasha tried using it to pay for her first semester at Berkeley when the government put a hold on it. Natasha called Leonard. Leonard called Todd.

"We went to high-burn security status," Skinner recalled.

According to Todd, Pickard leapt to the worst conclusion. Natasha would be deported. For three days, Leonard sweated it out at the Wamego silo, his imagination on overdrive. He ordered Gunnar Guinan to rent him a Ford Explorer with four-wheel drive, suitable for evasive off-road chases. He was 150 miles west of Wamego when he learned that Skinner cut another check and made good on Natasha's tuition.

Ultimately, the whole episode had been false alarm. Skinner

seemed to take it all in stride. There had never been any real danger. Kansas was one big snooze.

Leonard labeled all of it fiction. "Nat never tried to cash a check from the Mirage, and Skinner never paid her tuition," he said flatly.

The one Carneiro fact upon which both men could agree was the death of Skinner's landlord.

On March 27, a despondent Tim Schwartz paid a visit to Osage County an hour east of his home. Troubled over his recent divorce, the owner of the Carneiro silo found a remote fishing hole, loaded his rifle, and took his own life. He left his suicide note on his computer.

Skinner shed no tears, but had to wonder: when would Schwartz's heirs demand to tour their silo? That couldn't happen. The Control Center had flooded during recent winter storms. The lab chemicals set-up reeked and there was nowhere to safely hide equipment.

Skinner waited for a phone call from the Schwartz family, but there seemed to be no immediate threat. Within the month, things relaxed back to Skinner's version of normal. That meant manufacture, distribute, launder, repeat. Life went on.

Skinner maintained that he picked up another load of laundry in early April. Apperson met him at the San Francisco airport and they swung by the Kruglovas' new California Street apartment to pick up a briefcase containing between $176,000 and $197,000.

Once again, Pickard begged to differ.

"This is nonsense," he said. "Skinner would say anything, secure in his confidence that whatever he said would be believed."

According to Leonard, there were no funds, no briefcase, and no visit. Skinner never even knew where the apartment was.

When Skinner got back to Kansas, an indictment was waiting. The Department of Justice accused him of impersonating a federal official four months earlier at Harrah's Prairie Band Casino. The prosecutor assigned to the case was an ambitious young Assistant US Attorney out of Topeka named Gregory Hough.

Things looked grim, and yet, as in the past, Todd skated. Freed on his own recognizance, he was told to return to court with his plea in June.

Skinner's reaction to yet another close shave was celebration. He invited a dozen of his best buds to join him in Vegas, including Todd's mom. Following the death of his stepfather a year earlier, Todd had reconciled with Kathrine Magrini. They planned a Mother's Day bash like no other at the Paris Casino.

Krystle Cole and Emily Ragan were there. So were Leonard and Natasha. Billy Wynn came, as did Mike Hobbs, Todd's gofer-in-chief Gunnar Guinan, and a couple of silo gals who dropped by for a dose of Skinner's Eucharist from time to time.

"Our whole group paraded around the casinos like we owned the place," Krystle recalled in her self-published 2007 memoir, *Lysergic*. "We were decked out in expensive clothes, Armani, Gucci, etc."

Todd staked them all, enlisting each in his lysergic laundromat. Even Pickard gambled, winning $14,200 one day and $8,000 the next.

"I remember one occasion when Todd and Leonard went to play French Roulette," wrote Krystle. "We were staying at the Paris, in their best rooms of course, so all we had to do was take the elevator downstairs. Todd started playing with a large stack of plaques. They ranged in value from $1,000 to $10,000. He started throwing them down across the board, like they were pennies. After an hour of play he was up $64,000 and decided to stop. It was amazing! Afterward we all went over to the Bellagio for beluga caviar and wine, costing only a measly $4,000!"

Natasha didn't play. She regarded Skinner a tasteless buffoon, but fueled by innuendo from Skinner's gossipy smurfs, she began to suspect Leonard might be cheating on her. At every opportunity, she re-seduced him. During the first week in May, she booked a spa with His & Her massages at Big Sur's exclusive Ventana Inn and prepaid the $3,500 bill with cash.

Leonard preferred cash transactions. Skinner had gotten into the habit of springing for most of his credit card purchases. When Leonard snuck away with Trais for some R&R in St. Maarten, far from Natasha's jealous eyes, Skinner came through. When Leonard wanted Ann and Sasha Shulgin ferried to a psychonaut conference in Virginia, Skinner picked up the airfare.

Hotels? Car rentals? Restaurants? Only ask: Todd swiped his AmEx card. How he could afford such generosity was never discussed. Leonard figured Skinner's lavish lifestyle could be traced to Gardner Springs or Warren Buffett.

"We still thought at that time Skinner was as he claimed: heir to an industrial fortune," said Pickard. "And though an exotic drug abuser, also one who was intensely supportive of psychedelic research. We had difficulty turning down Skinner's largesse, or his credit cards, all of which made him believable."

Ever since Skinner first invited him to submit a grant proposal, Leonard held out hope for a Buffett-backed drug policy conference. While he remained skeptical, Leonard finally took the plunge. What did he have to lose?

His position at UCLA grew more tenuous by the day. He rarely showed his face in Mark Kleiman's office any more. As time went on, the prestige of a Harvard gathering seemed too delicious to ignore: sublime resolution to his constant juggling act.

A successful symposium might even lead to med-school admission . . . and not just some random also-ran like the University of Guadalajara. How did Harvard Medical School sound? If a doofus like John Halpern could cut it, why not a seasoned psychonaut like Leonard?

Lucille would have been so proud.

For weeks, then months, Leonard waited. When would he hear

from Buffett? Without wanting to seem too anxious, Leonard hectored Todd at every opportunity.

Patience, counseled Todd. Warren was a busy man.

During a brief sojourn in Chicago, Pickard arranged to meet the mysterious ET Man.

On May 8, he and Natasha flew there together, courtesy of Todd Skinner. They stayed at the Ritz Carlton, where James Edward Miller was to meet with Leonard. Miller showed up with another man Leonard didn't know and steered him to a secluded corner of the lobby. Natasha did not join them.

The meeting was no joke. According to Skinner, who watched from several yards away, their discussion surrounded the importation of $10 million in ergotamine tartrate. Todd might be footing the bill, but Leonard kept him at arm's length. No sense spooking his spooks with so much ET on the table.

After the ET Man left, Leonard rejoined Skinner. He laid out his plan: Apperson would pick up four boxes of precursor from a prearranged location, drive it to Kansas, and bury it near the lab until it was needed.

There were unforeseen delays. Apperson went MIA. Skinner offered to substitute a pair of his Gardner Springs employees to escort the ET, but Leonard shook his head "no." Apperson was usually very reliable, but Leonard suspected he had a tootsie in Albuquerque. Didn't everyone?

Apperson eventually turned up in Tulsa, rented a car in Chicago, and delivered the goods to Skinner a month later in Salina. Apperson wanted to buy a post hole digger to bury the payload, but Skinner said he'd take care of it. The ET never did get buried.

While he was in Chicago, Pickard also weighed Skinner's suggestion that he open an account with the venerable commodities trading firm ED&F Man. As Skinner explained it, the account made it possible to move large sums without being scrutinized by the Financial Crimes Enforcement Network (FinCEN). Under federal law, casinos, banks and brokerages had to file Suspicious Activity Referrals (SAR)[2] whenever fraud, tax evasion or some other crime looked like it was being committed. ED&F Man did not have to file—or so Skinner told Pickard.

"I neglected to open an account," said Leonard. "In retrospect, this was a prime example of Skinner building a record to implicate others in his laundering activity."

Todd had other business in Chicago, too. He incorporated Skinner Industries in Illinois and named Leonard vice-president. Unbeknownst to Leonard, he also granted him power of attorney over his Wamego Trust.[3]

Any doubt they were doing business together officially vanished.

Skinner bookended his Chicago visit by totaling two cars.

On April 30, he cracked up his beloved $225,000 four-wheel drive Boxster Porsche outside of Topeka. Two weeks later, he creamed a rental car in Berkeley. He had to be taken to the Alta Bates Hospital for treatment of minor injuries.

Leonard called Katherine Magrini from Los Angeles the next day. Todd seemed accident prone. Was he all right?

A few scratches and bruises, said his mother. Nothing to worry about.

Pickard hung up, mollified. Again.

Todd Skinner kept getting into trouble, yet led a Houdini existence. He had more lives than a Cheshire cat. An unlikely warlock in which to place one's trust, he was as smooth-talking a grifter

---

2. Bank employees who believe a Currency Transaction Report involves fraud or other criminal activity can check a box and turn the CTR into a SAR.

3. Todd testified he trusted Leonard to help his children if he died, but Pickard said Skinner just wanted to incriminate him. He evened the score by quit claiming the deed to a Skinner creditor in 2003.

as Leonard. Having him on Pickard's side seemed far better than having him as an enemy. Still, he worried Leonard.

On his way back to Vegas for another rendezvous with his new partner, Leonard made a pit stop in Anaheim. While they could no longer be called a couple, he and Deborah remained friendly. They would always have Melissa in common.

Pickard met mother and daughter on Main Street USA, smiling wide and long as he caught his leaping moppet mid-squeal.

For one May day in Disneyland, Leonard forgot about Skinner, Halpern, Wathne, and Petaluma Al. Guilders and ET and the swimming pool project were artifacts of another place and time. He remembered instead his vows as a Buddhist priest: to live in the now with his once true love and their little girl.

"Flying on Dumbo with Melissa," he remembered. "The whirl we took in Alice's teacups. Just as we were about to board, we were assailed by Alice in pinafore and blond hair. And the Mad Hatter himself, tall and in black waistcoat!"

Leonard was fifty-four. Melissa was five. In his memory, she wore saucer eyes, Mouse ears, and a grin of endless delight.

In *The Rose of Paracelsus*, Leonard wrote about an unnamed tot who serves tea to a stuffed toy angel and a crippled giraffe. She called the giraffe Gigi. In Leonard's telling, the angel bows its head in perpetual prayer over Gigi's broken limb. The scene is fiction, and yet it's not.

"Melissa actually had a Gigi, and I always promised that I would fix her leg one day," he said.

He never did.

The chief function of the Director of Cage Operations at the Paris Casino was to take note of suspicious activity. When a gaggle of Kansas yokels started raking in the dough during the month of May, Dave Ellis did just that.

He started by filing a SAR on Gunnar Guinan, an unlikely

winner who cashed in chips by the thousands. Ellis followed up the SAR filing with a four-alarm memo to all Paris cashiers: Beware of Guinan, the suspected ringleader Gordon Todd Skinner, his mother, and all those with whom they associated. They might be "gaming agents," the Vegas euphemism for high-end grifters.

Within a week, however, Ellis changed his tune. In the Director of Cage Operations journal, he wrote without explanation: "Heat's off Skinner—Let him do what he wants—anything he wants."

In his own personal journal, Pickard similarly ricocheted in his opinion about Skinner. A laptop file he labeled "Snowman" noted each *mitzvah* followed by every transgression. When caught stealing, Todd simply passed off each sleight of hand as a practical joke.

Take the Case of the Missing Mortgage. By the spring of 2000, Leonard's love life had evolved into French bedroom farce. Natasha was jealous and pregnant; Trais was pregnant but benign. All that his first baby mama demanded was security for herself and her impending child. To that end, Leonard ordered Skinner to use $225,000 in Guilders to retire Trais's mortgage.

It took a couple months, but Skinner transubstantiated the Guilders into $190,000 in clean casino cash. He blamed the $35,000 difference on descending Dutch exchange rates, a dubious explanation Pickard accepted without too much grousing. What happened next, however, was larceny.

Skinner forged Pickard a check for $190,000 then snuck into his hotel room and destroyed it. Next, he FedExed Pickard a real check for $190 and another to Trais for $130—three zeros short of the $130,000 she needed to pay off her mortgage.

It was all just an elaborate joke, said Todd. Trais and Pickard were not amused. No matter, Skinner said with a chuckle. The real checks would soon be in the mail. His quarterly retainer from Warren Buffett had just been late, creating a cash flow problem. Not to worry.

On June 16, Skinner pled guilty in federal court to impersonating a government agent. His sentencing was set for August.

Todd appeared rattled. It was the first time he'd faced real consequences for trampling the law since the eighties. Everyone around him seemed to take a deep breath and a step backward. Following the Trais mortgage fiasco, even gullible Leonard Pickard had grown chilly. Todd strung him along with the Buffett scam, but he was running out of excuses.

To top off his growing isolation, he'd lost track of Krystle Cole. During the weeks following his two auto accidents, Skinner's new gal Friday disappeared. She strayed after a rave one night in Kansas City and never returned.

Skinner dispatched Gunnar Guinan to investigate. Guinan found her shacked up at an extended-stay hotel with a cellular phone salesman and part-time deejay named Ryan Overton.

Todd had an undeniable jealous streak. He enjoyed the occasional orgy and thought nothing of an anonymous poke now and again, but took umbrage at poachers. Clearly Overton had been Cole mining, but Krystle knew how to handle Todd. She offered up Overton as a guinea pig.

Todd dosed him with DMT and Alfred Savinelli's MDMA. He shot him up with ALD-25, Vicodin, and Valium to see how he'd react. Overton spent the week tripping. He became Todd's latest convert. Overton even offered to add his own brand of MDMA to Skinner's pharmacy. Before month's end, Overton was a full-fledged member of the congregation.

He was also a hidden liability. Besides running Generation Telecom and emceeing raves, Overton also sold MDMA he imported from Amsterdam through a Polish national who mailed it right under the noses of US Customs.

Tanasis "Socko" Kanculis was well known to the DEA. He smuggled MDMA out of the Netherlands by taping tablets inside magazines, sealing them in plastic, then mailing them past dope-sniffing dogs[4] to customers in Kansas City.

A month before Krystle met Overton, Kanculis sent him just such a package, but to the wrong address. It contained three hundred pills. The addressee called police as well as Overton. When both showed up in the front yard at the same time, Overton denied knowing anything at all about the pills. Police had to turn him loose, but he was now on the DEA's radar.

And so was everyone with whom he associated.

On a sunny afternoon in early July, Pickard cooled his heels in the foyer of a thirty-room mansion in the San Francisco suburb of Hillsborough. He twisted his fingers into a knot, meditated, hyperventilated, and adjusted his necktie. In a nearby conference room, Skinner conferred with Warren Buffett's associates, who were reviewing Pickard's grant application.

After what seemed to be forever, Skinner emerged with a smile. He had good news and bad. Buffett hadn't been able to make the meeting, but he *did* approve the Future and Emerging Drugs Study conference! Confirmation would arrive shortly via FedEx. Skinner congratulated Pickard and gave him the tracking number. Buffett's wife Susie would handle all the details. Skinner handed Pickard a slip of paper bearing Susie's private number, but cautioned against using it except in an emergency.

Leonard left for London the following day for a chemical weapons conference, but he was so high on the Buffett deal he could have flown without the plane. How could he have known that he'd just been the victim of an elaborate hoax?

A couple weeks passed. Leonard returned from London. Skinner

---

4. To get around this problem, Krystle and Todd once discussed stealing two drug dogs from a cop who lived across the street from Krystle's parents in Kansas.

called him from Mendocino where he'd rented a summer getaway. Alas, there were problems.

Warren Buffett's rival, fellow billionaire Henry Kravas, learned that Skinner transferred $1 billion out of Buffett's secret Swiss account. Buffett had to distance himself from Skinner before Kravas blew the whistle. For the moment, that meant there would be no grant.

Leonard doubled over, gut punched.

Skinner brightened. Not to worry! He found a Tulsa-based Christian charity that agreed to pick up where Buffett left off. As proof, he had a $300,000 cashier's check from the J.E. and L.E. Mabee Foundation. The check was forged, of course, but looked convincing. As he later explained in court, Skinner observed the highest standards when it came to fraud:

"One way was to do it completely automated, which made a lesser-quality check," he said. "The better-quality check was to do it through multiple steps to where you would use a Selectric III typewriter that had a special font. And then we would actually stamp the numbers up on the top that would say 'official check' or 'cashier's check,' and those numbers would coincide with Federal Reserve numbers."

Leonard accepted the check, but not the explanation. Skinner had run his con into the ground. His mark was finally on to him. He belatedly began studying Buffett's biographies.

"When I asked Skinner the name of Buffett's most recent wife after Susie, he didn't know," said Leonard. "When I asked about Buffett's home in Omaha, where Skinner allegedly visited, he was unable to describe it, or to identify Buffett's old favorite car, or his history in trading or his daily habits. I added these discrepancies to 'Snowman,' along with the list of the many lies so far."

Each time Pickard heard from him for the rest of the summer, Skinner sounded a little more desperate, his excuses a little less convincing. If it weren't for Pickard's enduring dream of a Kennedy

School FEDS conference, he would have stopped taking his calls all together. His final "Snowman" entry was "GET RID OF THIS GUY!"

"He was unpredictable and kind of crazy," Pickard recalled. "From mid-July until October we had no contact. His life was unraveling. Then he called me."

Skinner wasn't alone when he phoned in late October. Sitting right beside him was a DEA agent named Karl Nichols.

XVI.

AMONG HIS PEERS, KARL NICHOLS was known as a Boy Scout. He liked to believe that he played by the rules, though a just end occasionally warranted all necessary means. He stood on the front lines of the War on Drugs and took great pride in nailing dope dealers.

Born the same year as Todd Skinner and John Halpern, Nichols hired into the DEA as a forensic chemist, then methodically worked his way up to Special Agent. He trained in the DEA's Richmond lab for four years before joining the California LSD task force in 1992, just in time for the climax of Operation Looking Glass.

Nicknamed Operation Dead End by Grateful Dead fans, who accused the DEA of targeting concertgoers, Operation Looking Glass resulted in nearly 3,000 arrests between 1993[1] and 1994. Some Deadheads went away for twenty years or more. The standing joke at the agency's San Francisco headquarters was:

Q—What do you call a Deadhead in a three-piece suit?
A—The defendant.

---

1.   The last big bust netted five suspects with 1.5 million hits on June 29, 1993. The four-year investigation climaxed with 160 officers and agents from twelve state and federal jurisdictions raiding nine different locations. The ring's leader was a thirty-seven-year-old Indian rug importer who went by the name "Sarah Bernhardt" and fled to Guatemala in 1990. The task force spent $120,000 on drugs but did not detail the total cost of the operation.

And yet, despite the success of Looking Glass, nobody was laughing. The Department of Justice hadn't shut down a single LSD lab since 1991. The drug kept coming from somewhere, but where?

The question obsessed Nichols as much as it did the old timers. The halcyon era of Owsley, Scully, and Sand was over. The acid underground had frozen solid. Nobody talked. Infiltration was a pipe dream. The DEA might not have learned the secret meaning of Ivy Mike, but its agents knew they were aiming at a silent, moving target, and consistently missed.

Operation White Rabbit almost didn't happen. Had it not been for Todd Skinner's desperate persistence to rat him out, Pickard might have continued unhindered, and no one would have been the wiser.

But by the summer of 2000, Skinner's long, slow slide into perfidy had become a toboggan. One trouble cascaded into the next:

- Ryan Overton entangled him in his MDMA import scheme, which the DEA was rumored to be scrutinizing. Under a nationwide party drug crackdown known as Operation Flashback, ecstasy dealers were prime targets.
- The Pottawatomie County Coroner officially declared Paul Hulebak's death suspicious. Too many needle tracks, too many conflicting stories. Sheriff's detectives named Skinner a person of interest.
- Spurred by multiple reports of suspicious activity, the Kansas Attorney General subpoenaed the Wamego silo's phone records dating back to 1997.
- Skinner's time was up at the Carneiro missile base. Tim Schwartz's heirs ordered him to move, but the silo was a swamp. The ventilation system had flooded, scattering flasks and drug debris everywhere.

Skinner tried to remain rational. He handled one thing at a time, beginning with the Carneiro eviction. He called Apperson, but "C" was in the hospital with an ear infection. Pickard was still in London, trolling for support of his Harvard future drugs conference. In their absence, Skinner rounded up several Gardner Springs employees and headed for Carneiro.

Skinner's crew bleached every surface and salvaged what remained, but not without problems. While packing up a box of beakers, Gunnar Guinan began hallucinating.

"It didn't look good, but I didn't perceive what it was," he said. "It wasn't Betty Crocker. It wasn't some type of food preparation. It was some chemical endeavor."

Skinner told him to drop a Valium or two. Gunnar slept for forty-eight hours.

Skinner's father drove up from Tulsa to help. Todd cautioned him not to duplicate Guinan's mistakes. Wear gloves, trousers, and long-sleeved shirts. Breathe through your nose.

In all, the emergency move took five days. On July 17, they caravanned everything from Carneiro to Wamego. Once again, Skinner counseled haste and care. He could ill afford hauling anyone to the same ER where he'd dumped Hulebak a year earlier.

While his makeshift crew hauled glassware into the grotto down below, Skinner hustled two twenty-canister cases of ergotamine tartrate into a metal barn on the grounds above. Each canister was worth $100,000. When he was sure that he was alone and no one was watching, Todd jammed both cases into a niche in the ceiling.

For the next couple of weeks, Skinner relaxed. He'd dodged the latest bullet in an ever-increasing volley. He rented a seaside place in Mendocino to get away from the maelstrom in Kansas. He even returned to Vegas with his usual squad of smurfs and partied hearty while cleansing cash.

His Waterloo didn't arrive until early August, when Krystle called from Kansas City with disturbing news. The DEA had intercepted an MDMA shipment from Amsterdam. They were questioning Ryan Overton and connecting the dots.

The second blow landed on Aug. 25, when a Kansas magistrate ordered Skinner to pay a $10,000 fine for impersonating a government agent. Todd shut his eyes. Running low on money and second chances, he left the court despondent. He stewed a day or two, then began calling the DEA.

The first agent he reached in Tulsa listened impatiently to his improbable story, then told Skinner he was nuts. The second one in the San Francisco office did much the same. Skinner made his third call to Topeka attorney Tom Haney, who advised him to pack his bags and accompany him to Washington, where he retained a DC law firm, to connect them with the right people at the Department of Justice.

By the first week of October, Haney and Skinner had hammered out a deal: in return for blanket immunity, Skinner admitted to laundering LSD profits, distributing thousands of doses, and securing lab sites. Asked why he was coming forward, he explained with a straight face that acid was a sacrament. The fact that Leonard sold it as a commodity so offended him that he decided he must be stopped. Pickard, he said, was a bad shaman—the ruthless brains of the outfit.

Todd's treachery carried a nice bonus. Haney negotiated witness protection and a $200,000 DEA stipend for Skinner's cooperation. He also got a guarantee of up to a third of any drug money the DEA might recover.

It was a dramatic reversal of fortunes for Todd. Suddenly, things were looking up. He wed Emily Ragan on Sept. 9. He and Krystle might canoodle now and then, but it was his pregnant girlfriend he took to the altar. He'd been gaslighting her for over a year. Echoing Kelly Rothe's experience,[2] Emily would soon annul the marriage

---

2. Kelly Rothe finalized her divorce from Skinner on Nov. 15, 1998, moved to Massachusetts, and became a genetic researcher at Harvard.

and fight to retain custody of their infant daughter, but not before Skinner had drawn her into a brief, unwitting role in Operation White Rabbit.

Before the wedding, Emily had briefly moved back in with her parents. They doted on their brilliant daughter. When she took up with Skinner, they objected, but didn't disown her. Emily was always welcome home. Which gave Skinner a swell idea.

How about putting Emily's old room to good use? The Ragans lived in Manhattan, just a fifteen-minute drive from Wamego. What a great place to store ET! Following their wedding, he transferred most of the canisters from the ceiling of the metal barn to a closet in Emily's bedroom, far from the eyes of the DEA.

Operation White Rabbit was underway.

Pickard got hitched that summer too. Natasha was twenty-eight and he was turning fifty-five. Following his London trip, Pickard rendezvoused with his fiancée on St. Maarten, in the same Caribbean resort where he'd trysted just a few months earlier with Trais. Leonard and Natasha flew on to Honolulu from St. Maarten, married, then headed back to the mainland just in time for Leonard to slip away to New Mexico to visit Trais and his newborn son Duncan.

"I feel blessed to have my children, born under any conditions," he said. "I don't feel serial monogamy, which this was to a limited extent, was indiscriminate. Nothing was casual. There were no others. And love has many forms."

His life might not have been quite as chaotic as Skinner's, but it ran a close second. Following the Warren Buffett debacle, Leonard knew he couldn't trust Skinner to keep the swimming pool project afloat. Moving to Kansas had been a mistake. He and Apperson put $5,000 down on a new Santa Fe rental and began looking for a different way to do their laundry.

Through Mike Bauer, Leonard recruited a young computer whiz

who showed promise as an offshore money manager. While Mike majored in history, Bauer's high school chum Kenichi Sakai studied investment banking. When Leonard asked if he knew how to hack, Kenichi perked up. He loved a challenge.

They began by breaking into the database of a south Florida tax dodge called Prosper International Limited League. Pickard was impressed. He was able to secure several PILL debit cards under his various aliases (Connor, Maxwell, Niemi) and deposit just under $10,000 in each account so that no misguided PILL employee might be tempted to file an SAR.

PILL[3] looked like it might be as good, if not better, for disinfecting Guilders than Skinner's ED&F Man trading account.

Leonard latched on to Sakai. He asked him to meet the first week of September at the Menlo Park office of web designer Deborah Lehman. Their purpose: to bring the swimming pool project into the Internet Age.

"I was extremely uncomfortable," Lehman later told investigators. "It didn't seem like what he was asking from us was a good match with what we do."

Leonard handed Lehman $5,000 in cash and told her he wanted to develop three new websites: the first would promote Pickard's UCLA research; the second would be called "futuredrugs.com," a high-security link connecting researchers around the globe; and the third was a hub for offshore banking and tax-free havens like

---

3. In 2006, a Florida federal judge labeled PILL "an alleged tax fraud scheme" operated by a father and son out of the Bahamas. Twelve years later, PILL had moved to Belize and advertised itself thusly:

    "Join 27,000 satisfied clients in 110 countries! An unsurpassed business opportunity—No selling—No buying—No inventory—No reporting—No accounting—No deductions—No paperwork—No forms—No office rent—No set hours—No overhead—Completely private—No equipment—Unlimited market—Operate anywhere—Very little competition—Instant access to income anywhere—Unlimited income potential."

PILL. All were part of Leonard's FEDS master plan to study international drug trafficking, he said.

"He grabbed my hand, thanked me, and left before I could tell him I didn't want to work with him," said Lehman. "He just left and I wasn't sure what to do next. My feeling was this was drug money. I was scared of it."

It was during this flurry of activity that Skinner, surrounded by DEA agents, recorded his first phone call. It began awkwardly. He needed Pickard's help moving a piano and some heavy boxes at the missile silo.

Pickard waxed sarcastic. If Skinner was so helpless, why didn't he get one of his flunkies to help?

Despite the chill he heard in Pickard's voice, Nichols sensed a big fish on the line. The cagey back-and-forth between Skinner and Pickard about a swimming pool project was proof enough that Skinner hadn't been lying.

The more he'd dug into Pickard's past, the more Nichols became convinced that he'd finally stumbled upon the psychedelic Wizard of Oz. The DEA had a file on him dating back twenty-seven years. While he was extremely careful, Pickard's big weakness seemed to be women. He'd recently left one to cohabitate with another, only to leave her for a third that he'd picked up during research in Russia. All three were at least twenty years younger than Pickard.

But it didn't end there. Skinner claimed in his debriefing with Nichols that Pickard hit strip joints and gentlemen's lounges everywhere he went. In San Francisco, he had his own harem. Four strippers in particular at the O'Farrell Club dithered with Leonard to a degree that made Nichols wonder whether they were angling for more than tips. Martina Schenevar, Deanna Luce, Athena Raphael, and Sita Kaylin looked like they did a lot more than dance and let Leonard buy them dinner. Nichols suspected they might be muling drug profits from the Golden Triangle to Los Angeles. Raphael's LA boyfriend, he believed, was doing the laundering.

At the end of that initial phone call, Pickard agreed to a face-to-face. On the evening of Oct. 23, he met Skinner at a Sheraton in San Rafael. While Natasha waited in the bar downstairs, Skinner bitched about the $10,000 he had to pay for the minor infraction of impersonating an Interpol agent. Hidden video captured the entire uneasy reunion:

> **Skinner:** "Did you see how much money it took me to get myself out of my little fucking bullshit thing?"

> **Pickard:** "It was more than the money; it was the risk to your life lived, and all your friends' lives . . . With that kind of public exposure, and scrutiny. . . ."

Pickard was far more concerned with the future of the swimming pool project than he was Skinner's $10,000 fine. Kansas was no longer acceptable. He'd sooner set up in Europe and do his laundry in Holland than remain in Wamego.

Skinner stopped whining and Pickard became more agreeable. He digressed, making small talk about Sasha's newest designer drug. Street named "Foxy,"[4] a ten-milligram dose boosted sex drive while delivering a three-to-six-hour trip.

Skinner had to agree: sounded like a fantastic way to fuck.

Then and there, Karl Nichols nicknamed Leonard the "Sex Maniac." He continued taking notes while Pickard gave Skinner his cell number. They agreed to keep in touch.

On Oct. 27, DEA agents did a walk-through at Skinner's silo. The only chemical Karl Nichols saw was an open can of ET[5] sitting

---

4. 5-methoxy-N,N-diisopropyl tryptamine
5. The ET turned out to be ergocristine, an ergotamine analogue that was legal under Schedule One.

atop a stereo. Skinner neglected to say he'd relocated ten more to the metal barn (a.k.a. "the Lester building") or that he'd hidden another three behind a deep freeze. He also failed to disclose that he'd carted the rest to Manhattan and put them in a closet in Emily's bedroom.

Nichols didn't seem to notice. He and his agents were too busy effusing over the 120 crates of lab equipment stacked five high along one side of the Lester building. Outside of his team, Operation White Rabbit was very hush-hush. Nichols liked to say that not even Attorney General Janet Reno was in the loop.

And yet Skinner and his minions had been hinting about super-secret doings down at the missile base for weeks. Most everyone in town knew something was up. When suits in Ray Bans began frequenting Toto's Tacoz on Main Street, both the sheriff and Wamego police took note. The one person who never had a clue was Leonard Pickard.

When Leonard flew into Tulsa on Thursday, Nov. 2, his agenda topper was sending flowers to Trais: blooms for baby Duncan with all his love. Only then did he get down to business.

He and Apperson rented a car, then met Skinner at the top of the Adam's Mark Hotel. He appeared nervous.

"I didn't want to go up because I was concerned they had found out I was working for the government," Skinner later testified in court.

Todd transformed fear into bravado. "I'm not afraid of the Mafia or the government," he boasted to Pickard and Apperson. "I'm more powerful than you realize!"

Leonard rolled his eyes. He paid Skinner lip service then silently thanked providence he'd soon be in his rear view. The following morning, he and Clyde hit the road.

Skinner had driven ahead. As recorded by a microphone wired to his thigh, he kept up a running patter with his new handlers while he was on the road to Wamego: "Oh, this is so much fun! Oh, this is so much fun!"

He was already waiting at the silo when Pickard and Apperson arrived. He steered them toward the Lester building. As they inspected the lab equipment, Skinner slipped inside the silo next door to make a phone call.

What do I do next? he whispered into the receiver.

Stall, he was told.

When Skinner returned, Pickard was upset. Where was the ET that "C" hauled down from Chicago?

Skinner tap danced. Not to worry. It was hidden for safekeeping. He'd deliver the missing canisters the following morning. In the meantime, Skinner gave them each three Valium, handed over the keys to the Lester building, and told them where to park when they rented their truck. He didn't volunteer to help. Skinner had pressing business elsewhere.

Pickard and Apperson picked up their rental from U-Haul and returned to the base at midnight, working till dawn dumping chemicals and loading the truck.

When Pickard's hotel phone rang the next day, it was already past one p.m. Still tuckered from the night before, he rubbed sleep from his eyes and thanked Skinner for the little blue pills. Any chemical hangover was minimal.

Skinner seized upon Pickard's gratitude to deliver bad news. He couldn't get the ET until Monday.

Why not? Pickard's voice rose along with his displeasure. He told him he'd better come up with the chemicals or "your ass is grass." He reminded Skinner that he and Apperson had a long drive ahead of them.

Patience, Skinner counseled.

Patience my ass, countered Pickard.

Early Monday morning, Skinner rang again. He had the ET. Throughout the day, he promised to meet, then cancelled at the last minute or simply did not show. The game continued into the afternoon, each conversation recorded by the DEA as Leonard's patience frayed.

Skinner's final call at dusk was delivered with regrets. He had an emergency. He had to leave town. No explanation, but he did leave the "records"[6] on a treadmill inside the Lester building. All they had to do was pick them up.

Pickard smelled a rat. Was this Warren Buffett redux? He demanded a face-to-face. Skinner refused, then turned Pickard's paranoia on its head. He had reason to fear the cops as much as Leonard.

Leonard considered then rejected Skinner's excuse. He'd be by to pick up the "records" a little later. Skinner had better be there.

When Pickard and Apperson rolled up, the compound was silent. No cars. No crickets. No llamas. No Skinner. The gate was unlocked. They drove in, parked, and adjourned to the Lester building to wait.

Time passed. The wind picked up as night fell. It looked like Skinner stood them up again. Everything was boxed, so they finished loading the truck. They worked steadily, perspiring despite dropping temperatures. They finished just before sleet began pelting the windshield.

Pickard's cell rang. It was Skinner. Still peeved, he lit into him. "My life passed before my eyes today," Pickard snarled.

Skinner protested that *he* was the aggrieved party. "You really frightened *me*."

Pickard thought a moment before admitting he overreacted. They agreed to bury the hatchet and meet later at a café in Topeka.

---

6. Leonard's code for the ET.

Pickard hung up and made his final round for anything Skinner had neglected to pack.

He used bolt cutters to get through the silo door, only to find a second one that wouldn't budge, even though it seemed to be unlocked. Apperson tried. Still wouldn't budge. They gave up. What they did not learn until much later was that Karl Nichols and Todd Skinner were on the other side, holding their breath as well as the door.

As they caravanned out of the compound and onto the redundantly named Sixth Street Road, Pickard twirled the radio dial in search of von Weber, Saint Saens, or maybe a little Tchaikovsky. He hummed a Van Morrison oldie as he ran over the slim pickings of the east Kansas airwaves. No classical music this night.

A smile played over Leonard's taut features as he mouthed Morrison's words:

We were born before the wind
Ah, so much warmer than the sun
And we shall sail as One
Into the Mystic.

A harvest moon peeked from behind the clouds blanketing the Flint Hills. Leonard heaved a sigh. It was good to finally be back on the road again.

PART THREE
What the Dormouse Said

XVII.

AN OWLISH MAN WITH WRY wit and a Missouri drawl, *Wamego Times* publisher Mark Portell belied small town stereotypes. Born in the "Show-Me" state, he chose the Kansas flatlands to ply his craft. He was a newsman, through and through, but not of *The Front Page* variety. Portell was more likely to cover a Chamber potluck or a 4-H hog auction than write the kind of metropolitan headlines that graced the *Kansas City Star* or the *Topeka Capital-Journal*.

Wamego was an anachronism and so was its newspaper. Not only did the tiny town (pop. 4,372) embrace *The Wizard of Oz*; it invested in billboards up and down the Interstate advertising itself as the inspiration for the 1939 MGM film classic. There was an OZtoberFest each autumn and an Oz museum on the main drag[1] featuring over 25,000 authentic Oz artifacts. A seven-foot Tin Man greeted visitors at the front entrance. Right next door was Toto's Tacoz, Wamego's premiere Mexican restaurant.

Wizardly reference was everywhere. Portell once published a photo of a pair of human-looking legs that extended from the cellar door of a two-story house at the edge of Wamego. Visible to motorists headed toward state Highway 24, the legs looked like those of the hook-nosed actress Margaret Hamilton. The clear

---

1.   Lincoln Avenue, a.k.a. on road maps, "The Road to Oz."

implication was that this was Dorothy's house after it landed on the Wicked Witch of the West.

Not much happened in Wamego. That's why Portell's ears perked up when he heard Police Chief Ken Seager's voice crackle over his police scanner while he worked late at the paper on the eve of Election Day 2000.

"He asked all reserve officers to assemble in front of Wamego City Hospital," Portell remembered. "I thought it was probably somebody who'd walked away from the nursing home."

But as he drove up, he saw helicopters hovering.

"I recognized the police chief and a few local officers and the sheriff," he said. "There were a bunch of fellows with dark blue jackets on with 'DEA' printed on the back. So I figured it was something a little more important than an assisted-living escapee."

Portell tried to listen in, but understood nothing from the huddle of lawmen. An agent he later recognized as Karl Nichols finally asked who he was.

"I told him I published the *Wamego Times* and he used an expletive and said 'Oh my God, the media!' Then he walked away and left me standing there in the cold."

The following morning, Portell visited Chief Seager first thing.

"He was upset with the DEA because they didn't tell him that they were in town," said Portell. "Then when they lost their suspect, they wanted the assistance of the local police. The chief grudgingly granted that request but he told me, 'They're not paying my salary, so what do you want to know?'

"So I asked him, 'Who are you chasing?' And he said, "Well, they busted an LSD lab and they lost one of their suspects.' So that's basically how I found out what was going on. But the DEA wouldn't say anything."

Operating under a general rule of, "What the public doesn't know won't hurt us," the DEA adopted the omerta of its sister agency, the FBI. Nichols took the tactic a step further, threatening anyone who got in the way, including local officials and newspaper reporters.

Embarrassed by Portell's detailed account of their bumbled sting and Leonard Pickard's near escape, the DEA gave Portell little more than a scowl during the first couple of weeks. Portell had to quote Chief Seager that the bust was possibly the largest in history. It wasn't until after publication of the weekly newspaper's Nov. 30 edition that the threats began.

"When the DEA came in and began cleaning up the lab, of course no one was allowed in," said Portell. "They asked our local fire department to have a fire truck on site just in case. Our fire chief, who's a good friend of mine, had a video camera sitting on the dashboard of the fire truck and he called me up and said 'Are you interested in some pictures of the LSD lab?' And I said, 'Certainly.'

"So he printed off a few frames and I put 'em on the front page."

The photo display depicted a platoon of DEA agents in moon suits outside the missile silo, looking more like *Star Wars* troopers than drug police.

"The following Saturday an agent walked through the door and demanded to know where I got the pictures and I said 'Well, I won't tell you.' And he yelled at me and finally he said, 'Well, you must have paid attention in journalism school, didn't you?'

"And I said, 'Yes, I did.'"

The agent tried intimidating the fire chief next, threatening Christmas in jail if he didn't turn over the video. The DEA argued that agents worked undercover and revealing their identities could endanger them. Without agreeing, the Wamego city attorney struck a deal.

"If we turned over the film, they wouldn't arrest me or the fire chief," said Portell. "So we got out of that one."

When sound engineer Chris Malone read about the arrests, he flew to Kansas bent on getting either his money or his $150,000 stereo system back. After checking in at the Manhattan Hampton Inn, he and his business partner drove to Wamego, but were stopped by the locked gates of Todd Skinner's silo.

"He was a great customer," recalled Malone. "Bought a high-end CD player from us once for $30,000."

At the birth of the Internet, Malone had shifted the focus of his Sacramento specialty sound business to the worldwide web. He reasoned that well-heeled stereo connoisseurs were far more likely to surf for top quality equipment than visit their local Best Buy. Todd Skinner turned out to be a prime example.

"Money was never an object," said Malone. "All he wanted was the best."

Usually Skinner settled right away and for cash, as he had when he invited Malone to wire Jerry Garcia's San Souci for his Sting party. But lately, Todd had been buying more and more on credit. His most recent acquisition was also his most expensive. Once Malone installed the speakers deep below the Wamego horizon, Skinner stopped paying his bills.

News of the LSD bust set off alarms and sent Malone back to Kansas. For a week, he drove daily to the silo but the gates were always locked. He and his partner poked around Wamego, asking about Skinner. None of the locals were much help. The DEA kept everyone in the dark, including the police.

But on the last day before they were to fly home, they returned to their hotel room to find that their electronic door lock didn't work.

"It was fused shut," said Malone. "Hampton Inn literally had to replace the entire door."

The following morning, they paid one final visit to the silo. The gates were wide open. An unidentified man stood by a trailer inside the fence. He seemed to be waiting for them. The guy struck a neighborly pose. Malone thought he might have been one of Skinner's employees. The man repeated meagre details reported in the *Wamego Times*, but had no idea where

Skinner was. Of course, he could not let Malone in to retrieve his speakers.

Defeated, Malone headed for the airport. On the way, his cell phone rang.

"It was the top prosecutor in the state," recalled Malone. "He says, 'Hey! I heard you were in town.' I'm like, 'Okay.' He's like, 'We'd like to talk to you.' I said, "I'm heading to the airport right now.' He said, 'How about tomorrow?' I said, "I'll be in Sacramento.' He said, 'Fine. We'll be there.'"

The following day, Karl Nichols and his partner Roger Hanzlik showed up. Malone expected suits and ties; what he got were a couple of duffers who looked like they'd just finished a round at the municipal golf course.

In what would turn out to be the first of several conversations, Malone learned that Skinner was their Number One snitch—Nichols's Rosetta Stone inside the acid conspiracy. He was a rare bird and had to be protected at all costs.

For all Malone cared, Todd could be the Drug War's Second Coming. He wanted his speakers back. Skinner was a deadbeat, and from what Malone had been able to learn about him in Wamego, probably a killer to boot. Just ask Paul Hulebak's family.

"I said, 'You guys are protecting this clown and someday he's going to kill somebody. And it may not be your kid and it may not be my kid, but it's going to be somebody's kid and it's going to be your fault.'

"I was pissed. I actually had my finger in Karl's chest I was so pissed. I said 'You need to do something about this guy.' And he goes, 'What *you* need to do is stop playing private detective.' And then I got really pissed. I said, 'You get my goddamn speakers back and I'll quit being private detective.'"

The DEA bullied most everyone during the first few weeks. Sasha Shulgin described agents as "very brutal" when they descended upon his Orinda home. Mark Kleiman professed consternation at his protégé's secret life. Even Buddhists were detained for questioning.

"I was pretty upset when I heard of his drug activities," recalled the Zen Center Abbess, Blanche Hartmann, who underwent interrogation like everyone else.

Based on the assumption that her mortgage may have been paid with drug money, Trais Kliphuis faced the prospect of losing her home. Natasha Pickard did lose hers.

Leonard contacted his new wife immediately after his arrest. He told her his bail was probably going to be set at $600,000. The only one who had that kind of money among the swimming-pool crowd was Stefan Wathne,[2] whom he advised her to contact through John Halpern. Before she could do so, the government came calling.

"There were so many DEA that they couldn't fit inside the apartment," said Pickard. "They displaced everyone on to the street, including my father-in-law and Kusia,[3] our Himalayan."

The DEA tore the one-room apartment asunder, confiscating Leonard's laptop and Natasha's day planner, in which she'd written, "Leonard's in trouble."

"It was about a week after my daughter was born," said Pickard. "Natasha sent me a photo. Newborn in arms, she sat crumpled in a corner. The door had literally been torn off its hinges."

Some, like Deborah Harlow, reached out to the DEA preemptively. She volunteered the contents of a secret stash in Roseville. According to the National Self Storage registration, a Deborah Connor first rented the locker on April 11, 1997. When agents opened it, they found two boxes: one contained Melissa's baby clothes; the other, $170,100[4] in $10s, $20s and $100s. For cooperating, the DEA allowed her to keep $20,000.

---

2. Alerted by Halpern, Wathne fled the US and did not return.
3. Russian for "cat."
4. Leonard testified that General Dostum gave him the money for safekeeping.

With limited phone access, Leonard did his best to sound the alarm: "I tried ringing Halpern, as a gesture to a friend, but he hung up. At the time, I thought he was just nervous."

Leonard arranged to have keys sent to Mike Bauer that would unlock two Planet Self Storage lockers near Boston, similar to the one in Roseville where Deborah Connor kept nappies and cash. There were other storage units in New Mexico, California, and Massachusetts too, all eventually looted by the government.

From Santa Fe to Harvard Yard, psychonauts panicked. Alfred Savinelli spoke to Skinner shortly after the bust. Ignorant of Todd's role as "Cooperating Witness No. 1," Alfred offered to help Natasha come to Kansas for the bail hearing. Alfred warned Todd to no longer call direct. No telling who might be listening. If he needed to get in touch, Skinner was to have a woman call Native Scents, place an order for "sweet grass," and leave a safe number.

Savinelli confided to Todd that he thought Halpern might be the weak link. The risk of losing his medical license might have turned the Harvard psychiatrist. One thing seemed certain: if Leonard made bail, he would surely skip the country.

Skinner also called another friend. On the DEA tape, it sounded like an absurdist game of kindergarten gossip. The friend told Todd that Natasha told Savinelli, who then told Ganga White, who next told the friend that Skinner had been responsible for the bust.

Nonsense, said Todd. He'd been sitting in a Topeka restaurant when the raid went down. He didn't learn about it until one of his employees informed him. Gunnar Guinan heard the drama unfold over a police scanner.

His friend sighed that he'd always figured it was just a matter of time before Pickard fell. Now that it had happened, he was sure Pickard would roll on Skinner. He advised him to be careful.

Todd concurred. That was why he was leaving the country. He couldn't trust anyone. Henceforth, they'd have to communicate only by email. "Bubba" would be their code word.

For all his rehearsing, the reality of winding up back behind bars caught Leonard by surprise. He told police he'd only been trying to be a Good Samaritan; that all he was guilty of was helping Todd Skinner dispose of *his* illegal lab. None of the equipment or chemicals belonged to Pickard. He and Apperson were just trying to help out a friend.

Leonard had suffered similar misunderstandings in the past. The San Mateo police once mistook him as a meth manufacturer. As a science buff, he'd come into some second-hand lab equipment tainted with illegal chemicals. He wound up in jail during the late eighties for being the wrong guy in the wrong place at the wrong time. That was why he'd counseled Skinner to let him and Apperson trash his stash.

While inside on the 1988 beef, Leonard said, he'd learned his lesson. He'd buckled down, became a Buddhist, went to Harvard, earned his Master's, and landed a position at UCLA. He was respectable, if financially challenged. He owned no car or real estate, dedicating his life and modest means to his children and furthering the cause of international drug diplomacy. They didn't have to take his word. Just look at his record!

Why had he run from police? Because he realized how bad it looked. It was impulsive and bad judgement, but nothing more. Appearances could be deceiving.

At the end of November, Leonard remained ignorant of Skinner's duplicity. He wrote Bill Wynn care of Gardner Springs, assuming that Wynn would pass the warning on to Todd, whom he identified in his letter as "J. B. King." Leonard wrote that he believed the case would get tossed for illegal search and seizure. He cautioned J. B. that "discretion is the better part of valor."

Leonard wondered in a postscript whether Skinner's mother might be able to help him get a lawyer. Wynn passed the letter on to Katherine Magrini, who faxed it to Karl Nichols.

For his part, Skinner remained in hiding. Even his own mother didn't know where he was.

In the person of Todd Skinner, Karl Nichols had landed an extraordinary stoolpigeon. He meant to milk him for all he was worth.

Just three days after the Wamego raid, San Francisco's US Attorney wrote Nichols's boss about Todd. In a terse one-page opinion, he deemed Skinner exempt from a routine DEA requirement that informants provide handwritten statements each time they met with their handlers:

> This Office believes it is generally unnecessary and cumbersome to require confidential informants to prepare written statements at each meeting with DEA Special Agents. In our experience, DEA Special Agents in this district accurately record or report informant information in DEA reports. . . .

The US Attorney gave Nichols free range to handle his golden snitch in an informal manner. The US Attorney's name was Robert S. Mueller III.

By the end of November, Nichols and Skinner had become tight. While they built the case against Pickard and Apperson, Skinner maintained a low profile. The DEA had already found lots of cash. Before long, Nichols expected to hit the Mother Lode: millions upon millions.

Immediately following the bust, Skinner relocated to Mendocino at government expense. Krystle Cole, Gunnar Guinan, and a half-dozen others went with him. Skinner hired a couple of caretakers to protect the silo from vandals during his absence.

No sooner had Todd & Company settled along the California coast than he began to imagine reporters behind every tree. He told Nichols he had no interest in Witness Protection with US

Marshalls hovering over his every move, but it seemed apparent that he had to move.

Nichols put Todd in touch with a Tucson realtor, who rented him a posh desert hideaway. Because the DEA referred him, Skinner didn't even require a credit check. He got away with renting under Emily Ragan's name.

In her 2014 memoir *Lysergic*, Krystle Cole recalled their new digs:

> So, with the DEA's help, we rented a luxurious house in the foothills of the Catalina Mountains. We overlooked the entire city. There was a huge heated pool and Jacuzzi in our backyard. The house was amazing. There were five bedrooms and two bathrooms. Todd and I got the master bedroom and bathroom, complete with our own hot tub. Lupe got a room next to some friends visiting from California. Gunnar took a room off the garage. And our other friends visiting from Kansas took the room at the opposite end of the house.

Leonard's new home was the Shawnee County Jail, where transcontinental trains whistled in the distance all night long and winter crept past central heating and settled like death into every cell. Pickard shivered in prison blues, sandals and socks, his silver shoulder-length mane contrasting sharply with the close-cropped gangsta cut of the typical tatted jailbird.

He had ample solitude to contemplate his dilemma. The Buddhist in him experienced *satori*: everything changed while nothing changed. He identified as Tim Leary's heir: martyr to a greater cause.

Years later, in *The Rose of Paracelsus*, he imagined a conversation about the pitfalls of leading a dual existence. He spoke with Crimson, first of the Six mystery chemists he would meet during his lysergic travelogue:

Crimson: "The occult life . . . is an exercise in cultivating two or more parallel worlds, and moving easily among them."

Pickard: "What are the rules of conduct?"

Crimson: "Let's call them 'Washington Rules,' as in DC, followed so one's demise is met with dignity, rather than walking abused in forlorn circles around a prison track."

In those early days, Leonard was not yet ready to accept Washington Rules. He kept faith. He needed only one reasonable soul with a passion for justice to hear him out. What he needed was a good lawyer.

Topeka attorney Billy Rork took up Pickard's defense. A flamboyant James Carville doppelganger, Rork had made his career fighting the Drug War. He loathed the DEA, its bigfoot tactics, and its holier-than-thou arrogance. Beneath the phone number on his business cards, he printed this advice to prospective clients: "Shut up. The police aren't your friends unless you are six years old and lost."

Pickard needed no such advice. Since his initiation into the acid underworld during the late sixties, he knew to zip it.

Rork sympathized. He'd been in plenty of hot water as a kid. He grew up in foster homes, lived on the streets, never graduated from high school. He'd spent time in juvie, got his GED, graduated college, entered law school, and passed the bar in 1980. His memories of feeling helpless fueled his passion for justice. He'd taken on every sort of criminal case from littering to homicide, as long as he was fighting for an underdog.

"You don't know what it's like to be locked up for something you didn't do," he said. "I've never forgotten that."

The court declared Pickard indigent and ordered the government to pay Billy's fees. The week before Thanksgiving, he bought his client a pair of shoes to wear at his arraignment. Natasha sent Leonard his one formal blazer—a well-worn jacket from Moscow's GUM department store. "Fitting, I thought," said Leonard.

He pled innocent. Billy believed him. US District Judge Richard D. Rogers did not. While granting Apperson bail at $200,000, he ordered Pickard held without bond, not because he was a flight risk, but because he was a danger to the community. Unlike Apperson's squeaky-clean record, Pickard's arrest history dated back to high school. When busted, he was using a half dozen aliases. He had a phony British West Indies passport and an impressive array of false ID. No bail was deemed high enough.

Leonard's sole consolation came during a weepy recess. Natasha handed him a bundle in a pink blanket. Guarded by marshals, he held his infant daughter, also named Natasha, for the first and last time.

"It was a glimpse of limitless joy," he recalled. "Surrounded by the sacred, I whispered what love and comfort I could, and vowed to return to them. I could have held them, and hold them even now, forever."

XVIII.

IN THE WEEKS FOLLOWING THE Wamego bust, Karl Nichols was forced to reassess Todd Skinner. It started with the Operation White Rabbit debrief in the DEA's Oakland office a week after Pickard's arrest. There were handshakes and "Atta boys" all around before everyone settled down to business.

Senior DEA research chemist Tim McKibben kicked things off with the news that they'd confiscated enough ET in Wamego to make 826 million hits of LSD. While the agents whistled and joked about cornering the market, Skinner piped up that they didn't know the half of it. Pickard hid even more ET in St. Louis.

Nichols demanded elaboration.

Skinner had been on hand the previous May when Pickard met with the mysterious ET man in the lobby of Chicago's Ritz Carlton Hotel. He watched them cinch a deal for a lot more ET than the piddly little haul the DEA confiscated in Wamego. When Apperson trucked that original shipment from Chicago to Carneiro, Pickard ordered him to stop over in St. Louis and squirrel a lot of it away.

Whereabouts in St. Louis?

Skinner didn't know, but he'd try to find out.

Three days before Christmas, Todd called Karl from his Tucson hideaway. Boy, was he embarrassed. He'd just learned that some of that missing ET had been hidden in Kansas, right under his nose. When he told Tom Haney,[1] his lawyer advised him to call Nichols right away. He didn't want his client violating his immunity agreement.

Skinner told Nichols that Gunnar Guinan would bring him the chemicals during the first week of January.

Most of January came and went.

After many heated phone calls, Skinner showed at Nichols's Northern California office Jan. 22 with a trunk load of ET and a confession. He'd been hiding the stuff all along. He had no excuse. On advice of counsel, he threw himself on Karl's mercy.

Nichols fumed, but he needed Skinner's testimony. He let it ride.

Another month passed. Skinner had a further confession. This time Nichols flew to Kansas City. He met Todd and his lawyer in the lobby of the Airport Ramada Inn, where Karl locked eyes with his snitch. Skinner offered a small red case that contained two canisters of ET.[2] He was abjectly apologetic. He'd forgotten to include them with the Jan. 22 shipment. He hoped to God he hadn't messed up his immunity agreement.

Nichols lost all conviviality. There had better be no more screwups.

And there were not, at least as far as Nichols could tell. All ET appeared accounted for.

And yet both Nichols and Asst. US Attorney Greg Hough had to wonder if they'd made a mistake. They began harboring serious doubts about their star witness.

By December, the Acid King saga exploded onto the national stage. San Franciscans in particular honed in on the unfolding story filtering out of Wamego.

---

1. At the end of 2002, Skinner had chalked up $280,000 in legal fees. A former AUSA, Haney sued for $175,000 plus $200,000 for injuries he incurred hopping a fence at the missile silo, but never collected.
2. Subsequent testing showed the contents to be ergocristine, not ergotamine tartrate.

During its raid on Natasha Pickard's apartment, the DEA confiscated a "To-Whom-It-May-Concern" letter from San Francisco District Attorney Terence Hallinan[3] that took on added significance following the bust.

"When I was in private practice, I represented Leonard Pickard on some legal matters," it read. "I always found him to be an honorable person who kept his word."

A progressive with a long history of defending marijuana suspects, Hallinan refused comment to both the *San Francisco Chronicle* and *Rolling Stone*. Leonard, too, wouldn't say how he knew the DA, though it appeared Hallinan may have played a role in negotiating Leonard past his 1976 MDMA arrest in San Mateo County. Hallinan was among the first, but would not be the last prominent name to crop up in the prosecution of Leonard Pickard.

In Kansas, the prospect of belated Flower Power in the Flint Hills tantalized newshounds like Mark Portell.

"I've read a little bit about LSD," said Portell. "I've never even thought about using the substance."

Nonetheless, he'd never heard of anyone dying from it either. Like marijuana, LSD seemed one of those relics from the sixties that got people loaded with no lasting effect. It made for a helluva news story, though.

"Anytime something like this happens in a small town, it adds a little excitement," he said. "The first night when they were going door to door and no one knew what it was about, I think it made people a little nervous. I'm sure a few pulled their rifles out of their gun safes and peeked out the window, but there was no panic or anything like that. People were just curious."

Before the bust, Portell had heard that Todd Skinner operated a spring factory in the old silo. Great feature story, he thought. Portell called Gunnar Guinan. Gunnar never called back.

---

3. Hallinan lost the DA position to Kamala Harris in 2004.

After the bust, everyone wanted to find Skinner. In March, Pottawatomie County prosecutor Barry Wilkerson talked a grand jury into charging Todd with the involuntary manslaughter of Paul Hulebak. The autopsy revealed "remote and recent needle injection sites of the upper body and lower extremities." Skinner appeared to have shot Hulebak up like a pin cushion in a desperate attempt to counteract the opioids in his system.

Gunnar Guinan, who witnessed the entire grisly episode, later testified to Todd's panic. His boss kept repeating over and over, "This is on me."

The Pottawatomie County Sheriff had his indictment in hand, but when deputies showed up at the silo, they were told Todd left with no forwarding address. The DEA offered little help in tracking him down.

Six months after Pickard and Apperson were arrested, a Kansas City jury acquitted Mark McCloud of conspiring to distribute acid—a charge that could carry a life sentence.

"Thank God the people of Kansas City can tell the difference between art and LSD," said the forty-seven-year-old Bay Area artist.

During a two-week trial, federal prosecutor Mike Oliver tried to link 33,000 sheets of blotter paper seized from McCloud's three-story Victorian in San Francisco's Mission District to acid distribution 2,000 miles away on the other side of the country. The DEA maintained that blotter acid confiscated during a 1999 bust in Kansas bore McCloud's distinctive original designs.

"Mark McCloud was the head of an LSD conspiracy that gained a new generation to the cause of LSD," declared Oliver. Despite losing, the Assistant US Attorney accused McCloud of conspiring with a fugitive acid dealer to sell psychedelics to schoolchildren.

Ten years earlier, the government failed to convict McCloud in

Houston on the same charge. That the DEA would try again in Kansas came to him as no surprise. To McCloud, there was no state in the union more hostile to hippies, including Texas.

"They spent a million dollars trying to kill me," he said.

When he read about Leonard Pickard and Clyde Apperson, he shuddered. Heir to an Argentine ranching fortune, McCloud could hire the best defense money could buy. All he could do was pity those who could not.

The same month McCloud was exonerated, the DEA honored Karl Nichols for the Wamego bust. As Leonard was being transferred from Shawnee County to Leavenworth, Billy Rork mumbled something about Karl's citation. Leonard made a congratulatory note a priority in his new digs.

The legendary federal prison loomed like a medieval fortress over the east Kansas plains, but it was the modern Correctional Corporation of America[4] pre-trial facility built beside it where Pickard would spend the next two years. The building was far from palatial, but more akin to a college dorm than the Shawnee County jail. At least he had a table where he could write.

Nichols ignored Pickard's note, but added it to his growing file. Before Leonard had figured out that Todd was Cooperating Witness No. 1, he'd felt compelled to tell his side of the story. When Nichols wouldn't respond in writing, Leonard finagled his personal cell phone number. Nichols answered in sotto voce, à la Sgt. Joe Friday.

"I immediately advised Pickard that I could not speak with him and that any communication would have to be made with the

---

4. Founded in 1983, the second largest for-profit private prison company in the US houses approximately 90,000 in its more than sixty-five facilities and employs over 17,000 nationwide. CCA changed its name in 2016 to CoreCivic amid recurrent charges it shortchanges both inmates and taxpayers.

concurrence of the AUSA," he recalled. "I stated that I was prevented from speaking with Pickard by the attorney/client privilege provision of the Sixth Amendment."

Either Pickard admitted guilt, said Nichols, or he could not speak to him.

No deal, said Leonard. He would fight the charges, but felt duty-bound to alert the DEA to a possible fentanyl epidemic that looked like it might hit within the next ten years.

Nichols hung up.

Before Nichols had a chance to hang his award on the wall, Skinner threatened to nuke the DEA's case. Todd failed a polygraph in April, admitted to squirreling away yet another can of LSD precursor, and confessed to hiding a pile of DMT labware. While the Hulebak homicide charges were pending, Karl had no choice but to suspend Skinner's immunity agreement, including his $200,000 stipend.

Undaunted, Skinner kicked up his spending. He moved from Tucson to a $4,200-a-month penthouse on the thirty-second floor of Seattle's Metropolitan Tower. He told Nichols a white supremacist threatened his mother after reading about the Pickard case. Katherine Magrini got a restraining order, but Todd had no such protection and was publicly branded a snitch in the newspaper.

During a brief return to Kansas, the Pottawatomie County Sheriff finally caught up with him. Todd was arrested on May 16, but convinced the court he was penniless. After he was released on his own recognizance, he hot-footed it back to Seattle.

In a series of hearings that summer, Tom Haney and the DEA argued for Todd's acquittal. Karl Nichols' partner Roger Hanzlik even took the stand, swearing that no one at the DEA knew about the Hulebak case until after the Wamego bust. By then, of course,

Skinner had immunity.[5] The Department of Justice notified Haney by letter the week of the silo sting that his client was not immune from prosecution for "acts of violence," but neither he nor Hanzlik mentioned that in court.

Meanwhile, Todd established a new persona in Seattle. With nurse Krystle at his side, he became Dr. Gordon Skinner, world-renowned AIDS specialist from the United Kingdom. If his King's English bore an Okie inflection, it was only because he'd spent a little time in Tulsa with his father, also known as Dr. Skinner. To his hi-rise neighbors, Todd was also a chess master and a military history expert. Much in demand, Dr. Skinner charmed everyone. Patients flocked to him at all hours.

Todd maintained his burlesque for the better part of a year before his facade began to crumble. According to Krystle, he ran a brisk MDMA business on the side, dealing as many as four thousand hits a week. To the unsuspecting public, however, he operated an exclusive rehab and holistic clinic where IVs of amino acid could counter most any ailment known to man.

During his brief sojourn in Tucson, Todd had met a young woman with a strung-out kid sister. In a dress rehearsal as Dr. Skinner, he introduced himself to Rain Tredway as her last best chance to save sixteen-year-old Tyra Tredway from heroin. Rain's little sister had been on the stuff since she was thirteen.

Todd left the desert for Washington state before Rain could get Tyra into treatment, but she told her mother and they tracked the desert miracle worker down to his penthouse clinic. The Tredways dispatched Tyra to Seattle. Her cure seemed to be taking until the local District Attorney charged Tyra with selling MDMA.

Dr. Skinner intervened on her behalf. He told Deputy District

---

5. Under terms of so-called Kastigar immunity (*Kastigar v. United States*, 406 US 441, 1972), a criminal's admission of guilt can't be prosecuted unless the government learns about it from sources independent from the criminal's confession.

Attorney Gary Ernsdorff that he and his father, also named Dr. Skinner, were treating the girl for heroin addiction. He'd injected her with amino acids, the same treatment he'd used on approximately 100 patients who'd come to the clinic with ailments ranging from AIDS to arthritis.

Combined with similar complaints from other families, the Tredway case triggered an FDA investigation. Special Agent DaLi Borden found that Skinner had been writing prescriptions at the local Bartell's pharmacy for Imodium, erythromycin, and Compazine, but that he was no doctor. When the state pharmaceutical board ordered him to cease and desist, the filing bore the names of twenty youngsters like Tyra Tredway whose families had been bamboozled with phony prescriptions.

Meanwhile, Pickard's defense team had tracked Skinner down and alerted his neighbors, as well as Chris Malone. Ignoring DEA warnings, the intrepid stereo salesman flew to Seattle, confirmed that Todd had installed his silo speaker system in his penthouse clinic, and called authorities. In mid-July, the Pottawatomie Sheriff issued a warrant. Seattle police executed it, Skinner surrendered, pled innocent to theft, and was released on $10,000 bail.

Malone was in Washington, DC, on business, browsing in a local bookstore, when Pottawatomie Sheriff Greg Riat called with the news.

"Chris, they arrested Skinner on Friday."

"Yeah, I figured they would."

"They let him out on Saturday."

"I figured he'd bail out."

"Well, he's not very happy with us," said Sheriff Riat. "He's not happy with you and he's not happy with me."

"So what? I'm not worried about Skinner. He's a big guy, but he's a coward."

"Yeah, but he's not above hiring somebody. Chris, we're taking precautions."

After hanging up, Malone weighed the sheriff's words. He flew home to Sacramento to assure his family's safety, then called Karl Nichols.

"Karl, this knucklehead is out there. It sounds like he's dangerous. You guys are protecting him and I might be in danger."

"Don't worry, Chris," Nichols assured him. "He's not going to put out a contract on you."

"How do you know that?"

"He's out of money."

"Wait a minute. The only reason he's not putting out a contract is because he's out of money? Karl, I happen to know he's paying $5,000 a month in cash for four apartments. And you're telling me he's out of money?"

"Yeah."

"Okay. Fine."

Malone immediately applied for a concealed weapons permit.

"I'm not a gun guy, but I did that," he said. "And I had my truck set up with a remote starter. I'm not a paranoid guy, but if a sheriff tells me he's taking precautions, I'm thinking I'd better take this seriously."

XIX.

John Halpern debriefed the DEA nine times between December of 2000 and May of 2002. His cooperation cost him friends, credibility, his marriage, and very nearly his career, but like Todd Skinner, he was immune from prosecution.

"The DEA went to Halpern first and he squealed like a little girl," said Savinelli.

He never divulged the level of detail, but Halpern did confess before a grand jury. He dove so deeply into *mea culpa* that he admitted to once shoplifting with his wife. Gabrielle Halpern (a.k.a. Yan Yang Chen) divorced him once she learned about his indiscretion and alleged money laundering.

Halpern put on his best façade for the DEA.

"They flew out their top CIA polygraph operator," he recalled. "Insisted that there is no way to beat the polygraph. But, *I knew!* I put on antiperspirant to counter my galvanic skin response and took something to keep my heart rate down. Every time I was told to relax, I'd tense up."

Halpern might play their game, but he held the DEA in contempt.

"Karl Nichols is a shrimp dick who has a Napoleonic complex," he snarled a decade after trial, when there was no more fear of reprisal. "One time, I was being interrogated by all these fuck wads:

DEA, Kansas Bureau of Investigation, FBI. I go to the bathroom, come back—there's dead silence in the room. Eight or nine people all looking at me at once. I'm like, 'Yeah? What's going on?' One of them says, 'We were talking about you while you were taking a leak. You're the smartest guy in the room.' I said, 'Thank you.'

"But then he leans forward with a sneer and says, 'Only thing is, there's all of us, and just *one* of you.'

"See, *that's* intimidation."

As with Skinner, the DEA kept Halpern's cooperation under wraps. His duplicity eventually leaked, often with Halpern's unwitting help. At a spring psychonaut symposium six months after his first debrief, Halpern ran into Dave Nichols and Sasha Shulgin at the MIT Faculty Club in Cambridge.

"It was the oddest thing," recalled Nichols. "John came to our table and starts waving his hands, shaking his head and says, 'I didn't tell 'em anything they didn't already know!' We had no idea what he was talking about. Sometime later, we heard he'd been singing like a canary."

Halpern excused his behavior as motivated by self-preservation. He blamed Leonard, then and now.

"He was a train wreck waiting to happen," he said.

In January of 2001, Alfred Savinelli got an anonymous phone call directing him to a back booth at a Taos coffee shop a couple blocks from Native Scents. When he arrived, he found only a cup of coffee and a sealed envelope next to it with his name written on the front.

Inside were summaries of the DEA's initial interview that Halpern, as well as a second interview with a redacted source that Alfred assumed to be Skinner. Alfred's name was sprinkled liberally throughout both documents. An unsigned cover letter suggested he leave the country. Savinelli speculated that the not-so-subtle message had to have come to him circuitously from Leonard Pickard.

"Leonard, John, and Todd all decided either on their own or as a group: 'Let's make Alfred the scapegoat,'" said Savinelli. "I was the kingpin. That's what the DEA thought. That's what they all wanted the DEA to believe."

Within the month, Alfred received a subpoena to testify before a San Francisco grand jury on Feb. 22, 2001. He was doubly panicked because his son had been living with Halpern while attending school in Cambridge. Alfred feared his boy would get caught up in the sting. To save himself and his family, Savinelli admitted to buying chemicals and glassware through his company, but only because Leonard told him he was using them for academic purposes. He wound up providing approximately four hours of testimony for the prosecution.

He believes it helped his case that half his legal bills were paid by pop stars Paul Simon and Sting. That he had strong connections with celebrity made him a far less likely target. His nexus for both singer/songwriters was yoga: he met Sting through Ganga White; Simon through Ashtanga yoga guru Danny Paradise. Like both pop star practitioners, Savinelli literally liked to tie his body into knots.

"They (Sting and Simon) stopped by to see me whenever they were in Taos," said Alfred. The two performers also shared a passion for ayahuasca.

"I watched Paul do the funky chicken once right there on my kitchen floor," he said. "He and I are exactly the same height."

Simon and Savinelli swapped stories regularly before the Wamego bust. Alfred points to his name listed among the credits of "You're the One," Simon's 1999 Grammy-nominated comeback following the failure of his Broadway debacle, "The Capeman." Referring to the lyrics of many of Simon's songs on "You're the One," Alfred proudly stage-whispered, "My mouth to his pen."

He connected the two rock icons when Savinelli began attending Sting's annual Rock for the Rainforest benefit concert each spring at Carnegie Hall. The year Simon was on the bill, Alfred shuttled back and forth between both singers' Upper Westside living quarters.

"They live in the same building in New York City," said Savinelli. "Paul's up on the twelfth floor and Sting's got an apartment downstairs."

Their names appeared together once more in newspapers during the buildup to the Pickard/Apperson trial. Among the thousands of pages filed in the case, the eyes of reporters like Mark Portell went right to the line reading "Sting/Paul Simon." When the media called their publicists, they got a standard "no comment," but Savinelli said privately that their combined help staved off bankruptcy, the threat of which is another government tool in pressuring witnesses like himself.

"There's no level to which they won't stoop," he said.

During the two years Pickard prepared for trial, he could never predict where help might come from. There was cautious encouragement from the Shulgins, Mark Kleiman, and colleagues at Stanford or Harvard, all of whom had much to lose if they raised their voices too loudly. But there was unexpected help too, including Skinner's girlfriend Krystle Cole, her other paramour Ryan Overton, and Todd's own father.

Overton visited Leavenworth once to let Leonard know that the DEA snared both Overton and Tanasis Kanculis[1] in the same Skinner web that would eventually bear the name Operation White Rabbit. Overton said he'd like to take the stand on Pickard's behalf,

---

1. Questioned under oath at the 2003 trial, Skinner denied knowing Kanculis:

    Q—Do you know a Tanasis Kanculis? T-A-N-A-S-I-S K-A-N-C-U-L-I-S.

    Skinner—No, I've never heard of that name before. That's a strange name.

but he'd been warned to "get used to wearing khaki" if he testified for the defense. He didn't.

A month before trial, Tulsa police opened an investigation of Gordon Henry Skinner on accusations of child molesting.[2] It was not the elder Skinner's first brush with the law, but it was the worst. He was ultimately exonerated, but the allegation came at a particularly bad time.

Whatever his own sins, Dr. Skinner (unlike Todd, Gordon Sr. was a licensed Doctor of Chiropractic) recognized his son's shortcomings. He contacted Oregon State Police and pinpointed Todd's narcotics cache in a warehouse on a pier near the mouth of the Columbia River. But when Todd graciously allowed police to search three days later, they found nothing.

Krystle told a very different story in *Lysergic*. When Seattle police arrested Todd for the theft of Chris Malone's $150,000 stereo system, there was so much stolen equipment that they had to make two trips to the penthouse.

"Ma'am, our van is full so we will be back in about an hour to load up the rest of the speakers," the lead officer told Krystle. "Do not touch any of the pieces to them while we are gone and wait here."

Breathlessly scattering exclamation points through her prose, Krystle related what happened next:

> I have never felt so relieved in my whole life! I waited for a few minutes to make sure they were gone, and then went directly to the closet. I couldn't believe it! They never looked inside the suitcases! Two of our rolling carry-on bags were packed with the largest assortment of psychedelics that I'm sure most people have ever seen. They held kilos of MDMA, MDA,

---

2. In 1992, Sandra L. Skinner—his wife subsequent to Katherine—had been granted an emergency protective order against him.

LSD, Mescaline and DMT. There were smaller amounts of many other rare tryptamines as well. They snooped around everywhere, but totally missed the jackpot! We would have been sitting in jail for life if they would have found them!

By the time the police got back for the second load of speakers, the suitcases had been removed to another, much safer location. Todd was let out on a $10,000 bail the next day and, thanks to the DEA, the case eventually went away....

Following their trouble in Seattle, Todd and Krystle turned up allegedly stone broke in Oklahoma. Katherine Magrini put them up at her place and gave them both jobs at Gardner Springs. They cleaned up nicely and bore the appearance of middle-class respectability.

But expensive habits die hard. Under the name Todd Rothe-Skinner, Todd leased the fifty-eighth-floor penthouse of the Citiplex Towers two weeks before Christmas. Monthly rent: $4,500.

Krystle, for one, had turned over a new leaf. She enrolled at the University of Tulsa. Katherine bought her a car. Todd's mother treated her like a daughter.

"It is good to be able to experience what having a mother is like, anyway!" Krystle effused. "Life is funny that way. I always seem to get everything I really need...."

Skinner's image was almost rehabilitated by the beginning of trial. Chris Malone wouldn't let up on his stolen stereo, but the Hulebak manslaughter charges went away. Once Roger Hanzlik testified that the DEA had been clueless about Skinner's guilt before granting him immunity, Kansas Judge Steve Roth felt he had no choice but to dismiss the charges.

"I wrote the judge that Skinner's immunity agreement excluded acts of violence, but he never wrote back," said Pickard. "With the manslaughter charge dropped, Skinner was sanitized to testify."

Malone alone refused to give in despite veiled threats and signs that he was under investigation. When he had home Internet cable installed, the phone company technician handed him a tiny epoxy device with four wires extending from its edges.

"I don't know what the hell this is, but it doesn't belong in your connection box," he told Malone.

Once Todd left Seattle, the theft charges Malone had leveled against him did not stick. Malone found another way to stick it to Skinner.

Inevitably, Malone had made Pickard's acquaintance, first by mail, then phone, and later in person during visiting hours at Leavenworth.

"Cagey is a good way of describing Leonard," he said. "He always tries to game the system and the situation, but he knows that I know, and I know that he knows that I know . . . so we have a good time."

Remembering that Skinner had given him power of attorney, Leonard asked Malone how he'd like to own a missile silo. With zero fanfare, Pickard quit claimed all twenty-eight acres to Malone.

By the summer of 2002, however, taxes, late mortgage payments, and over $700,000 in judgments[3] left Skinner so far in arears that the sheriff had to auction the property. Undaunted, Malone lodged the winning bid of $140,000—roughly the same sum upon which Skinner welshed when he originally bought Malone's stereo system. When he inventoried the interior of his new purchase, Malone found a hidden marijuana garden, contaminated ground water, and a 750 KVA (kilo-volt-ampere) transformer capable of powering a shopping center, but no stereo system. The closest he ever came to recovering his equipment was a visit that Krystle Cole paid him one day when she offered to sell him back the remnants.

---

3. Among his creditors were Ganga White's White Lotus Foundation ($80,000) and Skinner's attorney Tom Haney ($280,000).

"I gave her $14,000 or $15,000 in cash," he said. "You think she's just an innocent little thing, but she riffles through the money, checking for fakes, just like a pro. She put on that whole innocent act. Baloney."

In July of 2001, Karl Nichols ordered the most junior member of the swimming pool project to San Francisco. While Nichols used his carrot-and-stick technique to interrogate him, Mike Bauer's eyes drifted to several large binders sitting atop Nichols's desk, each labeled "Operation White Rabbit."

"I first learned of Operation White Rabbit through the observations of Mike Bauer," said Leonard. "The fun part was that OCDETFs (Organized Crime Drug Enforcement Task Force[4]) like White Rabbit are heavily funded, allowing agents to take junkets to NYC, the Caribbean, Mexico, Las Vegas, Chicago, New Mexico, California, and Russia. Certainly more appealing than Wamego. There was great hope of unraveling some mammoth international drug conspiracy based on Skinner's florid stories."

After graduating from Boston College in 1995, Mike Bauer translated English textbooks to Spanish and worked part time for John Halpern. While he visited Montana one summer, Halpern slept with his then-girlfriend. Heartbroken, Bauer sent his ex a dramatic selfie: he had a pistol in his mouth.

Against all odds, he and Halpern remained friends. Halpern introduced him to psychologist Andrea Sherwood, the future mother of Bauer's two children. He also introduced him to Leonard, with whom he registered instant simpatico. Leonard invited him to

---

4. Created in 1982 at the peak of the War on Drugs, the OCDETF combines resources of eleven federal agencies, including the DEA, to take down major cartels. Employing approximately 2,500 agents, the task force spares no expense. Responsible for some 44,000 convictions and the seizure of over $3 billion in assets, the OCDETF has executed hundreds of successful efforts in its brief history. Operation White Rabbit was not among them.

a psychonaut conference in Acapulco, cementing a friendship that lasted long after Operation White Rabbit wound to a close.

Todd Skinner remembered Halpern's former "stack rat" as a Boston College history undergrad whom Pickard hired to help research the Russian and Afghani drug trade during Leonard's final year at the Kennedy School. He also assigned Bauer to research Skinner.

"I think that he was sent to check me out extensively," said Todd. "He hitched a ride from Taos to Tulsa, and then he ended up going to Wamego and became almost a permanent resident.

"Early on, I told Mike, 'Get out of this thing,'" said Skinner. "'This is a giant LSD conspiracy and I don't want you getting hurt.' Halpern and Leonard said that I suffered from many psychoses and that I was totally nuts and that there was no such thing as this (conspiracy), and all the money that Leonard had came from an inheritance from his father and mother."

As Operation White Rabbit unraveled, most of Skinner's assertions proved false. The only sound advice he gave Mike Bauer was to "get out of this thing."

XX.

WHEN THE CASE OF THE Wamego Acid King finally came to trial in January of 2003, Billy Rork offered up Skinner's sustained malfeasance in defense of Leonard Pickard: the government's star witness was a pathological liar, a repeat felon, and a murderer.

Sorry, said Judge Richard D. Rogers. The jury would hear nothing of the Hulebak case, since Skinner's complicity amounted to "only allegations." Rork didn't even know about his appearances on behalf of the government at two previous federal trials, where Skinner asserted his Fifth Amendment right against self-incrimination (aliases, sources of income, etc.) fifty-three times.

Asst. US Attorney Hough forgot to tell the defense or the jury.

Skinner had blanket immunity, said Rogers. His misdeeds were irrelevant.

Appointed by President Gerald Ford in 1975, Judge Rogers was eighty-one, and long past the age of heavy legal lifting. He passed off most duties to two clerks, who had been with him nearly forty years.

"They'd hand him pieces of paper during trial and have him correct shit," said Billy Rork. "I don't think he had much of an attention span."

Rogers concentrated on looking magisterial. In *US v Pickard*, he smelled a career capper.

A corn-fed standard bearer of prairie populism, Rogers grew up in

Wamego. Before receiving his lifetime appointment, he distinguished himself first as Mayor of Manhattan then President of the Kansas State Senate. He took the "lifetime" part of his appointment seriously. Though long absent from the practice of law, on Nov. 25, 2016, he remained technically on the bench when he died at ninety-four.

Rogers was no progressive, but neither could he be labeled reactionary. In 1988, he demonstrated humanitarian backbone by ordering the early release of four hundred Kansas inmates because of prison overcrowding. He told the state legislature to build another prison or he'd release even more.

But Rogers had no tolerance for drugs. He and AUSA Greg Hough shared an epiphany in 1993 when a mild-mannered weed dealer went berserk in the Fred Carlson Federal Building.

Jack Gary McKnight, a thirty-seven-year-old railroad accounting clerk, blew up his car, then shot and killed a security guard before tripping a pipe bomb and imploding himself. Convicted of growing 100 marijuana plants, McKnight was "a very quiet, reserved person," according to AUSA Hough.

Not on Aug. 5, 1993, however. Had he gotten off the elevator on the correct floor, McKnight might have taken out the entire US Attorney's office, including Greg Hough. Instead, McKnight came out shooting on the top floor, where Judge Rogers had barricaded himself inside the law library. He and his clerks watched helplessly while McKnight's car exploded out in the parking lot followed by the sound of McKnight turning himself to hamburger out in the hallway

With stiff upper lip, Rogers told the *Manhattan Mercury*, "None of us were terribly frightened, but we were tense and worried."

Ten years later, Rogers and Hough shared a cynical view of drug dealers. Whether mild-mannered in appearance or not, pushers were diabolical, and had to be stopped.

The trial of William Leonard Pickard and Clyde W. Apperson began Monday, Jan. 13 and lasted fifty-six days, forty-two of them devoted to the testimony of twenty-nine witnesses and the introduction of over one thousand exhibits. It took two and a half days to select eight men and four women for the jury. It turned out to be the longest criminal trial in Kansas state history.

"At his advanced age, Judge Rogers relied heavily on his clerks for decisions on attorney motions, but he also ran a taut ship," recalled Mark Portell, one of only two reporters[1] who attended regularly.

"The federal courtroom was relatively small, with only three or four rows for gallery spectators," he said. "I don't recall any 'shady characters' among them.

"During my first day, I was reading a newspaper as jurors were brought in. A bailiff told me to put down the newspaper. In Judge Rogers's court, it apparently didn't matter if you were a participant or a spectator. You were expected to pay attention."

The defendants arrived daily in chains at four a.m. and cooled their heels in a holding tank until they were marched into court. Clyde Apperson never spoke a word. Leonard Pickard, on the other hand, talked frequently and at length.

Once, he turned and asked Portell if he was from the *Wamego Times*.

"I said, 'yes,' and he wanted to shake my hand, but the Marshals wouldn't allow it and shoved him back into his seat."

Pickard testified that the only reason he and Apperson came to Wamego was to help Skinner destroy a dangerous drug lab: they were Samaritans played for fools. Among other assertions, Pickard testified that Skinner "claimed he might have part of the clandestine laboratory of George Marquardt and some of Marquardt's ergotamine tartrate." In Skinner's amateurish hands, that could only spell disaster.

Leonard and AUSA Hough fenced throughout. When the

---

1. The other was Steve Fry, court reporter for the *Topeka Capital-Journal*.

prosecutor asked if Leonard could recall previous contradicting testimony, he'd taunt, "Use your mind."

"Don't be insulting," shot back Pickard.

Pointing to his fifteen different aliases, Hough asked him which he preferred.

"You may call me Mr. Pickard," answered Leonard.

When Pickard expressed concern from the witness stand over his wife and child, Hough baited: "Which one? With Trais Kliphuis or Natasha Kruglova?"

"I think that's reprehensible on your part, sir," said Leonard.

The bickering arose so often and with such bile that Judge Rogers weighed in. Siding frequently with Hough, he instructed the jury to ignore Pickard's sarcasm, but also cautioned the AUSA to be "less harsh" and give Pickard time to answer.

"I'm used to some of this in this trial," he said. "And I want you to stop! I want you to stop quarreling."

On March 4, days before taking the stand, Karl Nichols made his final entry in the Skinner file. Despite having to clean up Todd's messes during the previous two years, he wrote, "It has been determined that the potential benefit to DEA and the public interest outweighs the negative risks associated with this CS."

There had never been any question that the government's case hinged on Todd Skinner. In total, Pickard would spend five days on the witness stand; Skinner was there for eleven.

"Skinner was drugged out on benzodiazepines throughout his testimony," recalled John Halpern.[2]

Valium did not prevent him from lying under oath. In one particularly glaring exchange, Apperson's attorney Mark Bennet annihilated Skinner's credibility:

---

2. Halpern did not testify, but two days before the verdict, he submitted a grant application to the National Institute on Drug Abuse to study MDMA. NIDA approved the grant in September of 2004.

Bennett: Over the years of illegal activity, you've found it necessary to be quick-witted and untruthful?

Skinner: Yes.

Bennett: Have you made up stories to stay out of jail and out of trouble?

Skinner: No.

Bennett: Have you made up stories to stay out of jail?

Skinner: No, I don't think I've been in a situation like that.

Bennett: Have you developed an ability to look someone in the eye and lie to them about illegal activity?

Skinner: Yes.

Bennett: From age nineteen to the present, have you lied to authorities to conceal your drug use?

Skinner: I'd have to think a long time about that.

Bennett: You've lied to conceal possession of drug manufacturing equipment?

Skinner: Yes.

Bennett: You've lied to conceal your involvement in an illegal drug lab?

Skinner: Yes.

Bennett: You've lied to people about stealing hundreds of thousands of dollars?

Skinner: Yes.

Bennett: When you get right down to it, Mr. Skinner, you're willing to lie whenever it will benefit you, isn't that right?

Skinner: No, that's not true.

Bennett: But you're willing to lie to stay out of trouble?

Skinner: Yes.

Bennett: And you're willing to lie to stay out of jail?

Skinner: I don't know about that one. I need to ask a lawyer before I answer these questions.

Bennett: Mr. Skinner, you're willing to lie to this court, aren't you?

Skinner: Again, I'd like access to a lawyer.

While the jury was out of the courtroom, Hough admitted that Skinner perjured himself, but maintained that most of his testimony was truthful. In order to penetrate drug organizations, he explained, the DEA often had to rely on sketchy insiders.

The defense called for an immediate mistrial.

"It's a trial by ambush, judge, and that shouldn't be allowed," said Bennett. "This has been deliberate and intentional from the beginning. It's just not fair, your honor."

Rogers told Bennett to "sit down and shut up," then sided with the prosecution.

As the trial dragged on, Mark Bennett observed, "We've been together so long I told somebody we should have a float in the St. Patrick's Day parade."

Judge Rogers denied a defense final request for more time to examine prosecution exhibits and to call more witnesses.

"To suggest that you two very experienced attorneys need more time to prepare your final argument is not a good excuse at all," he said.

"Although we may be experienced, judge, there were over nine hundred exhibits and thousands of pages of reports and notes," said Rork. He threw up his hands. "I'm not Superman."

Rogers was unmoved. Final arguments began the next day. Hough went first.

"What you have here is two California men who want to sell you some ocean-front property in Kansas," he said. "The fact is, the ocean is not in Kansas. You see the defendants before you, stripped to the bone for what they are—LSD manufacturers with an LSD distribution network."

Pickard was "the chemist, the lead man," said Hough. "He's not the mild-mannered policy schmuck he would have you believe. Mr. Pickard was in charge all along. Mr. Apperson would have you believe he's stupid. Anyone—a fifth grade kid—has had enough science to know this was a laboratory.

"The defendants are gamesmen and gamblers. But the truth is . . . in this case, they've rolled craps."

In their own closing, the defense zeroed in on Todd Skinner.

"This was a setup, ladies and gentlemen," said Mark Bennett. "A setup in which Gordon Skinner was trying to get out of his own problems. The government, much to their chagrin, found out Mr. Skinner never met a lie he didn't like or embrace."

Apperson's lawyer advised the jury to weigh carefully each of Hough's assertions, as they were based on the self-serving inventions of a lifelong con artist.

"Challenge in your mind what he says. Don't just accept at face value what he says because the government's not always right and the government doesn't always do what it ought to do," said Bennett. "I told you in my opening statement we were going to prove that Mr. Skinner and the truth are total strangers, and we did."

Billy picked up where Bennett left off: "Would you buy a used car from Mr. Skinner?" Rork asked. "Mr. Pickard's misfortune was meeting him in 1998, and later becoming financially dependent on him. If it doesn't fit the government's case, you ain't gonna hear it,

I guarantee it. It's like the old Wendy's commercial: Where's the beef?

"Again, I can go on and on about dozens of pieces of evidence that don't fit the government's plan that you won't hear about. You have Skinner's version and you have Pickard's version.

"I'm not going to ask you to vote guilty. I'm not going to ask you to vote not guilty. I'm going to ask you to vote as if it was your loved one or brother facing this charge. Hold Mr. Hough—anything he says—to the record. It's not a contest. Did the government meet its burden of proof?"

In the Monday March 31 edition of the *Kansas City Star,* a headline summarized the marathon trial in the state capital as "One of a Kind."

> TOPEKA—The drug case unfolding in a federal courtroom here since January has a little of everything. Secretly taped conversations, false IDs, Las Vegas money laundering, a smuggler known only as Petaluma Al, testimony about Stinger missiles in Afghanistan and one of the biggest LSD laboratories ever captured in the United States.
>
> "I've been doing this work for 42 years," said Mark Bennett Jr., a Topeka lawyer who represents one of the defendants. "This case is one of a kind."
>
> Week after week, witness after witness, a judge and jury in US District Court in Topeka have listened to testimony about the shadowy world of international drug trafficking. After eleven weeks, the case went to the jury on Friday, and jurors are scheduled to return this morning to begin deliberations. . . .

In a little over five hours, the jury delivered guilty verdicts on all counts.

"We found the evidence was clear and convincing," said jury foreman Scott Lowry. "It was a pretty easy verdict to come to."

Six months later, Judge Rogers sentenced Pickard to life. Twice.

"Good thing the sentences were concurrent, rather than consecutive," deadpanned Pickard.

A first-time offender, Apperson got thirty years. Leonard got two life sentences because he was a Buddhist, quipped his critics. The second one covered reincarnation.

Pointing to his lengthy rap sheet, Judge Rogers justified Pickard's stiff sentence. Leonard immediately began planning his appeal, starting with a closer look at the elaborate DEA sting Mike Bauer identified as Operation White Rabbit.

"A Freedom of Information Act request followed," he said, "and here we are in the 10th Circuit arguing away about it nineteen years later."

In early 2004, Pickard and Apperson were flown to a squat old-style military prison in the central coast town of Lompoc, closer to their California roots.

"Clyde and I were in handcuffs linked to waist chains, and leg chains cuffed to our ankles," Leonard recalled. "We could hardly move. The air and light of the West lifted our spirits, but upon landing at Vandenberg Air Force Base, we were confronted by rows of implacable US Marshals brandishing shotguns.

"Taking small steps, leg chains cutting into my ankles, I was in a single line of sullen, tattooed faces, funneled into a narrowing tunnel of great coils of razor wire on all sides. Heading into the crowded madness forever, I thought: 'We're in serious trouble.'"

XXI.

Shortly after eight a.m. on July 11, 2003, Texas City patrolman Neal Mora pulled his squad car off the Galveston highway, slowed to a crawl and squinted up ahead at a desiccated wraith standing by the side of the road.

"Help me," it said. "Please."

Draped in a filthy blanket, Brandon Andres Green's hairless body was a roadmap of black and maroon, deep crimson scratches and hot pink bug bites. His eyes were as deep and dark as Auschwitz.

Brandon was an 18-year-old pizza delivery kid from Broken Arrow, Oklahoma. He'd been dumped five hundred miles from home, but not before days of torture, humiliation, and sodomy. Officer Mora got him to Mainland Medical Center, where ER doctors found a prolapsed rectum, mashed testicles, and hypodermic punctures adjacent to the festering wound along the side of his penis. His wrists and ankles were rubbed raw where he'd been hogtied. His skull, eyebrows, legs, and arms were razored slick.

After dressing his cuts, rashes, and scrapes, doctors admitted Green to intensive care and treated him for severe dehydration. He wasn't expected to live. Detectives recorded his intake interview. Green's recitation read like a Marquis de Sade fever dream.

His penis, testicles, back, arms, and legs had been injected with unknown substances. His groin was a swollen punching bag. His assailant sliced his phallus open with a razor blade, followed by a bleach bath. He hadn't been fed or given water for nearly a week. He'd been trussed up with duct tape. And perhaps most hideous of all, his genitals had been wrapped with a cord, then yanked until Green heard himself snap like a rubber band.

Green's sorry saga began three months earlier, when he hooked up at a south Tulsa rave with a stone-cold fox named Krystle Cole. He could not believe his luck. He'd been dating a Hooters waitress, but she had nothing on Krystle's milky complexion, Rapunzel hair, and maraschino smile.

Over the following weeks, he and Krystle swapped boasts, bodily fluids, and MDMA. She introduced him to her geeky old man, an odd-looking Neanderthal twice her age named Todd. Todd bragged about making MDMA in his own lab in Tulsa. As it turned out, he also acted as Krystle's high priest and psychedelic pimp. They were engaged, but Brandon didn't learn that until after he'd fallen beneath her spell.

Skinner had plans for Green. He told him he'd made a big-money deal to dredge harbors in the Caribbean, and he wanted Brandon to navigate the project. He and Krystle also indoctrinated him into the exciting life of international drug sales, promising to send him to Amsterdam as their envoy in a million-dollar MDMA transaction—a far cry from slinging dough for Mazzio's Pizza.

But there was something creepy about Skinner. Krystle confirmed it during their more intimate moments. When Brandon wasn't around, Todd beat her, then consoled her and begged for forgiveness.

" . . . Todd would cry uncontrollably at the feet of Krystle, expressing his undying love and dedication while Krystle would stand there stone cold and emotionless," Green recalled.

After secretly filing for his-and-her restraining orders, the couple set out to create a new life together. Brandon convinced Krystle to accompany him to the Tulsa DEA to turn Skinner in. During a recent Missouri road trip, Brandon got caught with meth and marijuana and concluded the best way out was to give the feds a bigger fish. Snitch out his rival for Krystle's affections, and he killed two birds with one stone.

When he and Krystle showed up on June 12, Green told agents Doug Kidwell and DuWayne Barnett that they were in love and desperate to get away from Skinner. In her written complaint, Krystle accused Todd of dislocating her jaw, throwing her to the ground, smothering, stalking, and threatening to kill her. She claimed they'd been separated since the notorious Acid King trial ended in Topeka three months earlier.

Todd was furious when he learned she'd double-crossed him.

"Skinner found out somehow," Krystle said. "He drugged me and kept me against my will for a day at the Renaissance Hotel, then he strangled me and almost broke my neck the day before Brandon was kidnapped."

An older, wiser Green remembered her being a participant, not a victim. "Krystle is the definition of wicked and manipulative," he said years later.

One memory upon which they could both agree was that Todd Skinner was the definition of jealous rage.

On July 3, Skinner dispatched Brandon to pick up an ex-Gardner Springs truck driver named Bill Hauck and drive him to the DoubleTree Hotel in downtown Tulsa.

Before he began muling marijuana for Skinner, William Hauck lived in New Jersey. He met Todd in the Gloucester County jail in 1989 while Todd was doing time for his Camden marijuana bust. Hauck was there for statutory rape.

Tough break, said Todd, but he liked Hauck. If he ever needed a job, he should come to Tulsa.

And come to Tulsa he did. When Bill Hauck wasn't legitimately driving a truck for Gardner Springs, he kept Todd Skinner supplied with long-haul sinsemilla he picked up for him regularly in Arizona.

But Hauck outgrew Todd's dope runs. He quit Gardner Springs for a real job with Trustee Trucking. He married and became a father. He had a different life when Todd sent Brandon Green to pick him up the day before the 4th of July.

They'd never met. All Hauck and Green had in common was Skinner's promise that they both could be in on the ground floor of his new and lucrative Caribbean dredging venture.

Hauck remained dubious, but Skinner did comp his room on the eighteenth floor. Todd shared a pair of DoubleTree suites on the fourteenth with Brandon and Krystle. Brandon told Hauck he'd joined the couple to make a new batch of communion wafers. Todd planned to celebrate Mass on the 4th of July.

Skinner and Krystle threw an Independence Day blowout in their DoubleTree suite and invited several of their best MDMA customers. They partied long past the public fireworks display they viewed from their hi-rise windows. Todd went through his transubstantiation routine, getting a half dozen twenty-somethings loaded to the gills. Still relatively sober, Hauck drove one of the more polluted guests home, then crashed himself.

The following day, he left the hotel to visit family for a couple days. When he returned on July 7, it was to a scene straight out of Dante's *Inferno*.

Hauck saw Brandon lying on the bathroom floor when he entered Skinner's suite, his denuded skull wrapped in duct tape and his hands taped to his feet behind his back. A KFC cup covered his genitals. As he watched slack-jawed, Skinner kicked the half-comatose boy in the groin—a maneuver Todd called "harpooning him in the nuts."

Brandon would pay for sleeping with his wife, Skinner muttered over and over. He next jammed a hypodermic of brown liquid into

Green's penis. Give him gangrene, he explained. His dick would eventually turn black and fall off.

Brandon later recalled his agony only in snatches. Mercifully, he nodded off for hours at a time. At one point, he began convulsing. He remembered Krystle looming over him in a white robe, conducting some sort of séance.

"While I was being tortured, she would chant prayers over my body, offering my soul up as a sacrifice to Satan," he said.

Krystle described the experience as one of psychedelic detachment, like watching a movie.

"His lips would start to turn blue and his lungs would sound sputtery, wheezy, like he had aspirated," she said. Then Brandon would sink back into unconsciousness.

Krystle came up with the idea of shaving him clean. She enlisted one of the other party guests in her project. At one point, she covered his face with a towel so he couldn't see what they were doing.

"Krystle told me that my retinas were burned and if I removed the towel, I'd go blind," said Brandon.

But Todd dreamed up the cruelty coup d'état. It began by wrapping a telephone cord around his scrotum, then using it to lever the full weight of his unconscious body off the bed. His fury unslaked, Todd next wrapped the cord around Green's penis. Bracing his foot on the boy's stomach, Skinner jerked the cord again and again until he heard the cartilage snap, crackle, then pop.

Despite the horror of that memory, Brandon came to fear Krystle more than Todd.

"I feel like Todd's ceiling is Krystle's floor," he said. "That is why I feel like she is more dangerous. I feel like she was able to consume everything Todd had, then pushed him out of the way and continued going."

Had he been conscious, Brandon would have been stunned to know that Skinner took time off to visit the same DEA office where Krystle and Brandon had ratted him out three weeks earlier. While

Brandon lay trussed up and drooling back at the DoubleTree, Todd and his lawyer demanded to know why the DEA was investigating him.

Skinner's visit to the Tulsa office prompted a call to the US Attorney which, in turn, prompted a call from AUSA Allen Litchfield to his counterpart in Topeka: AUSA Greg Hough. Litchfield told him that Todd had "popped up and walked into DEA claiming all kinds of immunity. Frankly, he sounds a little spooky."

Hough referred Litchfield to Karl Nichols, but Nichols said he'd washed his hands of his star witness once Leonard Pickard's trial was over. As a matter of fact, Nichols put out an APB that summer to all DEA offices across America: *never* use Gordon Todd Skinner as a snitch.

Brandon had only PTSD memory of the second week of July. When Hauck, Skinner, and Krystle loaded him in a box and wheeled him across the DoubleTree lobby, he went blank. He barely remembered being tossed in the back of his Sonata.

Driving six-and-half hours south to Galveston, Hauck remembered a zombie babbling from the backseat: "My dick hurts. . . . Todd shot me . . . why did Todd do that . . . Todd told me that you was going to kill me."

Mercifully, he slept most of the way.

Hauck met up with Todd and Krystle in Texas City. The plan was to dispose of Brandon far from home, but not until Todd "scrambled his brain." In a motel room at the edge of town, he picked up where he'd left off in Tulsa, injecting Brandon with brown goo, then force-feeding him vitamins to "heal up the needle marks." While Todd tortured, Hauck assisted. Krystle went to the motel pool to relax.

Shortly after sundown on July 10, Hauck loaded Brandon back in the Sonata. Todd ordered Krystle to follow in Skinner's brand-new silver Porsche convertible and bring Hauck back once he'd dumped the body.

Hauck drove around until he found a remote spot off County Road 1573. He parked beneath a tree one hundred yards from the pavement and arranged Green's body on a blanket along with two bottles of water and a candy bar at his side, should he ever come to.

After leaving the keys in the Sonata, Hauck walked back to the highway, where Krystle picked him up and drove back to the motel.

Todd bought the morning paper, scanning for obits. He never wanted to kill the kid, "just mess him up," he told Hauck.

Krystle phoned Brandon's cousin to feign concern over his whereabouts. He was in intensive care at a Houston hospital, she was told. He'd been found wandering naked down some country road near Galveston.

All three piled into Todd's Porsche and returned to the dump spot. While Hauck and Krystle searched for the Sonata, Skinner loitered near a farmhouse. A black guy materialized and told him an ambulance recently hauled off some buck-naked white kid.

That was enough for Todd. He paid off Hauck, told him to get home on his own, then headed north. He and Krystle planned to lay low for a couple weeks.

A week later, Hauck sat nervously in the same DEA office in downtown Tulsa, where Brandon and Krystle first described for agents Todd Skinner's limitless appetite for destruction.

Before he spoke, Hauck wanted a guarantee. Todd once asked him to kill a Columbian coke dealer. He had little doubt Skinner would do the same to Hauck if he knew he was talking. He would do so only in confidence.

On July 27, Todd Skinner tied the knot for the third time. In a brief ceremony at Katherine Magrini's house, Krystle Cole became Mrs. Todd Skinner. She professed to have been as out of it in her own way as Brandon Green was during his recent ordeal, but at least she wasn't comatose.

Over the remainder of the summer, the investigation of Brandon Green's strange and vicious kidnapping evolved into a solid case. One by one, Skinner's street recruits followed Hauck's lead, relating stories of overdose, ER visits, high living in low places. As he regained strength, Green himself became the prosecution's chief witness, as well as Exhibit No. 1.

Skinner remained oblivious. Following his brief panic in Texas City, he settled comfortably back into his routine of unbridled hedonism.

Karl Nichols might believe he was broke, but that showed how little Karl Nichols knew about his own snitch. In all, Skinner figured he'd stolen 1.2 million untaxed dollars from Leonard Pickard.

"I've never reported income in my life, from the day I was born to this day," Skinner boasted during trial.

By contrast, Leonard couldn't even pay his student loans.

"I still owe $50,000," he said recently. "I made minimum monthly payments from 1997 until my arrest. The loan currently is frozen, no payments are demanded, but interest still accrues. It must be $70,000 or more by now. Wouldn't you think I'd have paid it off long ago if we were earning $24 million a year making LSD?"

XXII.

Todd Skinner's luck ran out one hundred miles north of Reno on the last night of August in 2003.

After Krystle left him alone in their rented RV with $2,400 in cash and 25,000 hits of MDMA, an agent from the US Department of Interior swooped in and arrested her husband for drug sales.

Todd wasn't the only dealer hauled in. It was the final day of the annual Burning Man festival outside makeshift Black Rock City with over 30,000 die-hard psychonauts in residence. In a proudly pagan tradition dating back to 1986,[1] seekers and shamans alike gathered annually in Nevada's high desert to celebrate art, empathy, and the absurdity of human existence. With a bonfire visible from fifty miles away, they watched a forty-foot wooden effigy turn to ash while tripping, dancing, rocking, and rutting through the night. The Skinners correctly guessed it to be the perfect sales venue for their pharmaceuticals.

The theme in 2003 was "Beyond Belief," reflected in the religion-mocking names of over five hundred congregations assembled

---

1. Originally free and open to all, Burning Man evolved into a five-day hippie bazaar capped at 70,000 participants by the Bureau of Land Management. Operated by a non-profit, it charged $425 admission and a $100 per vehicle entry fee in 2019, but effigies grew to over one hundred feet high.

around the Burning Man effigy: Tyrannosaurus Rex Jesus Temple, Church of Stop Shopping, Black Rock City Bike Repair & Divinity School, the Surely Temple, and the Black Rock City Wedding Chapel ("Fake weddings on demand; real ones require advance notice.")

The atmosphere was relaxed. Everyone was high on something. But ecstasy entrepreneurs on Skinner's scale were not tolerated. The Bureau of Land Management issued 177 citations that year and made ten arrests, but Todd's was unique in that he was pretty certain he'd been set up by his new bride.

"Even though she was at Burning Man and left suddenly the day before my arrest and drugs were found in her purse," Krystle did not get busted, Skinner groused.

Todd, on the other hand, was told that his arrest was the least of his troubles. While driving him to the Washoe County Jail in downtown Reno, a sympathetic deputy told him that the Tulsa DEA was in on the bust. The cops from Oklahoma promised that Skinner would never see the light of day again.

In jail, his notoriety preceded him. Another arrestee roughed up the star witness from the Acid King trial, but there was no time for whining or filing assault charges. Skinner was quickly arraigned, then bound over to Tulsa for trial on the kidnapping and torture of Brandon Green.

In a *Slate* article published on April Fool's Day of 2004, psychonaut journalist Ryan Grim posed the headline question, "Who's Got the Acid?" He answered it in the deck: "These days, almost nobody." The reason, based on a DEA press release, was the Wamego bust.

In rare public praise for agents Karl Nichols and Roger Hanzlik, DEA Administrator Karen P. Tandy celebrated Leonard's double life sentence on November 25, 2003, while soliciting DEA funding from a Congressional committee:

DEA dismantled the world's leading LSD manufacturing organization headed by William Leonard Pickard. This was the single largest seizure of an operable LSD lab in DEA's history. On November 6, 2000, DEA agents seized from an abandoned missile silo located near Wamego, Kansas, approximately 91 pounds of LSD, 215 pounds of lysergic acid (an LSD precursor chemical), 52 pounds of iso-LSD (an LSD manufacturing by-product), and 42 pounds of ergocristine. . . . Since that operation, reported LSD availability declined by 95 percent nationwide.

From his new home inside Lompoc federal prison, Leonard ground his molars. He dashed off an angry letter to *Slate*: almost none of Tandy's self-congratulatory tribute was accurate.

"The idea that he was producing millions of doses that were getting into the market and he was a major supplier to the world was 100 percent bullshit," said John Halpern.

LSD availability did decline briefly, but only because acid alchemists around the world slowed production. As Leonard would later declare in *The Rose of Paracelsus*, each of the mysterious Six were capable of producing eight hundred grams a month—sixteen million doses, or roughly twice the lifetime output of Owsley Stanley.

"When Leonard got busted, they all stopped because they were afraid that Leonard was going to throw them under the bus," said Halpern. "That's why all the acid dried up for a year or two."

Without success, Karl Nichols continued trying to locate the millions Pickard allegedly earned from making all of that LSD. Petaluma Al didn't have it. Neither did the ET Man. The DEA tracked down Stefan Wathne to Moscow, but Russian extradition yielded only red tape and no drug money. The $3 million Wathne supposedly laundered never turned up and Wathne himself remained at large somewhere on the other side of the world.

"I think Nichols was absolutely certain that he was going to bring down this big organization but all he got was a chemist and a gofer," said Chris Malone. "This may have looked like a big deal, but in fact a lot of it was crap. I think Karl was pissed."

At *Slate,* Ryan Grim followed up on Leonard's letter. He quizzed analysts both inside and outside the government, as well as Karl Nichols.

"We found LSD," protested Nichols. "We found iso-LSD, we found all the equipment, the chemicals. Basically, we found everything."

Grim concluded otherwise. One year after publishing his first article, he wrote a second one, headlined:

Hey, wait a minute . . .
The 91-Pound Acid Trip
The numbers touted by the government in its big LSD bust just don't add up.

During Pickard's sentencing, DEA forensic chemist Timothy McKibben admitted as much: "The actual amount of all the exhibits containing LSD was 198.9 grams."

Working backward from each reported chemical quantity in the prosecution's exhibits, Grim concluded that the ninety-one pounds of LSD contained less than seven ounces, and possibly none at all. When he quizzed Nichols's boss, Grim got stonewalled:

The office of US Attorney Eric Melgren cooperated in the reporting of this story by allowing Agent Nichols to be interviewed. But when asked direct questions about the validity of Melgren's 91-pound press release claim, the office demurred. It would neither defend the number nor abandon it. A Melgren spokesman stated, "We've given you all the information we can on this subject."

John Halpern understood perfectly the government's intransigence. It was about saving face, but it was also about money.

"Look, you've got to understand, only two people are in jail for a vast 'conspiracy' and the government spent God knows how many dollars—scorched earth, leave-no-stone-unturned—on this issue," said Leonard's unindicted co-conspirator.

Once the pursuit of Pickard's millions began looking like a wild goose chase, Nichols's operating budget shrank.

"After the bust, Karl told local volunteers they'd be paid once the case concluded," recalled the *Wamego Times*' Mark Portell. "He later reneged, saying he was going to use the remainder of his budget to give bonuses to his agents.

"Of course, that didn't sit well with local emergency personnel, many of whom had taken days off work to be on-site during the dismantling of the lab. Nichols and Wamego Fire Chief Phil Stultz almost came to blows over the issue.

"In the end, by order of Judge Rogers, the DEA paid local volunteers for their time. Apparently, Nichols was unaware that Judge Rogers was a Wamego boy and that his nephew was assistant director of Pott County's Emergency Medical Services (EMS)."

Maintaining a low profile in the wake of the Wamego disaster, Alfred Savinelli had to agree with Halpern and Pickard, despite their DEA-fueled differences: Operation White Rabbit would better have been called Operation Whitewash. Nobody got rich off the missile silo caper except Todd Skinner.

"In short," said Savinelli, "Karl Nichols fucked up."

In May of 2004, six months into his sentence, Leonard came across an intriguing article in *Quarterly Interest*, journal of the Kansas State Bank Commissioner. It identified bank examiner Scott Lowry as a 1987 graduate of Washburn Law School, the same school from which AUSA Greg Hough had graduated in 1986. Funny thing, thought Leonard: neither man had bothered to point this out during the trial. During voir dire and all the way through to verdict, the jury foreman never volunteered that he and the chief prosecutor attended law school together.

Leonard alerted Billy Rork, who immediately filed for a new trial.

Judge Rogers wasted no time dashing hopes. There was no proof that Lowry and Hough colluded, regardless of how it might look. He denied a new trial in record time, setting the stage for appeal.

It didn't matter. On March 28, 2006, the 10th US Circuit Court of Appeals concurred with Judge Rogers, affirming both sentences against Leonard Pickard and Clyde Apperson.

In March 2004, a Nevada jury convicted Todd Skinner of selling MDMA. The judge sentenced him to four years.

Skinner howled before and after about the government immunity that got him off in Paul Hulebak's death. It applied in the Burning Man case too, he argued. When that failed, he claimed he was the victim of a government conspiracy fueled by Krystle's lies.

He was not entirely wrong.

On Feb. 20, 2005, Krystle called Billy Rork. If she testified against her husband, she'd do no jail time for her part in the Brandon Green kidnapping. She was prepared to start down that road by belatedly nailing Todd for Pickard's crimes. At Billy's urging, she filed an affidavit with the US Court of Appeals stating that Skinner had been the chemist and Leonard his patsy.

"In the last note I received from Cole, she said that the month before my arrest, Skinner brought out a horde of receipts he'd kept for years," said Pickard. "He arranged them all in order for presentation to the DEA. He'd been building his case for that rainy day since the first time he met me."

In June of 2006, an Oklahoma jury convicted Todd Skinner of kidnapping, assault, and torture of Krystle's boyfriend. Already doing time for his Burning Man felonies, Todd again tried to invoke DEA immunity, but Karl Nichols was no longer there for him. He got life for assault and ninety years on the kidnapping and conspiracy counts.

Successfully portraying the naïve Kansas farm damsel one more time, Krystle was ordered to pay $52,109 in restitution and placed on five years' probation.

"Unfortunately for society, Krystle has the capability to play or maneuver a person or situation just as someone would engage in chess," said a chastened Brandon Green. "One person Krystle played was Gordon Todd Skinner. She always had the upper hand in their relationship. Krystle was not controlled or brainwashed by Todd. Todd was enthralled and would have done anything for her."

Though never fully recovered from his injuries, Brandon improved enough to add a Krystle prediction:

"Just as (with) her predecessor/husband, each time she slides through the court system successfully, she will become more brazen and confident."

Four months pregnant when they wed, Natalya Kruglova knew nothing about Trais Kliphuis until she read about her in the newspaper. Trais gave birth to Pickard's only son, Duncan, on Sept. 22, 2000, just two months ahead of Duncan's half-sister Natasha. They have never met.

"When the two pregnancies occurred, I thought it best to wait until the children were born to make introductions," said Leonard. "I was certain to do so, having already introduced Deborah and Natasha at a picnic in a park in Sausalito. Trais also knew of Deborah, so inevitably we would share these blessings with growing peace. The matter may be more complex, and beautiful, than anyone will ever know."

Deborah was less sanguine. She cut off all communication after the trial. The last time Leonard saw her and Melissa was in Mill Valley in late October, "just before the world ended."

In 2006, Ann Shulgin sent a Christmas card in which she wrote about having Debbie and Melissa for Christmas dinner. The Shulgins joined in a toast to his health and well-being.

"We both hope you're doing well and keeping your courage up," she said. "Could you possibly ask for a Presidential pardon?"

"I have nothing bad to say about Len," Deborah wrote in a 2018 email. "I tried to help him before and after his arrest but Len doesn't listen, at least not to me. I hope that he can eventually win his freedom and enjoy his remaining years in peace and comfort."

Trais never married, yet she alone of his three baby mamas remains in regular contact and visits often. As with so many who fall beneath Leonard's spell, Trais remains fiercely loyal, choosing to overlook his breathtaking transgressions.

"One can only honor the mothers," said Leonard.

He and Natalya have had no contact since 2008; wife and child moved on. Pickard hears of them through others, but the best he can do is get a general impression.

"I know they are comfortable and doing well in school and career, and that Little Natasha is being brought up in the best way. They have a good life, so that is some solace.

"But the loss of Natasha and Little Natasha was and strongly remains, the greatest pain my heart has ever known. It began with the loss of hope then her assumption I would never return. There were years in which I could hardly send a Christmas card. Letters and gifts do seem to get through somewhere, but never any return mail. Not many have been made captive forever, in the flower of love, and watched it die."

XXIII.

IN 2005, PICKARD AND APPERSON transferred to a new home. Recently built near Victorville in California's Mojave Desert, the modern penitentiary did not look nearly as menacing as Lompoc. Nonetheless, gangs ran the place.

"With violent tribes and fear everywhere, it's a world most cannot imagine outside of war zones," said Pickard. "Blood clean-up crews on call; 'stars' carved into walls from the sharpening of homemade knives."

Leonard managed to survive, even thrive, until he could take no more and asked for a transfer.

"Due to the homicides and assaults at Victorville, I requested a gang-free environment."

Under Bureau of Prisons rules, an inmate can request a move once every eighteen months, but the system does not make relocation easy. His transfer began in solitary.

"The hole is a wall of sound," Pickard explained. "Screaming twenty-four hours a day. Four-point tie downs immobilizing arms and legs of recalcitrant inmates. Strapped to a cement block with little rings to attach appendages.

"For sunlight, you spend one hour a day in an actual cage. You can walk about two feet. People flood their cells and throw excrement. All the joys of home. Hole time tends to discourage people from blithely requesting transfers."

His transfer, he maintained, was voluntary. The hole, however, was not.

"You're allowed one phone call a month, squatting by a cuff port,[1]" said Pickard. "Actually, I found the solitude refreshing in a way, just writing all day, planning. Six months of it. While newspaper op-eds argue the destabilizing effects of such treatment—and for many isolation *is* disorienting—as a devoted reader and writer it was a transient blessing from the usual chaos above ground. The hole is literally beneath the institution, a prison within a prison."

But it can get cold down there.

Leonard remembers shivering through one December, pacing to stay warm while writing a paper for presentation at a Swiss psychonaut symposium. He used a four-inch pencil stub on scraps of paper in the dark. Titled "International Prevalence," his essay was to be part of a three-day birthday celebration in Basel where LSD was first discovered two years before Leonard was born.

Dr. Albert Hofmann was turning one hundred years old. Leonard sent his paper, along with his regrets.

Dr. Hofmann's birthday was the ultimate trip for hundreds of psychonauts who flew in to pay homage from around the globe.

Dr. Tom Roberts, a psychology professor at North Illinois University, staged a reenactment of Bicycle Day, the April 19, 1943, ride that Hofmann made from Sandoz through the cobblestone streets of Basel while loaded on LSD. Dr. Charles Grob described his new UCLA clinical study of psilocybin as a palliative for the terminally ill. And Ralph Metzner, the Harvard grad student who acted as Leary and Alpert's junior partner in the sixties, taught the entire assemblage a new dance he called the Bardo[2] shuffle—a kind

---

1. The slide opening at a cell door where guards can handcuff the inmate or hand him a tray of food.
2. Bardo: (in Tibetan Buddhism) a state of existence between death and rebirth, varying in length according to a person's conduct in life and manner of, or age at, death. (*Merriam Webster*)

of hokey pokey for heads. Among the youngest was a four-foot tall blue-eyed blond. Leonard's daughter, Little Natasha, giggled for the camera while hugging hard on to Ann and Sasha Shulgin.

Dr. Rick Doblin teamed with Dr. John Halpern at the MAPS[3] booth, handing out literature in furtherance of studies like Dr. Grob's. A general excitement seemed to grip old hippies and enlightened newbies alike: a new day was at hand where science could once more dabble in brain chemistry without fear of running afoul of the law.

But there were cautionary moments. During a panel discussion on the future of psychedelic study at the Basel summit, San Francisco acid artist Mark McCloud interrupted Halpern mid-pontification.

"Are you a DEA agent?" McCloud demanded.

"No," Halpern stammered. "No DEA."

As later commemorated in the *Entheogen Review* exposé "Halperngate," the Harvard psychiatrist protested his innocence. In the matter of Leonard Pickard and Clyde Apperson, Halpern was *not* a snitch.

"I'm doing work," he said, referring to his ongoing study of peyote among the Navajo and psilocybin therapy at Harvard.

"They're doing life!" quipped someone in the audience.

Halpern found no quarter among his peers that day, or for many days thereafter. His outing as a government turncoat made him a pariah among the hardcore. Sasha and Anne Shulgin both had their problems with Leonard's recklessness, but found bigger ones with Halpern. So did Dave Nichols, Rick Strassman, Stan Grof, Myron Stolaroff, and a host of other leading psychonauts. Nick Sand, who was seen at the Hofmann birthday bash carrying Little Natasha on his shoulders, turned and walked the other way when he saw Halpern approach.

Gary Walter "Doc" Dash, who was doing thirty years himself in

---

3.   Multidisciplinary Association for Psychedelic Studies

a federal prison for LSD manufacture, came to Halpern's defense: "I myself have on more than one occasion instructed friends to tell the DEA whatever they wanted to hear because they already had more than enough to get me. I never allowed any of my friends to jeopardize their lives, careers, or families in a pointless attempt to protect me. It may very well be that Pickard instructed Halpern to do the same."

Rick Doblin alone stood by Halpern at the Basel conference. The MAPS founder funded several Halpern projects and refused to throw him beneath the DEA bus. He correctly pointed out that virtually everyone associated with Todd Skinner's missile silo made deals with the government, from Alfred Savinelli to Deborah Harlow. No one was immune from Justice Department blackmail.

But Halpern lost more than reputation. After Dr. Hofmann's birthday celebration, he testified before a San Francisco grand jury that indicted his onetime childhood friend Stefan Wathne. Karl Nichols initiated a "Red Notice" to all 190 Interpol member nations asking them to be on the lookout for him. Using the alias Gunner S. Moller, Wathne was arrested in New Delhi on Sept. 24, 2007. The US Attorney's office in San Francisco started extradition, but he agreed to return voluntarily.

"The attorneys all trooped down to visit me in the hole after Wathne was detained," said Pickard. "I explained he was innocent and I told them I would testify to that if it went to trial."

But it never did. On Jan. 10, 2008, Wathne pled not guilty to money laundering, surrendered his passport. The wealthy Wathne sisters posted a $5 million bond. The family put up six apartments on Central Park South as collateral. If convicted, Wathne faced twenty years. Halpern watched the proceedings from afar.

"He pleaded guilty to a misdemeanor and paid a $100,000 fine," he said. "He didn't lose his green card, didn't cop to a felony, wasn't guilty of money laundering or anything, so I would say that's as good an outcome as you're gonna get."

Wathne and Halpern never spoke again.

Chris Malone sold his missile silo in 2006 to a military history buff who wanted a safe place to store his armaments. Prior to the close of escrow, Malone got a call from his property manager about a break in.

"I knew exactly what they were doing," Malone recalled. "Once they got through the doors, they went thirty feet down one tunnel, a hundred feet down another, right to the bathroom. Apparently they had a sledgehammer and broke through the wall. We found two holes with a pile of sand in front of each cavity. Each hole was about the right size to fit one of those metal briefcases that Skinner used to carry around, full of cash.

"We did the math. I think each suitcase could hold about $600,000. So basically I had $1,000,000 in cash hidden in my building for four years and didn't know it. Which kind of makes you sick after a while. You go, 'Hmmm, unmarked bills.'"

There were other hidden treasures in the silo. Mike Bauer once paid a visit with his grandfather, also a military history buff. While they were there, Bauer accessed a secret computer and removed its hard drive.

He never revealed what was on it.

Following Dr. Hofmann's birthday gala, Dave Nichols had a crisis of conscience.

"I have never considered my research to be dangerous, and in fact hoped one day to develop medicines to help people," he said. "I was stunned by this revelation, and it left me with a hollow and depressed feeling for some time."

Nichols' revelation was that, in the Internet era, secrets like highly simplified recipes for LSD, fentanyl, and hundreds of equally potent brews had become available to anyone, anytime, anywhere. To Nichols' horror, that meant any nut with a test tube and a credit card could cook up the most exotic mind benders and mete them out with impunity to friends, blind dates, or the family dog.

On one hand, Nichols reveled in the early twenty-first century psychedelic renaissance.

Following in Sasha Shulgin's footsteps, dozens of researchers had picked up the torch, calling for renewal of over five thousand studies from the 1950s and '60s. Before the War on Drugs, LSD, mescaline, and psilocybin showed promise as therapy for everything from alcohol abuse to hospice care. Tentatively, and then in increasing numbers, psychedelic clinicians were again investigating PTSD, OCD, migraines, terminal patient care, addiction, and even spirituality. Nichols himself discovered breakthroughs that helped schizophrenics and Parkinson's victims.

On the other hand, he recoiled from the unprecedented misuse of designer drugs.

In a *mea culpa* in the journal *Nature*, the Purdue professor publicly agonized over synthetics which he'd had a hand in developing. In an article titled, "Legal Highs: The Dark Side of Medicinal Chemistry," he acknowledged that unleashing untested drugs in the digital age carried a risk far greater than anything Dr. Hofmann ever could have imagined.

A few weeks ago, a colleague sent me a link to an article in the *Wall Street Journal*. It described a "laboratory-adept European entrepreneur" and his chief chemist, who were mining the scientific literature to find ideas for new designer drugs—dubbed legal highs. I was particularly disturbed to see my name in the article, and that I had "been especially valuable" to their cause. I subsequently received e-mails saying I should stop my research, and that I was an embarrassment to my university.

Along with Sasha's *PiHKAL* and *TiHKAL,* Nichols's formulae had become staples of the Internet's "grey market"—drugs that were not exactly forbidden, but not exactly kosher either. One of them that Nichols developed had been sold on the street in Europe as ecstasy and killed six people.

"I had published information that ultimately led to human death," Nichols lamented, adding: "This question, which was never part of my research focus, now haunts me."

From inside his cell, Leonard sympathized. He recalled a botched black-market opioid that once caused San Jose addicts to freeze up at raves. The toxic drug eventually tested out as a Parkinson's treatment similar to the one Dave Nichols invented, but that was small comfort to the paralyzed dancers of San Jose.

"Without actual animal and human studies, the risk is significant," he said. "Amateurs distributing laboratory oddities? I agree with Dr. Nichols. I am very concerned with the increasing array of unexplored substances."

Simply outlawing them, however, was not the answer—an opinion shared by both professor and convict. Human beings, especially the young and stupid, seek their drug of choice, law or no law.

As one of the Six warned Leonard in *The Rose*,

But our fear is that—in the absence of the sacrament—toxic alternatives will proliferate, with addiction and loss of lives. Opiates, stimulants, bizarre lethal hallucinogens will enter the void. Governments would be wise to permit a certain availability of classical psychedelics, lest chemical horrors abound.

XXIV.

ON JULY 31, 2008, BILLY Rork served Greg Hough with a 117-page brief accusing the government of hiding evidence. Todd Skinner, not Leonard Pickard, was the Wamego Acid King, and they knew it all along.

"I don't mind trial by ambush," said Rork. "You get used to it. But the records on Skinner? Twenty-three different instances since the mid-eighties where he'd been working with DEA, and they gave us *one* case!"

The US Attorney's office balked. Hough hedged that "any cooperation by, or investigation of, Skinner by unrelated agencies were unknown." He blamed the DEA for his ignorance of Skinner's long, tawdry record as a government informant, accused murderer and unrepentant drug thug. Caught amid denials, the government conceded it "was unaware of these matters," but added the excuse that "each of the alleged matters involved agencies not involved in this investigation."

"This is the worst case I've ever seen in my life of withheld evidence, of altered evidence, of witness tampering, and I think we've just touched the beginning," Rork fumed.

After the Brandon Green case, Skinner himself accused Karl Nichols of "prepping witnesses." He and his partner made the evidence fit the crime.

"You see, I can't give a witness money or I'd be charged with bribery," said Rork, "but the government can pay them, put them up in nice hotels and give them something more valuable than money: their freedom."

Alfred Savinelli was Exhibit A. Before Karl Nichols began bullying him, Savinelli agreed to testify that Skinner, not Pickard, made and sold LSD among other drugs in both Santa Fe and Wamego.

"They scared Savinelli to death," said Rork. "He held out for about a year, a year and a half, then at some point he gave in."

After the DEA threatened to jail his wife and son, Savinelli switched sides and testified for the prosecution.

"Fact is, the prosecutor was sold a bill of goods and even in the face of defeat, wouldn't admit it, and even went so far as to alter exhibits and evidence to support their case! Why did they do it? They wanted to make this case out to be what they *thought* it was, and it wasn't. Pickard was never given a fair shot. Never."

Every year that Leonard spent behind bars, another piece of Hough's case fell apart, but the dirty pool didn't end with the government. The lawyer who steered Skinner into the arms of Hough and the DEA approached Billy once with an offer to reveal the government's fatal flaw.

"He wanted $20,000," Rork scoffed. "How thoughtful of him to offer assistance!"

Billy never charged Leonard a dime. Appeal after appeal, he remained on the case. He explained his charity as compulsion as much as it was compassion.

"The facts cry out for help. They just scream repeatedly. If you read the transcript, you would not *believe* what went on. All Leonard ever asked from the very beginning was, 'Billy, can you help me get the truth to the jury?' I told him I'd do everything I could."

The year following the filing of his appeal, Leonard discovered the existence of a second Operation White Rabbit.

Headquartered in Kansas City, Operation White Rabbit-East commenced on Oct. 23, 2001, almost a year after the day that Todd Skinner gave Karl Nichols and Roger Hanzlik their first tour of his missile silo. It ended Nov. 25, 2003, the day Leonard Pickard got life in prison.

The original Operation White Rabbit based in San Francisco began May 17, 2001, and continued through 2008. What it turned up was never revealed. For years, the DEA stubbornly refused to acknowledge that either operation even existed. Neither Nichols or the DEA's San Francisco office responded to the author's written requests for information on White Rabbit or Pickard's prosecution. Were it not for Mike Bauer's curiosity and Karl Nichols' vanity, all might have remained under wraps.

"Strange the government pretended these didn't exist," said Pickard. "They could have simply been honest."

Both he and Billy Rork figured the Justice Department wasn't forthcoming because nobody wanted to explain where the money went. One Operation White Rabbit yielded a DEA bonanza under the well-funded Organized Crime Drug Enforcement Task Force program, but *two* Operation White Rabbits?

"One can only imagine," said Leonard.

The problem for Karl Nichols and Roger Hanzlik was that their golden goose laid an egg—just not the right kind. They'd been conned by a con man and were too humiliated to set things right.

"The guy didn't have any money and the government never found any assets," said Billy.

The only dividend the DEA ever got from its investment was a 212-page slide presentation Karl Nichols cooked up as a training aid to instruct agents on how to bust an LSD trafficking organization. There is no evidence that his seminars ever resulted in a single arrest.

When Leonard went inside, marijuana was illegal. Though it remained a Schedule One drug fifteen years later, all but seventeen states (including Kansas) had legalized pot possession.[1] Recently, Oakland[2] and Denver approved possession of psilocybe mushrooms. Grow kits could be purchased over the Internet.

Though still illegal, LSD microdosing had been rampant in Silicon Valley for the better part of a decade, and ayahuasca was legally available through the North American União do Vegetal Church. Attitudes towards psychedelics had shifted dramatically since the turn of the century.

Leonard adapted to the times. His first prison job was teaching GED night classes where attention spans were short and boredom was the enemy.

"Soon I learned that the class would focus much better if I couched lessons on the metric system in terms of kilograms of crack," he said. "If I drew a sailboat filled with pot and discussed how many hours and kilometers it took to arrive in San Diego, I got the idea of triangulation across a lot easier than if I just talked about angles and hypotenuses."

Nowadays, drug allusions don't carry the same clout with jaded inmates as they once did. Were he still teaching, he'd have to find different references. Times change, fears fade, and new ones take their place.

Leonard waxed sardonic: "How interesting that one can now publicly talk about psychedelics all day long, and socialize at conferences relentlessly, and publish and receive lots of donations, and be a media darling, without ever having any legal exposure. What an excellent idea!"

For himself, he's past entheogens. Like Tim Scully, he's on to the next stages of neuropharmacology:

"Biotech and gene editing for enhancement of cognitive traits,

---

1. Only 11 states allow recreational use. The remaining 22 restrict possession to medical use.
2. Oakland went even further, legalizing all plant-based entheogens, including peyote and ayahuasca.

and, to a lesser degree, erotogenics. I think about the proliferation of unregulated custom IVF clinics in third-world settings, with selection for eye and skin color, gender, personality, and intelligence. Now *that* will be a phenomenon, as we consciously select our next species."

Which is not to say that Leonard has lost all interest in drugs. Take fentanyl, for example.

The National Institute of Drug Abuse couldn't pinpoint a date, but it was clear by the end of President Barack Obama's second term that the US was mired in its worst drug crisis since the crack cocaine epidemic of the 1980s. The culprit wasn't LSD or any other psychedelic memorialized in Schedule One of the Controlled Substances Act of 1970. As Pickard predicted while still at Harvard, America faced an opioid crisis and more specifically, an epidemic of George Marquardt's deadly synthetic heroin. It took the overdose deaths of celebrities like Phillip Seymour Hoffman, Tom Petty, and Prince to set off alarms.

"In 1996, fentanyl procedures weren't available except in academic journals," Pickard recalled.

Nonetheless, he began tracking the drug from Harvard as a potential time bomb, especially if the recipe were to fall into the hands of Mexican cartels. "I knew we had a problem when a simplified procedure was discovered scribbled on a piece of paper that was found in the pocket of a Mexican auto accident victim."

Both its inventor, Paul Janssen, and Sasha Shulgin warned of fentanyl abuse, but Pickard made the first prediction of impending pandemic. In a 1996 slide show at the Harvard Faculty Club, he explained in detail how, why, and when the synthetic would join other overprescribed opioids seeping into the American mainstream, along with Leonard's preemptive prescription on how to stop it.

Billy Rork resurrected the slide show seven years later for Pickard's trial. Leonard spent two days on the stand, explaining to the court that an opioid plague was on its way. His words fell on deaf ears. Cassandra had better luck predicting the outcome of the Trojan War.

As his worst fears began to materialize nearly fifteen years later with over forty thousand deaths reported annually, Pickard began a prison email exchange with an old friend on the outside: former *Mother Jones* publisher Mark Dowie.

> Lennie—You know, of course, that the gas pumped into Moscow's Dubrovka theater during the 2002 Nord-Ost Siege (intended to incapacitate the Chechen terrorists and save the 400 or so hostages trapped inside) was almost certainly Carfentanil, a gaseous form of fentanyl. The gas did end the siege, led to the death of all 40 terrorists, but also killed 204 of the hostages.
> They should have listened to you.
> Mark

> Hi Mark—Yes, my research and concerns about fentanyl date back to my time at the Kennedy School. The fen prediction from my testimony in the trial: "We are going to have a big problem." I am constructing a package containing all the relevant testimony. It was not simply a prediction, but offered methods to prevent or delay such an epidemic. Note I was first to recommend naloxone be widely-distributed. Of course, in 1996 there were only relatively small outbreaks, dependent on one lab, and the idea of an epidemic was science-fiction.
> Len

True to his word, Pickard compiled charts, documents, letters, trial exhibits, and reports from his failed FEDS program at both

Harvard and UCLA and sent off an inch-thick "Fentanyl Proposal" to every Senator and Congressional Representative in Washington.

In the cover letter, his attorney wrote, ". . . my client wishes to offer his assistance and analytical expertise to individuals and organizations concerned with the opioid crisis in an effort to reduce the death rate from fentanyl overdoses and to anticipate the future of the current crisis."

It was also worth noting that the venerable RAND Corporation published a history and analysis of fentanyl abuse in the autumn of 2019: *The Future of Fentanyl and Other Synthetic Opioids.*[3]

"My work in 1996 was cited six times and featured in the bibliography," Pickard said triumphantly.

But Congressional ears were as deaf as they had been a quarter-century ealier. There was an inmate registration number in front of Leonard's name and his return address was USP Tucson.

He got no responses.

Billy Rork was found dead in his apartment May 31, 2017. He was sixty-two. Known around the Topeka courthouse as F. Lee Billy, he was fondly eulogized as a fierce, fiery advocate for the abandoned, dispossessed, and forlorn. He advised his clients to tell police, "No, I do not care if we did go to high school together. I still do not wish to speak to you unless Mr. Rork is present."

Billy did not live to see the results of his appeal against the government juggernaut that railroaded Leonard Pickard and Clyde Apperson. On Nov. 17, 2017, a Kansas appellate judge ordered the DEA to unseal its four-hundred-page file on Todd Skinner. Leonard was exultant.

---

3.   Among other findings, the RAND authors cited a tenfold increase in fentanyl deaths between 2013 (3,000) and 2018 (30,000); a growing preference for fentanyl over heroin among addicts; and an epidemic headed toward pandemic without government intervention—a prediction both Pickard and Sasha Shulgin had made decades earlier.

"Nothing like this in jurisprudence has ever been seen before! DEA has refused to release even a single word for ten years, and is likely to continue to do so. But there's the rub."

As Billy explained his strategy, the government could choose to defy the court and hold on to the damning file, but they would have to release Leonard. Rork had bet that Skinner's DEA relationship dated back so far and was so toxic that the agency could not afford to let the public see the sleazy way it operated. If Billy was correct, Pickard would walk out of prison a free man, time served.

A month later, the Ninth Circuit dashed his hopes. Skinner's file would stay sealed. Leonard would remain Prisoner #82687–011.

On June 23, 2017, Dr. Michael Bauer got drunk, put a gun to his head, and squeezed off a permanent solution to a temporary problem.

"I saw him a month before," said Alfred Savinelli. "We'd had a very normal relationship for the past three or four years. We'd go mushroom hunting. He came up for the weekend with the kids. Didn't make sense."

"Maybe something from the Pickard saga caught up with him, but I don't think so," said John Halpern. "I think he committed suicide."

Both psychonauts knew Bauer from the earliest days of the swimming pool project, when he all but apprenticed himself to Leonard Pickard. Leonard, who encouraged him to become a physician, remained a father figure long after he went to prison. Indeed, Pickard may have taken the news hardest of all. For a year following Bauer's death, Leonard began evening prayers with a paean to his fallen friend.

"There always will be an emptiness in me, and in many others, that Mike once occupied," he said. "I wish I had known of the seriousness of his difficulties, but I only heard of his love for his wife and children."

Mike's mother is not so sure.

"Michael was most certainly a victim, as have been many young starry-eyed students whose parents send them to so-called prestige universities where they come in contact with these people who are protected by the university, and who do real harm," said Linda Bauer.

Since her son's death, she has turned her home office into a war room, convinced that there is far more to Mike's passing than simple suicide. Her son became chief physician for the vast Kiowa Pueblo reservation in the years after Pickard's imprisonment, but among other oddities, Bauer developed an obsession with Afghanistan that his mother lays to Leonard, along with Mike's lifetime lust for psychedelics.

"It all started the day he met Leonard Pickard," she said, comparing Leonard to the protagonist of TV's *Breaking Bad.* "The Leonard story is equally twisted. It's a picture with no edges."

On the one hand, Leonard maintained prison estranged them ("I hadn't seen Mike for twenty years. In the twelve years I've had email, he wrote me twenty or thirty times; perhaps five phone calls.") On the other, Bauer remained close enough to invite Leonard's son Duncan on rounds when he made house calls to remote cabins in the desert.

"He was the only doctor in Albuquerque who made house calls," said his mother. She quickly adds that he was also apparently the only doctor in Albuquerque with ties to both Central Asia and the CIA. "They tried to recruit him when he was going to Boston College," she said.

So completely did Bauer and classmate Kenichi Sakai fall under Leonard's spell that both risked jail time over Operation White Rabbit. The DEA held Michael for four days in San Francisco in 2001, accusing both men of money laundering. Ironically, Bauer could have claimed the name Ivy Mike. He proudly stood by Leonard long after others squealed. Like Leonard, Mike led a secretive double life.

But if Mike was mixed up in foreign intrigue or the international drug trade, Leonard maintains he knew nothing about it. He is equally clueless about the mystery surrounding Bauer's suicide and flinches at the suggestion he might somehow be responsible. Linda Bauer is looking for answers where none exist, he insisted. "We will grieve her pain."

Though he wasn't present, Pickard painted a vivid picture of Bauer's memorial, ". . . packed with physicians and residents and those who loved him.

"At the very end, after all the speakers, a Roadman for the Native American Church suddenly appeared, unannounced, moving through the assembly to the dais. Victor had guided Mike through many all-night ceremonies. He began singing in Navajo a death song for Mike, with his long, earnest prayer filling the room. He sang of Mike's vision to become a doctor, and how he was a great healer among his people, among the dispossessed and poor. Everyone's heart was taken skyward. At the end, the prayer descended into silence, and the crowd quietly parted to let Victor pass. Mike would have loved it. Pretty good story, yes?"

No sooner did he lose a young friend than word came that Leonard had lost an old one.

Nick Sand suffered a fatal heart attack at the age of seventy-five. After he did his ten years following the Canadian bust, Sand retired to California, unrepentant.

"Nick and I were quite different. He was eager to discuss his exploits, and did so at conferences and to media," said Leonard. "I, on the other hand, have always disavowed any experience or involvement with LSD, privately or publicly. I never mentioned the substance during my Cambridge years; my research was on fentanyl.

"Nicky admitted to being responsible for thirteen kilograms over his lifetime. The DEA accuses me of two hundred forty kilograms[4] or one kilogram a month for twenty years. Of course, that can only be fanciful."

He wrote Sand an elegy that was read several times at his memorial service.

"Just a personal thing, really," said Leonard. "A feeling. I hope he heard it, dancing in the sun."

As the years passed, so did other psychonauts whose friendship Leonard secured during his long, strange trip. Ram Dass died just before Christmas of 2019 and Leonard's longtime Harvard mentor Mark Kleiman passed away the previous summer. The former Richard Alpert was 88; Kleiman was 68. In poor health since Leonard's Kansas arrest, he died of complications following a kidney transplant. Pickard never faulted Kleiman for failing to step up in his defense during and after the trial. Like the Shulgins, Kleiman stayed in touch and tried to make prison life tolerable.

"My email and phone calls were taken care of for over a decade by Mark, who appeared at Lompoc and volunteered to help," said Leonard. "Otherwise, I wouldn't even have had mail."

After self-publishing *Lysergic*, her first-person account of the Wamego acid bust, Krystle Cole became a minor Internet celebrity. She starred in Vice TV's "Getting High on Krystle" episode of the popular psychonaut video series, "Hamilton's Pharmacopeia" registering more than 15 million views on YouTube. Her psychedelic advice website Neurosoup launched her second career as a psychedelic artist.

Todd's other exes also flourished. Emily Ragan remarried and

---

4. During a 2016 MSNBC broadcast commemorating the Wamego bust, former DEA agent Guy Hargreaves claimed Pickard made 3.2 billion doses, enough to intoxicate "the Western hemisphere." A semi-retired Arizona real estate agent, Hargreaves worked the case under Nichols and Hanzlik and later wrote a memoir, *Operation: Trip to Oz.*

taught chemistry at the University of Tulsa, then Metropolitan State University in Denver. Kelly Rothe moved to North Carolina and became a well-respected osteopathic physician.

But the Skinner curse persisted.

On Feb. 6, 2019, his son Morgan Rothe-Skinner murdered his uncle at Katherine Magrini's home in the New Orleans French Quarter. For no apparent reason, the 26-year-old Tulane design student stabbed Daniel Magrini to death, then held his 76-year-old grandmother at knifepoint.

"This has undone me," said Katherine. "He told me he had just killed him. Things went downhill. He was just very manic."

Her "agitated" grandson eventually rolled his uncle up in a rug, his feet poking out. That was how police found the corpse when the standoff ended and they arrested Morgan for second-degree murder. Katherine vouched for him the way she had once vouched for Todd: a good boy who wouldn't even break the speed limit.

"I love my grandson very deeply, no matter what happens," said Katherine.

In 2019, Morgan's father remained in residence at the Joseph Harp Correctional Center. He has been moved at least 10 times according to one of his visitors, and bounced around his cell at least once, requiring extensive stitches. The balding loon known among fellow inmates as Dr. Lecter will be eligible for parole in 2044 when he's 80.

At 5:45 a.m., Leonard walks the tier to shake off aches acquired from sleeping on a thin mattress over a steel cot. Next, he's out on the track for an hour walk. He watches the sun rise past the guard tower while listening through his earbuds to classical music broadcast from the University of Arizona. The day begins, mostly spent reading, writing and corresponding, meditating, and helping others with legal advice.

"Old black man just walked up to me and said, 'Thank you,'"

Leonard wrote in an email. "Over seventy, no teeth, rail thin, polite, he's done thirty years. Perfect record, not literate, a rarity. He didn't know about the Compassionate Release program, so I approached him one day and wrote his petition. That's flying well now, though we may have to go into federal court one day. He may go home. That made the morning, if not the week."

Compassion and gratitude contrast sharply with the more typical resentment and anger that echo everywhere, always, throughout each day.

But if hope is the thing with feathers, Leonard Pickard keeps it well fed and watered.

Richard Shelton, Regents' Professor Emeritus of English at the University of Arizona, directed the University's creative writing program before he began his prison writing outreach in 1970. It started with Charles Schmid, "The Pied Piper of Tucson,"[5] who wrote to ask for his feedback on his poetry. It was surprisingly good. With funding from the Arizona Commission on the Arts, Shelton launched a lifelong commitment to help inmates express themselves.

"Their deprivation seemed to increase certain sensitivities," he said.

When Shelton extended the program to include the federal prison on the outskirts of Tucson, Pickard bowled him over.

"I was stunned," he said.

During the years that followed, Pickard's prose became a staple

---

5. A charismatic serial killer, Schmid murdered at least three young women in the mid-sixties, was sentenced to death, and briefly escaped from prison after posting his poetry to Shelton. "For all the wrong reasons, I critiqued his work and discovered that he was quite talented," he said. In 1975, fellow inmates stabbed Schmid forty-seven times, including once in the eye. He lingered three weeks then died. He was thirty-two. His crimes became the basis for one of Joyce Carol Oates's earliest short stories, "Where Are You Going, Where Have You Been?"

of the annual *Rain Shadow Review*,[6] a compilation of the best of Arizona's prison writing. With his 2015 publication of *The Rose of Paracelsus*, Leonard graduated to the top rungs of Shelton's students.

"It's fascinating," Shelton said. "Not for everybody, but fascinating. I told him he would reach a smaller audience, but he was fine with that."

"*The Rose* was written, not for the public, but for the experienced," said Leonard.

John le Carré bought a copy for his son Nick. Jeremy Irons's secretary wrote that the actor would love to read *The Rose*, so Leonard sent him two. He began a sequel in 2017.

"I may call it 'Songs of the Rose,' for it concerns memories of the Six: their efforts across the earth to explore novel substances, and to contain addictive compounds."

In 2018, he orchestrated a four-hour podcast (https://psyche-delicsalon.com/podcast-609-the-rose-garden-introduction/) with readers recruited from among psychonauts and admirers around the globe.

"This week I received photos of *The Rose* being read on board the Queen Elizabeth II," he said. "Social circles are expanding.

"Writing is the perfect art for these elder days. It brings the greatest pleasure and a sort of tranquility. The Life Force will carry us 'til pen drops from hand, yes?"

He worries about saying all he needs to before it's too late. Sasha[7] is gone now, along with Nick Sand, the Bear, Tim Leary, Petaluma Al[8] and most of the first generation of psychonauts, but even at this late date, Leonard ponders the possibilities of higher education.

"Before dying in prison, I hope to contribute to society," he said. "I'm seeking a faculty sponsor to oversee a dissertation in absentia

---

6. Known as *Walking Rain Review* before 2011.
7. Alexander Shulgin died of liver cancer June 2, 2014. He was 88.
8. Dead at 80, Al Reid passed on July 4, a month after Sasha.

on the topic of their choice, or on one of several issues: the future arc of the opioid crisis, potential outcomes of medicalization of psychedelics, or monitoring advances in biotech related to enhanced cognition."

The thing with feathers roosts outside his window, always just beyond his reach, but it springs eternal.

Shortly after Christmas, Leonard's email account went dark. At 9:22 a.m. Dec. 27, 2018, the only message displayed in the prison email system for William Leonard Pickard read:

This is a system generated message informing you the above mentioned federal inmate temporarily does not have access to messaging. You will receive notification when they are again eligible for messaging.

Epilogue

To live outside the law you must be honest ...

—Bob Dylan

JUST AS MYSTERIOUSLY AS IT switched off, Leonard's email switched back on in April of 2019. He and USP Tucson's other cyber literate were allowed to return to their CorrLinks[1] accounts.

"They use me as a dictionary, for they are unfamiliar with spell check," he said. "Today, I was asked to spell 'regular,' but my favorite was some years ago when a young kid turned to me and said, 'How do you spell "pray"?'"

Like all aspects of daily existence, prison censorship is vague, arbitrary, and routine. In June 2019, guards told Pickard he could not receive the Art Issue of the *New York Review of Books* because it was a threat to institutional security.

"My favorite recent rejection is the bio of Percy Bysshe Shelley by Claire Tomalin," he said. "A scholarly work containing a chaste drawing of Shelley as a boy wearing a suit, from about 1812 or so."

The drawing didn't meet the "educational exception," according to prison censors—an argument Pickard might easily have won in

---

1. A privately-owned computer company operating since 2009 that allows inmates to communicate with the outside world.

court if he had the $300 filing fee and didn't mind waiting six to twelve months.

"The author of the prohibited work is a prolific British biographer of Victorian writers and a former *Times* editor," he said. "I've worked my way through her writings on Thomas Hardy, and on Dickens's companion in his later years."

Not that Leonard didn't understand the general logic of censorship. Prison is lousy with pedophiles, as illustrated by an incident some years back, when staff screened *The Mission* (1986) for inmates. The story of eighteenth-century Jesuits evangelizing the Amazon starred Robert DeNiro and Jeremy Irons and featured several scenes of naked and near-naked native children. Whether by threat or coercion, the inmates got the projectionist to replay those scenes to hoots and whistles, over and over again. A warped audience can interpret the most innocent portrayal as porn, and majority usually rules.

"While a *Transformers* movie or *Swamp People* or *The Walking Dead* is watched by all, the most popular show on TV for forty years is not," he said. "In twenty years, I've never seen *60 Minutes*.

"Pity about Shelley being rejected though. Love his poetics (e.g. "The Witch of Atlas") and the Byron/Mary Wollstonecraft/Shelley triangle. I was just writing a scene set near Shelley's sightless marble bust in the common room at Eton.

"I live in the nineteenth century as much as possible, while captive in the steel horrors of the twenty-first."

Life is arbitrary.

"So tomorrow we are (all twelve hundred men—sorry, I mean 'inmates') to move one cell over, carting all belongings. My legal files alone are hundreds of pounds. No explanation."

His companions range from the tattooed ("many full facial, often with skulls underlying the tissue . . . one whose sclera is dyed deep blue") to pet lovers.

"They train small snakes and tarantulas to crawl across hands and over shoulders," he said.

Some raise pigeons in their lockers while others construct "mouse wheels": cardboard contraptions which rotate vertically as rodent treadmills.

"The mice seem to find it pleasurable and can run for hours until they're flushed by staff."

An entrepreneur nicknamed Spiderman created a Black Widow gymnasium by linking empty medicine bottles and peanut butter jars in an elaborate terrarium he furnished with sticks, a plant, shallow water and all the comforts that Wolf Spiders, et al, might desire. He assembled his arachnid army from the chain link fence in the exercise yard, fed them ants, and hosted great battles, betting on the outcome.

Everything comes back to money. Pets sell for "books" of postage stamps, the de facto exchange for gambling debts, drugs, food, personal services, etc. Even in prison, capitalism trumps all other brands of commerce.

And yet, there are sublime moments. One moonlit night years ago, Leonard witnessed a huge, silent white owl with an eighteen inch wing span swoop to an eave just a few feet away from his cell. He and his roommate watched by moonlight through the four-inch slit that serves as their window.

"We turned off the lights, invited others in to visit, and communed for hours until it spied a mouse in the yard. Our first and last glimpse of the quiet majesty of nature."

Coming in this cool, overcast morning from walking/running around the dirt track at six a.m., then at the loudspeaker's command passing under the gun tower and razor wire and military fence and locked gates and through metal detectors and guards in anti-stab vests, I was listening on headphones to a piano rendition of Tchaikovsky's "Sugar Plum Fairies." Reminded me of my father playing the Tin Soldier to

Tchaikovsky's Nutcracker. *I could only smile and offer a little prayer of thanks for a moment of grace at the start of the day.*

I wonder what almost twenty years now in a maximum-security environment does to a man. After a day in the chiller (wearing mittens and knit cap due to the coldness), compressed among the tattooed faces and eyeballs, we were let onto the track for an hour. Few go, for most remain mesmerized for decades by TV. But wandering alone was an elderly friend, a native Sioux from South Dakota.

He has a fine old dark brown and deeply craggy face that Edward Curtis would have photographed. Gray hair to shoulders, easy, slow walk, the rhythm of his language—that which older Native Americans often speak.

He told me of riding his horses who still wait for him: bareback with just a blanket and no halter (for they sense his wishes and the way), along the ravines and isolated magic pools and streams of remote places, then watering his horses and building a fire and just sitting and feeling the peace and beauty. He's going home soon to his sons and horses. Best conversation I've had in a long time.

Postscript

Until the 24th of July 2020, the final pages of *Operation White Rabbit* ended in the imprisoned voice of William Leonard Pickard, Inmate # 82687-011, speaking with weary but unbowed resignation from inside Tucson's maximum-security federal Penitentiary.

He held out hope. He worked tirelessly for his own freedom, as well as that of dozens of others, instructing all comers on how to navigate the impenetrable federal appeals system. But the system hadn't worked for Pickard. Even with his minor legal triumphs, such as forcing prosecutors to release more of the voluminous yet dubious evidence they used against him than they ever revealed at trial, he could not reverse Judge Rogers's draconian sentence. In writ after writ, appellate justices conceded mistakes may have been made, but none absolved Pickard of his crimes.

Then, late on a Friday night in July, five words rocketed across the internet, shifting tragedy to triumph.

Leonard Pickard had been released.

Everything changed in a tweet. The headline: William Leonard Pickard's latest appeal for compassionate release had been granted.

The verdict stood. He was still guilty of manufacturing and distributing 90 percent of the country's LSD supply, and would have to submit to five years' probation. But his age (seventy-four) and health (stage three chronic kidney disease, hypertension, iron deficiency anemia, hypothyroidism, cataracts, pre-diabetes, prostatic hyperplasia, posterior vitreous detachment and Vitamin D deficiency) prompted the closest thing that the government offers as mercy.

Leonard would immediately leave prison after nearly twenty years. The normally glacial justice system moved with such speed that there was no time to close out his email. All texts bounced back with an alarming note that this inmate no longer existed. Most of those who'd championed his cause for two decades had no idea how to even contact him, let alone where he would wind up when he walked out the gates for the final time. He later confessed to friends that he felt like a virgin in this brave new technological world—one that he'd left behind when Bill Clinton was still in the White House.

"As you can imagine, matters are overwhelming but a continuing delight," he told me a few days later.

Without fanfare or much in the way of a helping hand, guards handed him a pair of jeans and a one-way bus ticket that left around midnight, then sent him on his way. He barely had time to call Trais Kliphuis to let her know he'd be arriving the following day. She and Duncan met him at the Albuquerque bus depot the next afternoon. After hugs and tears and a gathering up of Leonard's meager belongings, they drove home to Santa Fe, where Leonard reacquainted himself with the luxury of an actual mattress with pillows, sheets, and box spring. When he switched off the lights – another small privilege he'd never again take for granted – he could actually hear the sound of his own breathing, and nothing more.

His family and friends set him up with a MacPro laptop and cell phone—twin toys that simply did not exist when he went inside at the turn of the century. His millennial son Duncan taught him the rudiments, while Trais hooked him up with WiFi.

Leonard boggled.

"Have sorted out some of the new world of electronica and am somewhat functional," he reported after a few days of practice. "Remain amazed at the rapidity of communication, and fullness thereof. Evolutionary."

When I had finished writing *Operation White Rabbit* some months earlier, Leonard pulled one of his many strings and had a friend on the outside deliver a magnum of Moët & Chandon to my front door. A master of the grand gesture, he never let prison limit his good will. The day after Mike Bauer's apparent suicide in 2018, he saw to it flowers were delivered to Bauer's widow. While a self-trained expert at manipulating words, Leonard knows full well that actions always speak louder.

I reciprocated the day following his release with roses. A dozen appeared on his doorstep with a note attached, apologizing that they hadn't come from Paracelsus. As with all the gifts and simple pleasures now at his disposal, flowers were as cherished as fresh blueberries and yogurt ("Heaven!") at his breakfast table.

"The week has been quite a transition, as you may imagine, but I now do long pre-dawn walks beneath the Sangre de Cristo mountains and watch the sun rise over vast ranges of pinon, sage and juniper," he said. "Flocks of joggers all wave or say 'Hi,' some towing herds of goats (only in Santa Fe).

"Not many have survived two life sentences, Dennis," he continued. "There are many in there (Tucson penitentiary) my age and with Covid exposure, so I expect the fentanyl issue was the definitive force, though the Court hardly could admit it."

Since the pandemic struck in March, Leonard and his cellmate had been locked down twenty-three hours a day. The virus still managed to sneak inside, indiscriminately infecting five guards and eleven inmates. The isolation was meant to flatten the curve and save lives, just as quarantine is supposed to do on the outside, but prisoners can't even get out to walk the dog or visit the grocery store. Forget about binging Netflix for days on end. Most of the time in solitary, Leonard couldn't even communicate through CorrLinks, the Bureau of Prisons-sanctioned email system. He had to resort to pen and paper and wait for weeks for a reply.

In ordering his release, the chief judge of the U.S. District Court in Kansas, J. Thomas Marten, made few concessions. Leonard had been found guilty and went to prison twice on drug convictions before the Wamego bust. Three strikes and he was officially out.

Thus, letting him go could not be characterized as absolution. Nor did his early (1996) warnings at Harvard about fentanyl being the next deadly drug on the horizon figure into Judge Marten's decision. Age, health, and rehabilitation tipped the scales in Pickard's favor.

"Pickard's offenses were serious but having spent two decades in prison he has been seriously punished," wrote Marten.

Ironically, President Trump's unpredictable impulse to commute sentences of his friends and favorites also played a role. In December of 2019, the President signed into law the First Step Act, easing strict mandatory sentencing for the first time since Richard Nixon and Ronald Reagan declared war on drugs. Kim Kardashian's successful campaign to free convicted Tennessee cocaine dealer Alice Marie Johnson in June 2018 led to broad prison reform legislation. The trend toward commuting harsh sentences like Pickard's seemed to have played a role in Marten's decision.

"The government has not challenged the defendant's contention that, at 74 years of age, he does not pose any significant risk to society, or that he has not engaged in substantial efforts at rehabilitation," wrote Judge Marten.

Leonard turns seventy-five in October. He's rail-thin, but relatively healthy for a man his age. Despite the alarming catalogue of chronic medical issues that appear in Judge Marten's release order, he's already managed to land a job at a law firm, putting his years of paralegal training inside Tucson USP into practice.

Leonard wants to spend his remaining years making up for lost time with family. He reveled in the send-off he was able to give Duncan when his son left Santa Fe recently to study neurology at a nearby university.

But in a broader sense, all the time he has spent behind bars has not tempered his resolve about the fundamental freedoms denied by a government that seeks to "protect" its citizens from drugs. Leonard Pickard was sent away forever for making a drug that arguably has never killed anyone, while opioid mills like Purdue Pharma, McKesson, and Cardinal Health continue killing thousands with impunity. Don't get him started on the millions of legal deaths from nicotine and alcohol sanctioned by the federal government.

I've had to "stop the presses" a few times in my long career as a newspaper reporter, but this is a first in my incarnation as a book author.

And I can say unequivocally that far from being an unforeseen chore, this last assignment for Operation White Rabbit has been a genuine pleasure.

—Dennis McDougal, August 2020

Bibliography

Books

Bakalar, James B., and Lester Grinspoon. *Psychedelic Drugs Reconsidered.* New York City, The Lindesmith Center, 1997.

Brown, David Jay. *Frontiers of Psychedelic Consciousness: Conversations with Albert Hofmann, Stanislav Grof, Rick Strassman, Jeremy Narby, Simon Posford and Others.* Rochester, Park Street Press, 2015.

Caulkins, Jonathan P., Angela Hawken and Mark A.R. Kleiman. *Drugs and Drug Policy: What Everyone Needs to Know.* New York City, Oxford University Press, 2011.

Cole, Krystle A. *Lysergic: 2nd Edition.* San Bernardino, 2007.

Dobkin de Rios, Marlene. *The Psychedelic Journey of Marlene Dobkin de Rios: 45 Years with Shamans, Ayahuasqueros, and Ethnobotanists.* Rochester, Park Street Press, 2009.

Epstein, Edward Jay. *Agency of Fear: Opiates and Political Power in America.* New York City, G.P. Putnam's Sons, 1977.

Fort, Joel. *The Addicted Society: Pleasure-Seeking and Punishment Revisited.* New York City, Grove Press Inc., 1981.

Gissen Stanley, Rhoney, with Tom Davis. *Owsley and Me: My LSD Family.* Rhinebeck, Monkfish Book Publishing Company, 2012.

Grim, Ryan. *This is Your Country on Drugs: The Secret History of*

Getting High in America. Hoboken, John Wiley & Sons Inc., 2009.

Hargreaves, Guy. *Operation: Trip to Oz*. Brownsville, Sarah Book Publishing, 2013.

Jarnow, Jesse. *Heads: A Biography of Psychedelic America*. Boston, Da Capo Press, 2016.

Ketchum, James S. *Chemical Warfare: Secrets Almost Forgotten*. Santa Rosa, James S. Ketchum, 2006.

Kilmer, Beau, and Jonathan P. Caulkins and Mark A.R. Kleiman. *Marijuana Legalization: What Everyone Needs to Know*. New York City, Oxford University Press, 2016.

Kleiman, Mark A.R. *Against Excess: Drug Policy for Results*. New York City, Basic Books, 1992.

Kleps, Art. *Millbrook: A Narrative of the Early Years of American Psychedelianism, Recension of 2005*. Sacramento, Original Kleptonian Neo-American Church, 2017.

Lattin, Don. *Distilled Spirits: Getting High, Then Sober, with a Famous Writer, a Forgotten Philosopher, and a Hopeless Drunk*. Berkeley and Los Angeles, University of California Press, 2012.

Lee, Martin A., and Bruce Shlain. *Acid Dreams: The Complete Social History of LSD, the CIA, the Sixties, and Beyond*. New York City, Grove Press, 1985.

Mullis, Kary. *Dancing Naked in the Mind Field*. New York City, Vintage Books, 1998.

Pickard, William Leonard. *The Rose of Paracelsus: On Secrets and Sacraments*. Sub Rosa Press, 2016.

Pollan, Michael. *How to Change Your Mind: What the New Science of Psychedelics Teaches Us About Consciousness, Dying, Addiction, Depression, and Transcendence*. New York City, Penguin Books, 2018.

Ram Dass. *Be Here Now*. New York City, Harmony, 1978.

Savinelli, Alfred. Plants of Power: Native American Ceremony and the Use of Sacred Plants. Summertown, Native Voices, 2002.

Schou, Nicholas. *Orange Sunshine: The Brotherhood of Eternal Love and Its Quest to Spread Peace, Love, and Acid to the World.* New York City, Thomas Dunne Books, 2010.

Shapiro, Harry. *Waiting for the Man: The Story of Drugs and Popular Music.* New York City, William Morrow and Company Inc., 1988.

Shroder, Tom. *Acid Test: LSD, Ecstasy, and the Power to Heal.* New York City, Plume, 2014.

Shulgin, Alexander, and Ann Shulgin. *PiHKAL: A Chemical Love Story.* Berkeley, Transform Press, 1991.

Stevens, Jay. *Storming Heaven: LSD and the American Dream.* New York City, Atlantic Monthly Press, 1987.

Stickney, John. "The Commune Comes to America: Youthful Pioneers Leave Society to Seek, from the Land and One Another, a New Life." *Life,* 18 July 1969, pp. 16B-23.

Waldman, Ayelet. *A Really Good Day: How Microdosing Made a Mega Difference in My Mood, My Marriage, and My Life.* New York City, Alfred A. Knopf, 2017.

Periodicals

"An Epidemic of 'Acid Heads.'" *Time,* 11 Mar. 1966, pp. 44–46.

"Personality Characteristics Which Differentiate Creative Male Adolescents and Adults." *Journal of Personality,* Parloff, M., Datta, L., Kleman, M., & Handlon, Jan. 1968, pp. 528–552.

Court Cases

In Re William Leonard Pickard, 681 F.3d 1201 (10th Cir. 2012)

William Leonard Pickard vs. Dept. of Justice, 06-cv-00185 (N.D. Cal, 2006)

William Leonard Pickard vs. Dept. of Justice, 653 F.3d 782 (9th Cir. 2011)

State of Oklahoma vs. Krystal Ann Cole. Pre-Sentence Investigation Report, No. CF-2003-4213. Tulsa County District Community Corrections. 29 Jan. 2007.

Gordon Todd Skinner v. State of Oklahoma, 210 P.3d 840 (Okla. Crim. App. 2009)

Gordon Todd Skinner v. Addison, 527 Fed. Appx. 692 (10th Cir. 2013)

United States of America vs. William Leonard Pickard. No. 00-40104-01-RDR. United States District Court for the District of Kansas. 7 Dec. 2000.